DALIT WOMEN IN INDIA
Issues And Perspectives

DALIT WOMEN IN INDIA
Issues And Perspectives

By

P.G.JOGDAND

GYAN

ISBN : 978-81-212-0493-4

Published, 2018

Published by

Gyan Publishing House
5, Ansari Road
Daryaganj, New Delhi-110002
Phone: 011-47034999, 9811692060
www.gyanbooks.com
E-mail: books@gyanbooks.com

Printed at: G. Print Process, Delhi.

Dedicated to

Savitreebai Jotiba Phule (1831-1897)

who dedicated her life to the cause of women

FOREWORD

It can be said without any fear of contradiction that Sociology of Weaker Sections in India has achieved a recognition as a distinct branch of sociology. A great deal of scientifically done research material in this area is available now, some of which has been used and can further be used as policy input. Vast creative writings in the forms of poetry, novels, autobiographies, historical accounts, plays and the like, depicting the living conditions and problems and voicing protest, and aspirations of the Dalits have enriched the literary heritage of Marathi and other languages, thanks particularly to the Dalit literature movement which was primarily initiated and nourished by Marathi litterateurs. This literature, both scientific and popular has created new revolutionary consciousness not among the Dalits alone but among the thinking community in general.

Despite all this, one must concede that not much systematically done research work has been done on a section of the Dalits among the Dalits, namely 'Dalit Women' so far. Admittedly, one gets realistic and authentic glimpses of the life of Dalit woman through the creative writings of Dalit writers, particularly through the autobiographical accounts of both male and female writers. One even with a little human sensitivity gets stunned with the realistic and authentic accounts of life conditions of the Dalit women, her suppression, humiliation, sufferings, dilemmas and exploitation. Her sufferings are twofold. She has her own share of universal sufferings as a woman and additionally, she is a victim of a variety of exploitations, social, religious, economic and cultural as a Dalit woman. Her experience of patriarchal domination is qualitative more severe than that of the non-Dalit woman and opportunities and avenues available to her for voicing her grievences and agonies are very few. There is no denying of the important role the women's movements have played in India in the awakening of women to the rights and in redressal of the traditionally inherited grievances. However, barring in certain note worthy exceptions, the plight of Dalit woman as such has rarely been there as a priority item on their agenda. This is in no way a value judgement but a very general observation. One can also make similar comment on the obvious gender bias in the Dalit movements also.

I do not know how far it will be realistic to say that Dalit woman both brought up and living in a traditional family in rural areas learns to cope up with agonising experiences which she has to have in her day to day life. But I can certainly say that an educated urban Dalit woman experiences torturous and agonising moments continuously in her day to day life, when she is reminded constantly of her 'Dalit' status by others despite achievements and accomplishments of her own or those of her husband or father.

Keeping in mind these considerations and with a view to bring out different dimensions of the plight of Dalit woman; our Department and its Women's Studies Centre had organized a two day Seminar on 'Dalit Women'. This volume contains some of the scholarly presentations made in this Seminar. These scholars have tried to throw light on different aspects of the life of Dalit Women. These articles cover a wide spectrum of themes related to the Dalit Woman and would give readers a reasonably clearcut and realistic portrait of the Dalit Woman. The conceptual articles among them hopefully would provide atleast some kind of theoretical framework for the scholars who would be inspired to do further research in this area.

We had organised this Seminar with a modest objective of generating some consciousness about the plight of Dalit Women and this publication itself marks an achievement of that objective.

I am personally grateful to all the scholars who had participated in the seminar and also those who later on made available their contributions for inclusion in this volume.

I would also like to record my appreciation of efforts my all colleagues, particularly Dr. P.G. Jogdand had put in organising this Seminar and in preparing this volume.

U.B. Bhoite
Head,
Department of Sociology,
University of Poona, Pune-411 007

PREFACE

During the pre-independence period two movements which affected the position of women were the social reform movement of 19th century and the Nationalist movement of 20th century. The Status of Women was an issue of great concern to social reformers in India. The early social reformers were concerned with two major problems: the emancipation of women and the amelioration of the condition of Depressed Classes. Their first efforts were directed against certain customs like Sati, prohibition against widow remarriage, female infanticide, the observance of purdha etc. In fact, the debates were all based on the upper caste religious texts and the forms of violence being addressed were all primarily upper caste Hindu practices.

The lower caste women who were being marginalised were absent in these debates. Caste bondage had gender specificities and specific caste biased atrocities against Dalit women were not taken up in these debates. This is mainly because the category of 'Indian Women' was treated as a homogeneous category and read as 'middle class' 'upper caste women'.

The women's movement as a new social movement in India gathered momentum in 1970s and it included different shades of feminist perspectives subsequently. In the first phase the women's movement laid great stress on women's rights and in the second phase it emphasized more on women's liberation and autonomy. Some attached to mass based organisations, some party based and other autonomous women's groups and the issues taken up by them were varied. Issues of women's paid work, their unpaid domestic work and unionisation were taken up by mass based women's groups while the autonomous women's groups focussed on the issue of violence within the home and outside. Consciousness raising activities had emerged. But the specificity of the Dalit women's oppression remained hidden.

In 70s Dalit Movement as a New Social Movement expressed itself through radical literature and action. But even this upsurge did not give vent to the mute voices of Dalit Women located either in rural or in urban India. In the social sciences too the interconnection between caste and gender was not brought to the fore and category of 'Dalit women' figured neither in women's studies nor in caste studies. Hence, we will have to take into account the specificities of Dalit women in India.

Dalit women constitute a lower segment in Indian Society and suffer from dual disadvantages: (a) of being Dalits i.e. socio-economically and culturally marginalised group and (b) being women share the gender-based inequalities and subordination. With a view to discussing and documenting all India social reality of Dalit women to assess various theoretical positions on the issues and to understand region-specific socio-cultural practices impinging on the question of Dalit Women, a two day seminar was organised on "Dalit women in India: Issues and Perspectives" by the Department of Sociology, University of Poona on 10th and 11th September, 1993.

This book is an outcome of this seminar.

The problems of women in general and the issues related to their actual life situation deserve something more than our attention and intellectual intervention. However, it would not be realistic to presume that the women in any society are a homogeneous lot-culturally, socially and economically. The problems of women vary from one social stratum to another, one cultural group to another and also from one economic stratum to another.

Undeniably, those who are involved in women's studies as well as who are activists have looked at the intricacies of the above mentioned problem. However, it can be said that not enough attention has been focussed so far on the life condition and problems of women belonging to the Scheduled Castes and Tribes.

Further, it is being argued that the Dalit women are 'thrice alienated' by class, patriarchy and caste. The Dalit women subjected to severe exploitation at the work place also suffer on caste ground and gang rape from upper castes, while at the same time they may be beaten up in their own houses as well.

In addition to this, the process of rural development has played a decisive role in forced migration of Dalit women from rural to urban areas. Although the state sponsored developmental activities have brought some awareness to Dalit women, it has led to overburdening and self-exploitation. It is principally due to new agricultural technology and other modernization programme that the Dalit women have been adversely affected; displacing them from active labour force. As a result, Dalit women have to struggle harder to secure basic necessities of life viz.; food, fuel and water. Here, a mention should be made of Maharashtra Government's recently announced policy for women's empowerment. It seems, the urban based and better placed women will be benefitted out of this policy while the women belonging to the weaker sections will be left high and dry.

Admittedly, the above mentioned problems of the Dalit women have not received adequate attention of the mainstream women's movement. Contrary to the believe of the mainstream women's movement, the liberation of the women is not a uniform or undifferentiated domain. Notions of liberty vary from community to community. Hence, we will have to give due attention to the very difference in upper caste and Bahujan conception of liberation. Regarding the tribal women, it is being argued that they have an alternate mode of life. At the same time, a set of people maintain that the tribal women are being uprooted as a result of growing modernization and development and hence they should be brought under the purview of Hindu Code Bill. To arrive at a concrete conclusion it needs further probing. If we look at the complexities of caste and gender, we might hope that Dalit women's consciousness might have a revolutionary potential. The way Dalit women are located in the caste hierarchy they might challenge all the three structures viz. patriarchy, caste and class. They are fighting for establishing their own identity in society and their protest is directed towards breaking the cultural and material servility. This was evident from their active participation in Dr. B.R. Ambedkar's movement and even later struggles.

Is Dalit woman a separate category? Do they have typical problems as compared to other women in our society? What are the contemporary challenges before Dalit Women in particular and women in general? Why the Dalit leadership have had a cavilier approach towards the Dalit women? Do Dalit women face any cultural and social dilemmas? To explore these and other crucial issues concerning Dalit women we invited scholars, activists, lawyers and teachers, while extensively deliberating upon varied facets of this theme they discussed the issues and perspectives in the light of contemporary situation. All the papers presented in the seminar are not included in this book due to certain reasons. However, a few papers were solicited from scholars though their papers were not presented in the seminar. There is a dearth of material on Dalit women - which is crucial both for dialogue between women's movement and Dalit movement - and theoretical approaches on caste and gender.

A number of persons have helped me in many ways in bringing out this volume. I am highly grateful to all the contributors who have prepared their valuable papers despite their pre-occupations.

I owe thanks to D.N. Dhanagare, Ram Bapat, S.P. Punalekar, Vidyut Bhagwat, R.N. Kulhalli, Sharmila Rege, C.K. Purandare, Sadhana Natu, Nalini Pant who have helped me in a number of ways to complete this book. I take this opportunity to thank. Uttam Bhoite for writing a forward to this volume in spite of his pressing engagements. I am grateful to him for his kind advice and support.

I owe thanks for help and co-operation to Rev. N.L. Karkare, Director, Village Medical Service, Kamalnagar.

Finally, thanks are also due to Shri. B.P. Garg, Chief Executive, Gyan Publishing House, New Delhi, for bringing out the book in a record time.

Last but not the least, I am highly obliged to my colleagues in the Department of Sociology, University of Poona for reposing their confidence in me by giving this opportunity to edit this volume.

I am also grateful to our office staff (Mrs.) Agarkar, Sadhana Kulkarni and Sandhya Dubal for extending their cooperation in this endeavour.

Department of Sociology
University of Poona
PUNE-411 007

P.G. JOGDAND
Editor

CONTENTS

CONTRIBUTORS

1. Bhagwat Vidyut	Reader in Women's Studies Centre, Department of Sociology, University of Poona, Pune
2. Bharati Vizia	Deputy Director, Telugu Akademi, Hyderabad, (A.P.)
3. Dolas Avinash	Lecturer, Milind College of Arts, Aurangabad
4. Fr. Leo Sequeira	Papal Seminary, Pune
5. Gaikwad Jaideo	Advocate and social activist, Pune
6. Gorhe Neelam	Chairperson and Founder Member of Stree Aadhar Kendra and works as member of Maharashtra State Women's Commission
7. Jadhav A.S.	Lecturer, Department of Geography Shivaji University, Kolhapur
8. Jadhav Ujwala	Lecturer, Gopal Krishna College, Kolhapur
9. Jondhale Surendra	Reader in Politics and Public Administration, University of Poona, Pune

10. Kamble Saroj	Social Activist, Dhule
11. Lanjewar Jyoti	Lecturer in Marathi, S.B. City College, Nagpur
12. Minz Shashi	Deputy Collector, Custom and Excise, Pune
13. Omvedt Gail	Social activist, Kasegaon (Maharashtra) and has been researching issues of caste, class and gender
14. Pawade Kumud	Lecturer in Sanskrit, Nagpur College, Nagpur
15. Prabhavathi M.	Advocate and social activist, Bangalore
16. Punalekar Devyani	Coordinator, Examination Reforms Unit, South Gujarat University, Surat
17. Punalekar S.P.	Senior Fellow, Centre for Social Studies, Surat
18. Purandare C.K.	Research Scholar, Department of Sociology, University of Poona, Pune
19. Rege Sharmila	Lecturer, Women's Studies Centre, Department of Sociology, University of Poona, Pune.

1

DALIT WOMEN : ISSUES AND PERSPECTIVES

SOME CRITICAL REFLECTIONS

Vidyut Bhagwat

The theme of Dalit women is of a crucial importance in the contemporary Indian situation, particularly in the context of new social movements silenced today by narrowing their democratic space. By using the term *'dalit women' we are creating an imagined category. This imagining is necessary because we hope that Dalit women in the near future will give new critical dimensions to Indian feminist movement as well as to Dalit Movement.* As Gabriele Dietrich in her extremely balanced article "Dalit Movements and Women's Movements" points out while discussing the interrelationship between *caste and patriarchy,* that caste should be looked at as a marriage circle and *endogamy which is related to patriarchal controls over women.* Scholars like Gabriele Dietrich and Gail Omvedt point out that Morton Klass and Babasaheb Ambedkar both give most comprehensive and coherent explanations of the caste system. Dietrich further states that "in his early writings of 1916 Ambedkar comes very close to Morton Klass" version of *seeing caste as a "marriage circle"* which regulates access to resources as well as exchange of services based on territoriality and kinship". (Dietrich: 1992; 90) Her conclusion is that ".... neither Morton Klass nor Dr. Ambedkar go into an analysis of how the closing into endogamous marriage circles is related to patriarchal controls over women" (Dietrich: 1992; 92). She further states ".... intermarriage and even fantasies about intermarriage and interdining are major factors in triggering off caste riots in Tamil Nadu today. There is a need to work on a feminist position on this issue by Dalit women themselves since otherwise the debate deviates into the rape fantasies of men" (Dietrich: 1992; 91). I would only make an addition here by saying why talk about intermarriages even marriages within kinship by choice are opposed vehemently by the dalit-caste panchayats to chop off the heads of young couples e.g. The recent case in U.P. (August 1993). As we are all aware that the term dalit is meant to skip from the negative connotations of the word 'untouchable' and from the Gandhian framework of the word 'Harijan'. Though the term dalit is chiefly used for those who are ex-untouchables, now Buddhists or lower castes, Dalits really are a part of Indian counter-culture. The core of dalit consciousness is made of protest against exploitation and oppression. In short, the term dalit stands for change and revolution. *By using the term Dalit women we are trying to say that if women from dalit castes and of dalit consciousness create a space for themselves for fearless expression i.e. if they become subjects or agents or self, they will provide a new leadership to Indian society, in general and to feminist and dalit movements in particular.* Inspite of Dalit Panthers and Republican Parties, inspite of Dalit literature marking an authentic break-through in the white collared Hindu culture, and inspite of strong women's movement since 1975, *we feel that voices and protests of Dalit women are almost invisible.* This invisibility is so deep that leaders from left politics and leaders who are trying to build up new 'Hindutva' do not take due *cognisance of 'dalit women' at all.* In fact when we use phrases like, marginalisation of women in the development process, or feminisation of poverty or women's contribution in the unorganised sector we are referring to dalit women without even being conscious about their specificity. Dalit women were actively participating in the Ambedkar led movement in the pre-independence period. Today we see no protest against so-called 30% reservations for women in the local self government which further denies the possibility of dalit women getting any representation. Women who are part of toiling masses are leading their life as beasts of burden and often as victims of dominant caste onslaught. It is but natural that they are mute. But dalit women living in urban centres, taking care of their homes and children at times teaching in schools and colleges or most of the times playing the role of housewives have not yet come out. We do know how *they perceive themselves and the world around them*. Particularly, wives of political leaders, professors, doctors, executives are strangely silent. On the contrary, to take an example from Maharashtra, we can surely say that women from Brahmin and related castes are visible in various professions as well as are taking leadership in various social movements by showing their readiness to pay heavy price inside and side the household. We also witness some mobility on the part of dominant caste women and Jain women. *But what is happening to dalit educated women is peculiar and it is destroying their potentials.* Though there are some autobiographical writings, and some literary texts dalit women's writings has not become a force as yet. Malika Dhasal's autobiography *Mala Uddhvasta Vhayachay* was in a sense a significant contribution, however critics read it as an outburst and questioned its authenticity in the light of continuance of her marital life in the same Dhasal family. Today dalit women are working in various government offices, they are active members of Zilla Parishads but they are still bearing the burden of a double-day, sexual division of labour and overall patriarchal ideology and not saying any thing about it. Why is it so? It is not sufficient to answer it only in terms of political economy or brahminical ideology.

Amongst other social movements, women's movement is unique in many ways. Feminist consciousness not only makes one aware of the forms of power relations that men and women have with each other but is also adds to our understanding what it means by the common saying that *'all women constitute a caste'* i.e. *'baichi jat'*. This truth or reality is camouflaged by glorifying womenhood on Hindu patriarchal terms and dividing women into different castes. Male dominance or patriarchy is so deep rooted in us that both men and women in India will readily say that patriarchy is a western phenomenon and a western problem. Women in the developed world are living in a degraded status because of "their" permissive value system, market orientedness and consumerism. It is generally argued by many social thinkers that in India women are protected by community, caste, kinship and family networks.

This neglects the fact that women are the gateways of caste-system and the crucial pivot on whose purity - sanctity axis the caste hierarchy is constructed. Every caste not only controls "their" women's sexuality and labour power but in the process of reform or upgrading the community or the caste a new agenda of morality and efficiency is designed at every stage of history for women in such a way that at one level women from each caste are coerced into as if consenting for this change in fact "trapping" and at another level they are further divided and estranged from the collective consciousness of "baichi jat".

Moreover, the growing communalist and casteist forces today have mobilised "Hindu Women" who are given a promise of *'Ram Rajya' as a fantasy of a happy family. This is of course in direct counter position to the women's movement* which had pointed out the cracks and violence against women in 'happy families'. 'Stree Shakti' was counterposed to marginalise 'stree mukti' and *'Sita'* and *'Durga' were picked up as symbols to appose the 'liberationist ideology'* of the 'western' feminists. This poses a threat for both the women of the majority community who are being shown carrot of restricted mobility within a Hindu patriarchal order and for the women of minority community it means the postponement of issues like uniform civil code because of the ever impending threat of rape and violence from the majority community and increasing restrictions from the fundamentalists of their own community who seek to reinstate the communal identity through women.

The participation of women in the anti-mandal agitations and caste - based violence (Gothala/pimpri-Deshmukh) has implications for both the women's movement and the Dalit Movement. The women's movement has in its enthralment of 'sisterhood' failed to note the 'caste' factor while *the Dalit Movement has remained patriarchal and sees the dalit women's oppression merely as a caste oppression.* At this juncture we need to go deeper into the new construction of a concept of 'Hindu Religion', which is fundamentalist and patriarchal in many ways. Sandeep Pendse in his incisive article "Sadhvi Ritambhara Va Jamatvad" (Sadhvi Ritambhara and communalism) given us clues how women's leadership within the framework of neo-Hinduism is perverted and vicarious and how women like Ritambhara are further pitted against any space of emancipation or transcendence for "all" women. (Pendse: 1993; 11-20) Sadhvi by being "Sadhvi" i.e. one who has controlled her sexuality is not only uncommon but is "allowed" to incite the manhood of men who are young, confused and frustrated. In Dr. Pendse's opinion when the new capitalism in India is facing a race of hurdles, when people are entrenched in bargains, sales, indulgence, leaders like Sadhvi Ritambhara encourage a kind and convenient religiosity which does not disturb any one at the root. The ruling party has also not criticised Ritambhara who in a sense serves to hinder any mobilisation among the disenchanted youth by this opiating religiosity. Ritambhara creates a fear of castration in the minds of young men constructing them as Hindus sweeping all the caste, class consciousness in them. In her framework she promises men of virility and also puts a fear in their minds of turning than into eunuch if they do not listen to her and act. The othering process of Muslim community, positing them as backward, animal like or non-cooperative, cruel has made use of gender in subtle and open ways. Hinduisation of dalit youth in Bombay riots is an extremely alarming situation. In this context again we will have to make a conscious effort to build up our understanding of interrelationship between caste and gender.

Technically speaking Hindu religion is a natural religion which was not found by a single person. It is not based on a single text and it possesses no single church. Therefore it speaks in multiple ways, in multiple voices. At the philosophical or rather than metaphysical level it sees the ontological reality in terms of Prakruti-Purush dialectics. At this level it ascribes creative, dynamic role to women. This has inspired scholars like Vandana Shiva to build up a new paradigm in the form of ecofeminism. It is true that both the elite and the populist currents of Hindu opinion and sensibilities regarding woman carry a deep impress of mother-goddess cults and forms of worship. As a religion of a great agricultural civilisation it stands in awe, respect and yet fear and an anxiety about the role of a woman as a source of fertility and creativity. But barring the various modes of ritual and worship like Vamachari, Tantrik, Shakta all the so-called higher traditions of Hinduism ascribe to Hindu woman a complimentary or supplementary role. At the level of social reality Hindu religion has so far functioned within the context of a caste society.

The woman of the so-called higher castes pays for the dominant role gained by her male counterpart over the rest of the society. A rigid control over higher caste women in the context of their body and granting a lot of room for lower caste women not as freedom but as a space for brahminical male licentiousness are results of brahminic patriarchy. Women from lower castes were considered so lowly and degraded in life that their body was a free terrain for colonisation.

This process has given rise to various complicated situations for the practices of women's movements in the Indian context. Women from Devdasi or Kolhati castes might find marriage and the legitimacy that is granted through it as a liberating space from their trapped situation. Brahmin woman while analysing family and marriage as patriarchal structures will have to understand this need as a historical stage. Similarly those women born in Dalit castes will also have to produce their *own critical interpretations* of the issues prioratised by the other feminists in India like *securing control over body, sexuality, fertility and labour and the need to practice the slogan of 'personal is political'*. We must keep in mind that both the *dalit and non-dalit women are on the margin of Indian society.* The upper caste women have put up resistance and made some space, but we all know that this is not sufficient. Moreover, in order to create a challenge to patriarchal structures we in India need to know all the details of patriarchy's open and subtle modes. Feminist scholars not belonging to dalit castes might not be able to carry this task. Conscious women from dalit castes will produce this critique more ably. This research has to come from within and with critical consciousness.

Dalit Panthers particularly in their initial phase were extremely aggressive in their expression. Their dissatisfaction about their placement in the caste hierarchy came out in open through literature and politics. But dalit literature constructed dalit woman in the similar patriarchal framework of *'glorification of Motherhood'* and overall subjugation of women. Similarly dalit politics also looks at the issues of *empowerment of women as a non-issue. Women in dalit politics figure only in number and are also caught in a trap of 'our women' framework.* This *results into further marginalisation of dalit women.*

All those who are on the margins of social milieu will have to come together for creating an alternate world-view through ciritical perspectives. *Dalit women's agential collectivity is a fundamental necessity to build up a feminist movement in the Indian context.* Otherwise 'all women' coming together will end in privileging and *empowering high-caste Hindu women and degrading women from dalit,* muslim and other minority communities. The process will subjugate all women in many ways but this will affect the working class, dalit caste women the most. This is the time when we need very strong and firm and broad-based women's movement *which will subvert the populist essentialising meaning of "Baichi Jat" and create unity amongst all women in India, giving new meaning to the reality of baichi jat!*

References

1. Dietrich Gabriele; "Dalit Movements and Women's Movement" in *Reflection On The Women's Movement in India,* New Delhi: Horizons India Books; 1992.
2. Pendse, Sandeep; "Sadhvi Ritambhara Va Jamatvad" in *Stree-Uvach* 7th issue, Bombay: 1993.

2

ON DALITISM AND GENDER

S.P. Punalekar

Dalit Women in India is an extremely volatile and sensitive issue. Indeed this theme is very much relevant in current times, especially in the context of current debate on deregulation and liberalisation of Indian economy.

Though the terms Dalits and Dalitism have come into currency in the recent times, they have much longer historical context. And therefore we cannot ignore the past developments that have contributed in shaping the present day realities. Dalitism essentially implies conditions of subjugation; economic, political, social and cultural. Dalitism also embodies different degrees of marginalisation, legitimised through social institutions and their legal or quasi-legal structures. Dalitism has multiple forms and expressions as is evident from the current discussions among social scientists in India. Dalitism includes not only marginal status in economic sphere but also similar marginal statuses in cultural, political, religious and other domains.

If we accept that Dalitism symbolises marginalisation and hence denial of basic human rights and social justice, one should imagine the conditions of women belonging to Dalit groups or communities. They suffer on two counts being Dalit and being women. I do not think that I should press this point further. Many studies have eloquently brought out these features of multiple disadvantages suffered by Dalit women in India.

Let us briefly look into the major trends and tendencies concerning Dalit women in India in post-Independence era. For this, we have to make distinction between Dalit women in urban areas and those living in rural and tribal areas. Though, there can be similarities in some spheres between these two groups, the differences are equally valid, vital and also strategic. Urban Dalit women are found engaged in relatively secular, monetized occupational activities. A small percentage among them has risen to a relatively better status through salaried or service sectors, thanks to reservation policies and programmes of the union and state governments and also persistent efforts of enlightened sections within these communities.

Here we can also acknowledge the role of Mahatma Gandhi, Dr. Babasaheb Ambedkar and many others who through their reform as well as emancipatory movements helped in raising the economic status of some Dalit women in the urban areas. This is evident among few social groups like Kolis (who are OBC), Vankara, Mahars, etc. (who are SCs) and Chaudhari, Dhodia, Gamit, Mahadev Kolis etc. (who are STs). Years of social reform activities and also self mobilisation have enabled this miniscule section to come up.

It must also be noted that this urban strata of Dalit women (and also men) largely belong to landowning families, though it cannot be definitively said that women from all landowning Dalit families have been able to achieve this status. What problems this stratum of upcoming Dalit women are facing in the urban environment? Have they been accepted as socially equals by their co-workers belonging to higher social status groups? How do these Dalit women from urban areas look at their counterpart who are engaged in the low paid, low status occupations? We must find answers to these questions in order to discover *the levels of unities and disunities* among different sections within urban Dalit women.

Now about Dalit women working in organized and unorganized sectors of urban economy. According to one estimate the organized sector accounts for approximately 10% of the female labour force. A document "National Perspective Plan for Women, 1988 - 2000 A.D." has noted that "Employment opportunities in the governmental and public sectors and the private corporate sector are limited in view of the general constraints on resources for region, expansion and dependence on the dictates of market mechanisms which are prejudicial to women. Given these realities and based on the performance of previous decades, it is unlikely that this sector can offer much relief by way of expanded employment potential to women.

Given this assessment, it appears that *employment prospects for Dalit women in particular are too grim.* Entry into organized sector depends much upon contacts and social connections in addition to educational qualification and previous job experience. There are other negative features also. They include: (i) *segmentation in the labour market* which works against Dalit women, (ii) adverse implications of technological growth and (iii) *lack of unionization of female workers.*

In addition there are two other handicaps, namely (a) absence of a meaningful human resource development policies aimed at improving Dalit women's employability and productivity through training and (b) absence of national labour policy encompassing the needs of Dalit women in the organized sectors. *It appears that participation of Dalit women in organized sectors is considerably low or negligible. How this participation rate can be increased?* What social, legal administrative and technological measures are needed to step up this rate? These questions assume strategic significance.

In urban areas the Dalit women are found concentrated in the unorganised sector. This sector can be divided into two: (i) self employment, and (ii) wage employment. The first covers activities like hawking, scrap collection, petty trade or home based production or service activity. Dalit women mostly staying in slums or hutment colonies carry on these activities for survival and family support. These self-employment activities generally provide very meagre financial returns and also have uncertainties and insecurities.

Dalit women suffer the most if they are without kinship support and other social and political linkages including contact with municipal bureaucracy, police etc. There are health risks also which often cut into their already meagre earnings. Survey of bottle collecting women in Poona (who consisted largely of Dalit women), and studies of women hawkers and vendors by the SEWA, Ahmedabad amply demonstrate that self-employment activity is perennially insecure and unstable. *What can be done to make these self-employment activities secure and stable? What arrangements are needed to provide protection to Dalit women engaged in these activities? We must find answers to these questions.*

Now about *wage employment activities.* This is a complex sector encompassing variety of manufacturing and servicing activities. In this sector, we find a large concentration of urban Dalit women. The activities cover construction labour, land levelling, earth work, domestic labour, beedi-making, Aggarbatti and candle making, garment-apparel industry, jari and embroidery, toy-making etc. The labour market is highly fragmented with dispersal of labour force in all parts of the city. In this wage employment sector, there are non-Dalit workers also and they too suffer from variety of disadvantages. Women working in this sector are victims of low wages, irregular employment, absence of social security benefits and many other handicaps. They are dependent on whims of the employers including sexual harassment. Child labour is also pronounced in this sector.

In the recent years, Dalit women are found assembling at casual labour markets which are called Chakla barars in Gujarat and Addas in West Bengal. In these markets, the women members compete with men to secure purely casual employment. They work in the cities for land levelling, gardening, masonary assistance, building construction, loading and unloading of goods in transport godowns etc. Their employers are Mukadams, Contractors or Transport agents. These women earn between Rs. 20 to Rs. 30 per day for about 10 to 12 hours work. And for this they have to leave their home by six o'clock in the morning and if they find work they reach back after seven in the evening. Working conditions are extremely arduous. Prof. Ranade and Ramchandran have brought forth vividly the uneasiness and tensions faced by those women construction labourers.

In our own inquiry in Gujarat we came across several such instances of lower wages, unlawful wage deductions, summary dismissals and, also on some occasions, sexual harassment of women labourers. Most of them were tribals from Panchmahals, Bharuch and Vadodara districts. Report of the Core Group set up by the Ministry of HRD (1988) has also noted that the condition of women construction workers is pitiable. It has stated, "they (women workers) face instability and insecurity of employment, low wages, non observance of labour laws, bondage to the middle men who employ them without providing the facilities enjoyed by legislation. Their way of life is perpetually in a state of flux as they have to keep migrating from site to site. The average wages for women construction workers are generally lower than their male counter parts".

As in Gujarat and West Bengal, in many other states such casual labour markets have now emerged. They consist of migrant men and women largely from lower caste and tribes. It appears that there is some linkage between deteriorating rural conditions and expanding casual labour markets in urban areas. Generally, famine and drought conditions are responsible for large scale migration to cities and for entry into casual labour market. This needs further investigation.

It also means that we have to seriously examine the nature and direction of our rural development which in my view have played decisive role in involuntary or forced migration of Dalit women from rural to urban areas. Once such shift occurs, it is most difficult for them to avoid further drift into marginal status and dehumanisation. However, this aspect needs a careful probe.

Let us now turn our attention to social situation of Dalit women in rural and tribal areas. *In rural areas Dalit women are closely identified with their caste status and associated social disabilities.* Therefore, these women suffer all deprivations which their caste group as a whole suffer. Besides, they have to undergo additional hardships because of their gender. Here again, economic situation has important bearing on the life of rural Dalit women.

There are reports which indicate that in rural areas the hardships of Dalit women have increased over the years. Though there are some hopeful signs of upward improvements in health, housing and education of Dalit communities, such instances are comparatively fewer. There is *increasing stress on female labour in agriculture and agro-based industries. Burden on Dalit women is increasing.* The state sponsored developmental activities like *IRDP, RLEGP, DWCRA,* etc. have certainly brought some awareness to Dalit women in the rural areas but simultaneously it has led to overburdening and self-exploitation. Often there is withdrawal from school education at an early age. Also, because of fierce competition for scarce resources like firewood and fodder, the Dalit women have to struggle harder to secure basic necessities of life. Some IRDP evaluation studies have brought out these aspects clearly.

However, we must find out whether Dalit and non-Dalit women have differential experience with regard to access and utilization of village resources. My hunch is that though there are some commonalities, there is likely to be some major differences in experiences and perceptions of Dalit and non-Dalit women. The latter group is likely to enjoy some privileges and status. May be they can rely on their caste linkage and vertical solidarity to minimise their disadvantages in this regard.

That this is so is brought out eloquently by Baba Adhav in his book Ek Gaon, Ek Panavatha which discusses the conditions in rural areas of Marathwada and Konkan regions in Maharashtra. In Gujarat also, similar experiences are recorded in the studies by A.S. Patel (Narsands), Amrapali Merchant (Anand Taluka), Arjun Patel (Olpad and Navsari Taluka). This aspect needs to be carefully looked into through village level studies in different states.

One more point which needs serious attention is that of *availability of water*. It is now increasingly realised that women in general have to struggle hard to secure water for domestic consumption. Particularly this situation is explosive in dry, arid zones and in places which are now perennially drought prone areas. Dalit women have to suffer more because of caste distinctions and less or remote access to village community resources. *Water scarcity situation seems to have affected adversely the education among Dalit girls. This point needs to be explored more thoroughly.*

All this discussion suggests that the nature and *direction of rural development* have a lot to do with the prevailing conditions among Dalit women in rural areas. Mechanisation in agriculture, commercialisation of traditional services (which provide wherewithal to women in artisan families), introduction of technology, etc. are useful devices for growth and development. But their impact on marginal groups and especially the female labour need to be ascertained carefully and appropriate steps taken to safeguard the needs of the vulnerable sections.

Now about women in Tribal areas. Tribal community is not homogeneous socially and economically. Culturally also they have significant differences among them. In general, the conditions of Dhodia, Chaudhari, Gamit, Mahadev Koli women are certainly better than those belonging to STs like Dublas, Varlis, Bhils, Tadvis, Naikas, Katkaris, etc. Largely these differences are due to geo-economic factors, better land assets, early exposure to modern institutions etc.

Those tribes who lived in *Ranee Vistar* or interior forest villages lagged behind in economic development. Their infrastructural endowment was also poor. After Independence there has been some improvement in these backward, hilly regions. But the *Rastee* (Road-side) village (where Dhodias, Chaudharis, etc. lived) also received tremendous developmental inputs during this period. So differences between the two groups have not decreased; they have rather increased.

Tribal women do not suffer such caste rigidities as those suffered by scheduled caste women. They live within their own ethnic groups and hence enjoy relatively better social security and support. All the same their situation also calls for sociological investigation because of their isolation from mainstream society and hence greater control over their lives by their community and leaders who are male members. Some of their customs and rituals and social practices need to be examined as they are suspected to be perpetuating male dominance through cultural hegemony.

One significant point that has now arisen is their forced migration to irrigated villages within and outside tribal region and towns and cities for earning their livelihood. We have already mentioned about the pitiable conditions of tribal women in casual labour markets in urban areas. Similar has been the status of tribal women who are seasonally migrating to brick-kilns, salt pans and sugarcane fields. Jan Breman, David Atwood and my own studies inform us that *tribal women suffer from severe handicaps during such seasonal migration.*

Away from village and safer community environment, these tribal women in sugarcane fields live sub-human existence, devoid of basic facilities and perpetually facing tensions in their day to day existence. Their men-folk too encounter similar hardships but often they tend to forget their worries by drowning themselves in liquor consumption or gambling. Their wives and daughters have to worry for every day meals, water and such elementary needs of life. Stories of wife beating are not absent either. Their children are deprived of school and other social entitlements. Studies by Subhash Patil, V.B. Jugale, Vidyadhar Auti and others fully demonstrate these predicaments. Shramik Vichar, a daily from Poona (now closed) carried a good deal of information on the conditions of *these migrants* including their women-folk, suggesting that deeper investigation is the need of the hour to obtain better insights into the problems of Dalit migrant women.

One more area relating to tribal woman is that of emergence of large projects like Dams, industrial complexes, etc. This is a new area which merits closer attention of the social scientists. Dams are built for water and electricity which are needed to support agriculture and industry. They are called development projects for their supposed contribution to growth of national economy.

But what about those families (who are mostly Dalits, tribals) who are displaced and dislocated from their social and cultural moorings? It is a common experience that a displaced family is provided with meagre financial compensation and some supportive services. Recently there is some relaxation and land for land is being accepted as a rehabilitation package. But does this adequately take care of social and cultural needs and interests of displaced tribal women? *Do they participate in equal terms along with their men in decision making process?* These questions assume importance in the current context of *massive inputs into large projects.* It is from this angle, movements led by Medha Patkar, Baba Amte, B.D. Sharma and others need to be assessed.

By way of conclusion, the following points can be emphasized for their social relevance.

(i) It is imperative that *economic factors must be given full weightage in order to uplift Dalit women from their prevailing marginalized, dehumanized status.* This requires consideration of all issues that have bearing on the development perspectives and strategies of our nation.

(ii) As a corollary, rural development and urban development should be considered together and not in isolation. Similarly, organized and unorganised sectors should be examined together because they constitute two sides of the same coin, that is, the national economy paramater.

(iii) It is therefore urgent that all aspects of the present debate on liberalisation of Indian economy should be thoroughly examined. Dalit women have been contributing to growth and development throughout history. And even then they have remained at the lowest rung of the society, lowest of the low. What has contributed to this state of affairs? Which are the forces responsible for the present insecure, unstable, dehumanized status of the Dalit women?

(iv) There is a *cultural domain which requires deeper scrutiny.* This also includes structure of relations between Dalit women and non-Dalit women. *What are their perceptions of each other?* To what extent they are helpful and sympathetic? What causes apathy and alienation and social divisiveness among them?

(v) Further, the role of Dalit family and especially *the adult male members among them needs examination.* It is often found that the Dalit family is itself exploited from external agencies while *the Dalit women in the family is further severally exploited by the adult males* (and also females). *What are the forms of such family exploitation*? Baburao Bagul, Uttam Bandu Tupe, Daya Pawar and Laxman Gaikwad tell us vividly about *such family-centered exploitation of Dalit women.*

(vi) There is a need to closely look into conditions of women belonging to nomadic tribes. Their situation is intensely critical and often at times bordering on crises of survival. Conditions of women of Kaikadis, Kanjarbhat, Vaidu, Murali Makadwale, etc. need to be comprehensively documented. They are living at the margin of existence, perpetually moving from place to place and often harassed by village chieftains and the police. Indeed their struggle for survival defies our Sociological imagination. Laxman Gaikwad, Ramnath Chavan, and Motiram Rathod have helped us in realising the hardships encountered by Dalit nomadic women. Laxman Mane and others are struggling to acquaint us with the grim realities they are facing in thier day-to-day life. It is urgent that their problems too get sufficiently highlighted.

3

CASTE AND GENDER : THE VIOLENCE AGAINST WOMEN IN INDIA

Sharmila Rege

Let us review the different ways in which the issue of violence against women has been addressed in the last two hundred years in India. The basic questions that rise then are those pertaining to the forms of violence, the location of individuals and groups addressing the issue and the specific contexts of their addressal. The missionaries, the orientalists, colonial administrators, social reformers and the post-independent Indian nation-state have all addressed the issue of violence against women as a part of either their 'civilising mission', 'revival or modernisation of Indian tradition' or 'women as weaker sections' projects. The Edwardian and Victorian feminists addressed the issue as the white women's burden while the first wave Indian feminists lobbied for amendments in the Hindu law of property and marriage; for 'status' rather than 'survival'. All these discourses, in universalising the category of Indian women, often encroached on the customary rights of the lower women. Much of the American and British, second wave, white feminist discourse on the third world women carries the notion of third world women as 'always and already victims'. The second wave feminists in India who formed autonomous women's groups in the 1970's, had broken away from the 'larger/mass' movements which overlooked gender for the fear of dividing the movement. The autonomous women's groups politicised the issue of violence against women and attempted to build a sisterhood in struggling against violence. The divisions by caste and religion that threaten this sisterhood have become apparent in recent times. Steven Lukes' 'Radical View of Power' (Lukes, 1974) and Harding's 'Epistemology of Rainbow Coalition Politics' (Harding, 1991) provide relevant theoretical framework for the analysis of violence and the strife in sisterhood. The violent practices against women reveal definite variations by caste; while upper caste are subjected to controls and violence within the family, it is the absence of such controls that makes lower caste women vulnerable to rape, sexual harassment and the threat of public violence. To varying degrees these different practices are 'accepted' as given and some of them like 'sati' and 'devdasi' practice may even be glorified. Lukes has argued that the supreme exercise of power is through compliance, by control over the thoughts and desires of the other. The collusion and contestation between patriarchies and 'brahmanism' (upper caste practices and ideologies) reveals the exercise of such power through the differential definitions and management of gender by caste. Gender was and is crucial to the maintenance of reproduction of caste inequalities. Further Lukes has argued that power presupposes human agency and that agents consist in a set of expanding and contracting opportunities. Together these constitute the structural possibilities which specify the power of agents varying between time and over agents. (Lukes, 1974). Women's agency needs to be located in the context of the structural possibilities of class, race, caste and community. The state has in all its programmes assumed the women to be 'free agents'; outside the boundaries of caste, class and religion. The contradiction between the state's explicitly stated commitment to the annihilation of caste and upgradation of women and the increasing violence against women and the lower castes, is legitimised through the maintenance of caste and gender as separate issues on the political agenda, precisely because of the important links between the two. The 'real inte-rests' of women must be conceptualised from the perspective of the marginalised; in this case the perspectives of the Dalit women. Centring from the perspective of the marginalised prevents the distortion of both; those at the centre and at the margins. (Harding, 1991). Further such an analysis need not amount to speaking for the marginalised or speaking for the 'Dalit' women for the multiple and contradictory subject agent of feminism is also logically the subject of every other libratory project. In following Harding, we agree that this is not only an epistemological but also a moral and political issue.

The first major challenge to the women's movement in India had come from the state sponsored programmes of modernisation. But in recent times, a major threat is being posed by the Hindu fundamentalists who spread insiduous propaganda that not only 'others' the muslims but provides a utopia of 'Ramrajya' (rule of the divine). To the educated unemployed and the educated upper caste women confined to the domestic sphere, the Hindu fundamentalists provide a public forum. Women's power as in the Hindu religious mythology is being posed as opposed to the 'western' concept of women's liberation. The IMF guided liberalisation of the economy and the near acceptance of the Dunkel draft by the Indian government as against alternative paths of development, pose a major threat to the women workers and peasants. In such a context, the left, the anti - caste, ecology, tribal and women's movements in India are realising the need of interlinkages of 'rainbow' coalition politics. Social activist groups working in diverse areas in different parts of India are coming together, attempting to work out a political agenda. This paper is a part of such attempts; exploring the essential links between caste and violence against women. The first section attempts to give a brief summary of the issues that the contemporary women's movement in India has to confront. The second section traces the ways in which the debates and reform or legislation against violence has in fact realigned patriarchal interests with changing political formations. The third section presents cases of violence against upper caste women; the continuum ranging from everyday practices of verbal abuse to the cases of widow burning, the cases of rape of lower caste women which reveal the links between 'virtue' and the right to protest against rape and the recent cases of violence against lower caste men; in which upper caste women were reported to have not only incited their menfolk into violence but also participate publicly in the acts. In the last section, the impasse that the women's movement faces and the need to form coalitions, the important links between caste and gender that can help form such coalitions are outlined.

Vast differences distinguish the lives of women in different parts of India and within different caste, class, religious and ethnic groups. Eighty percent of India's population lives in the rural areas and more than seventy percent of India's female labour force falls in the category of landless agricultural labour. The struggle for these women revolves around procuring food, fuel and water for their families. The number of female headed households have been on the increase and there has been a growing deterioration and privatisation of the country's common property resources on which the poor in general and women in particular depend. (Agarwal, 1989). Food allocation in the family is heavily biased in favour of men and even in the agriculturally prosperous state of Punjab, women's average consumption of calories is only two-thirds of that of men; despite that fact that women in this region perform at least fifteen hours of arduous labour. This contributes to a higher mortality rate among women. For the women of the rich peasant and upper castes, it is a struggle against seclusion and torture within the family. (Kishwar and Vanita, 1991). In urban India, the female labour force is concentrated in the informal section; mainly as domestic servants, construction labour and casual labour. Only ten percent of the female labour force is employed in industries. There has been a visible improvement in the lives of the middle class, upper caste, educated women, in terms of their participation in education and employment. Several studies have revealed that employment for women of these classes has not brought much change in the power axes of the family. (Standing, 1990). Women's labour in fact remains a flexible resource. (Banerjee, 1992). There is therefore, the paradoxical co-existence of constitutional guarantees of equality and brutal expression of violence and the relative powerlessness of women. The population of women in India has been declining and the sex-ratio has declined from 972 females to 1000 males in 1901 to 927 females to 1000 males in 1991. Only 24.8% of the women are literate and only 5.7% can ever reach the university. More than 70% of the female labour force is in the unorganised section which means long hours of work, wage differentials and no security. Despite child marriage being a legal offence, 10% of the females in the age group of 10-14 are married by the age of 18. Birth of daughters is unwelcome and new forms of female foeticide are emerging. The birth of a daughter means the liability of guarding her virginity and debts in paying the dowry in marriage to the bridegrooms family. This payment, however, does not guarantee and security for the women as there is always a demand for more in the form of festive offerings and gifts. In the capital city of New Delhi, two women die of burns every day; the cases being either of 'suicide' or dowry murders. In 1991, the number of women who faced the torture of rape, were estimated at 2 million, and the majority of the victims were tribal, Dalit; the incidence of rape being higher in areas declared to be turbulent and where the army or the police have been stationed. (Gandhi and Shah, 1992).

The women's movement in India has been in a lull after the declaration of independence and the granting of constitutional guarantees of equality and freedom for all irrespective of caste, creed or sex. Disillusionment with the rhetoric of socialist democracy and planned development set in, during the mid-sixties and women began to participate in large numbers in the tribal, working class, Dalit and student's movements. The declaration of emergency and withdrawal of civil rights in 1975 had led to several atrocities. As the emergency war lifted, civil liberties groups brought to light several cases of gang rapes of lower caste women in northern India. Against such a background the autonomous women's groups emerged as the political force on the issue of violence against women. Nation wide networking of women's groups emerged on the issue of rape and dowry murders and the state was pushed into legal amendments. (Gandhi and Shah, 1992). As feminist groups in urban India began to focus on the violence outside and within the home, the media projected them as'western' and disrespectful of Indian tradition. The left and the anti caste movements labelled the feminist focus on violence as 'middle class' and saw the women's centres as being 'welfaristic' and not 'revolutionary' enough. All political parties were quick to catch on and re-vitalised or created a women's wing, taking care to draw on symbols of female power from popular Hindu mythology.

The state sponsored programmes of redistribution of land and modernisation had begun in the 1960's and by the 1980's, it was apparent that these had led to increased inequalities in income and wealth. For the first thirty years after Independence, women figured in the planned development as only 'mothers' in the 'mother and child welfare programmes'; despite the fact that more than 50% of the agricultural labour was provided by women. (Towards Equality, 1975). The development projects such as the green revolution project and the large dam projects have marginalised the poor and especially women. In the so-called prosperous green revolution region, the inequalities in income have increased and the number of dowry deaths and malnutrition of women have shown a steady increase. (Agarwal, 1986). In the industrial sector, in the free trading zones, women have been exploited as cheap labour and have been made to work under conditions of strict supervision and physical abuse. Attempts at unionisation have been brutally squashed with police assistance (Trikha, 1985).

The family planning programmes and population policies under the cover of 'cafeteria' approach have made political grounds of women's wombs. (Something Like a War, 1992). International organisations such as IPPF and the Population Council, have promoted the use of hormonal implants and injectibles and the MNC's who produce them, invoke the demands of the women's movement (control over body and fertility) as they market these drugs. Women's groups and health activists have opposed these on three grounds; side-effects, inadequate public health services to meet the demands of such implants and the fact that these drugs have not been standardised for women in India and that biochemical and epidemiological studies are essential before their introduction in India. Women's right to choose and freedom are invoked while the politics of the private and health care is sidetacked. (Tharu and Niranjana, 1992).

For the majority of women in India, the uppermost porblem is of survival. Poverty, dowry murders, widow burning, female infanticide have assumed new forms with modernisation and technological advancement. These contexts of fatal aggression seem to normalise the everyday practices of violence by the family, community, state and global economy. This reality of oppression is being measured, codified, as struggles are reduced to manipulable data to be filled into neat theoretical frameworks. Baxi comments that women's studies seem to be harnessed to producing a third gender-men, women and Ph.D's in women studies. (Baxi, 1987). Deprivatisation of the knowledge seems to be the first step in developing an approach towards violence against women and collective political violence in India. (Baxi, 1987).

To recall the questions that were raised at the on-set in the last two hundred years, what were the different forms of violence against women that have been addressed? Who were the individuals or groups engaged in the public debates on the issue? and most significantly, who is the 'Indian Woman' on whose behalf they plead?. The status of Indian women occupied a prominent position in the 19th century discourse. The need to reform Indian Society was incorporated into the reform of Indian woman's position and Indian woman like Indian tradition was defined across a particular axis of religion, class and caste. (Wolf, 1992). From the late 18th century, the missionaries had begun to attack a range of 'degenerate' Hindu practices, majority of which were directed expressly against women. The missionaries brought out a volley of tracts and pamphlets directed at the British government and public, giving dramatic and empirical details of practices like widow burning and proclaiming Indian men to be moral monsters. The aim was to contrast Hinduism to Christianity, the location of women's position at the centre of such a critique is seen as part of an ongoing process of creating and projecting a superior national identity of Britain, - of which the English woman was a central motif along with the English art, rural life, literature and character. (Wolf, 1992).

The appeals made by the missionaries led the colonial administration to intervene through social legislation. This intervention was varied in the different regions of India and reveals a complex inter-relationship of contest and collusion between indigenous patriarchal norms and those held by the British administration. This is largely, but rarely noted visibly in the colonial regulation on agrarian relations. (Vaid and Sangari, 1990). Several western educated, Indian intellectuals, concerned, no doubt, with the plight of Hindu women entered the arena of reform. These social reformers fall into two categories; those who saw reform as a revival of the 'Golden' period of Hinduism and those that sought the modernisation of 'Indian' tradition. The debates were all based on the upper caste religious texts and the forms of violence being addressed (widow burning, child marriage, seclusion, enforced widowhood) were all primarily upper caste Hindu practices. The lower caste women who were being marginalised by the new land legislation and exposed to the threat of sexual violence under the 'Zamindari' system of land legislation and the distress sale of women following the new land settlements (Vaid and Sangari, 1990) in the 18th century are absent in these debates. The 'Indian woman' in the reform debate was essentially Hindu, upper caste and symbolic of the emergent middle class; women being tied to the very process of cultural homogenisation of the middle class. (Banerjee, 1990). Such a reform movement had very little reach but served to provide a model of Indian womanhood. The position of the Indian woman had occupied much of the early and the mid 19th century debates; towards the close of the century this issue disappears from the arena of public debate. The overwhelming issues are directly political ones, concerning the politics of nationalism. (Chatterjee, 1990). It has been argued that nationalism resolved the 'woman's question' in accordance with its preferred goals. This resolution was built around a separation of the domain of culture into two spheres, the material and the spiritual. It was in the material sphere that the colonised were to imitate the West in order to overcome the domination but in the spiritual domain, the East was considered as superior and this was to be the spiritual essence of the national culture. This distinction of the material/spiritual was condensed into the ideologically superior dichotomy of inner/outer, home/world. (Chatterjee, 1990). This spirituality of the inner sanctum, the home was to be maintained by the woman as the torch bearer of tradition (All violence within the family was thus rendered invisible), and by reverse logic all those women (lower caste and working class) who 'did not' were designated as 'impure'.

British feminism had matured during the age of the empire but as Burton has argued the British feminists participated in the assumptions of national and racial superiority. She argues that Josephine Butler's campaign on behalf of Indian women is an example of imperial feminism. Her review of the feminist periodical literature of the 19th century reveals that British feminism constructed the image of the helpless Indian womanhood, on which their own emancipation in the imperial nation state relied. Burton concludes that not only did the Victorian and Edwardian feminists reproduce the moral discourse of imperialism but embedded western feminism deeply within it. (Burton, 1990). Ramusack has referred to the British feminists as the 'maternal imperialists' (Ramusack, 1990) while Paxton argues that for the feminists the choice was limited, between being racist and loyal or being disloyal to the civilisation. (Paxton, 1990) India remained an imaginative landscape for the British feminists who addressed the issue of violence against Indian women.

The first wave feminists in India (20th century) were women related to the reformers or the nationalists, mainly upper caste women who lobbied tirelessly for the right to property and amendments in the Hindu law of marriage. These first wave feminists were preoccupied with issues of 'status' rather than 'survival'. It was therefore, the uppercaste, middle class women who drew the benefits from the constitutional guarantees and legal measures (Omvedt, 1985). The second wave feminists in India who formed autonomous groups politicised the issue of violence against women, both inside and outside the home. Free legal aid centres and counselling groups were set up and consciousness raising through street plays and posters on the issue of violence became a regular practice in urban areas. As a result of several such campaign, the law against Rape and Dowry Prohibition Act were amended. The issue on Uniform Civil Code was taken up on a national wide scale; however, the ruling Congress Party fearing the loss of minority vote banks backtracked on the issue. Those second wave feminists who did not accept autonomy and separatism and had to remain in 'mass' movements argued that violence against women was no doubt an important issue but the campaigns for legal amendments and crisis centres were urban and middle clas: and that the economic issues were more urgent for the masses of women. The recent upsurge in caste and communal violence and the participation of the women of the dominant groups in this violence points towards the impasse facing the women's movement in India. (Tharu and Niranjana, 1992). In the next section cases of violence are presented, before undertaking an analysis of the impasse.

For most of us the issue of widow burning or 'sati' was a historical issue, till we saw a revival of the practice in 1987. The women's movement later unearthed the fact that after independence, there had been thirty eight cases of widow burning in India. Historically, the custom had been prevalent only in certain regions of India and among the upper castes and the landed. In regions where the widow had a right in the deceased husband's property, the practice became prevalent in the 12th and 13th century. (Laud, 1987). The custom can be seen as the ultimate resolution of the management and control over the widow's sexuality. The anxiety over controlling the widow's sexuality was so high that in certain regions the practice of 'cold sati' was devised for ensuring the commitment of 'sati' by the child widows. The child widow would be poisoned in course of a festive celebration of her declaration to become a 'sati' and then the cold body placed on a pyre of the husband. The lower castes did not practise this custom and the lower caste widows could remarry freely, until the colonial intervention through the Widow Remarriage Act of 1856. (Choudhary, 1990).

The debate on widow burning began in 1780's when the missionaries first took up the issue. The colonial administration first intervened in the civil society on the issue of 'sati'. A debate ensued between the colonial officials and the western educated Indian intellectuals on one hand and the conservatives on the other. The entire debate is pre-occupied with preserving true tradition. The widow is either the victim or the heroine and both parties intercede on her behalf to save her from 'true tradition'. The reformers claimed that the high traditions did not endorse the practice and that this was the true tradition to be followed while the conservatives argued that true tradition demanded that for her own salvation and that of her family, a widow must commit 'sati'. Mani had argued that in this debate women are neither the subjects nor objects but become the grounds for debate (Mani, 1990).

The revival of the practice in 1987 led to a nation wide controversy. There were mainly two positions taken; the liberals saw the practice as barbaric and a failure of modernisation while the conservative pro-sati lobby defended the practice as 'Indian' tradition. What is important to note is that the region which saw the revival of the practice, has never had a history of widow burning. Since 1954, the region has seen the upper castes build 105 temples dedicated to the 'satis'. The custom had been systematically used to revive the identity of the uppercastes (Rajputs) who had faced a downfall after the state sponsored land reform programme in which some of the middle castes had benefitted and had consolidated their political position. The protesting feminists came to be portrayed as a threat to the Hindu identity and an all India association for the preservation of sati as a religious duty was formed. The state fumbled, there was no comment for 11 days, as pressure from a progressive coalition built up the Sati Prohibition Act of 1829 was amended. The new act is again an upholder of 'true tradition' as it declares that the custom is banned since no religion in India endorses it. Moreover, the new Act treats the women as a free agent, by making her act punishable (Dhagamwar, 1988). the upholders of the practice brought forth the issue of the widow's will and voluntary 'sati'. Feminists argued that one can hardly conceive of the widow's will and voluntary 'sati'. Feminists argued that one can hardly conceive of the widow's will when widowhood imposes social death and its own regime of misery for women. By raising the issue of women's agency, in the Indian context, one walks on a tight rope. If widow burning is at the extreme end of the continuum of violent practices within upper caste families, a critique of the day to day life practices in the upper caste homes would reveal the different intermediate forms of control that operate. Firstly, there are linguistic clues; both verbal abuse and the reinforcing of stereotypes. There are also severe controls over women's labour in that under the ideology of 'grihalaxmi' (the woman as the goddess of the household) the burden of domestic work is glorified and often women begin to view this burden as their privilege. It must be noted here that the arduous tasks of domestic work are performed by the lower caste women who constitute the majority of domestic labour. Attempts of unionisation by domestic workers have been viewed negatively by their upper caste women employers; strikes have resulted in loss of jobs for most of these women.

In the upper caste families, women are denied the right to work outside the home and it has been observed that elevation in caste status is preceded by the withdrawal of womenfolk from work outside the family. Among the urban middle classes, (upper caste) more flexibility seems to be operating than implied by the categories of public and private. Women's labour is used to meet the increasing inflation but to ensure that this does not erode its own control, private patriarchal authority brings into use ideology which on one hand highlights women's total commitment to the needs of the household and on the other consistently reiterates taboos against sexuality or reproduction outside family and caste mores. (Banerjee, 1992). There are then the controls exercised through actual physical abuse; wife beating, enforced seclusion, denial of basic necessities are common methods of exercising control, the elder women of the family, generally the mother-in-law being the enforcing agent. The unmarried girls are closely guarded and any transgression of norms results in their being withdrawn from public life; they are brought up to believe that their husbands' extended family is their final destination and that their parental home is only a transit lounge. (In all regional languages in India, unmarried girls are reflected as property that does not belong to the family). The post-independence Indian state has offered women equal facilities for education and training but in no way has it questioned or bypassed the household's authority to decide whether or not women can avail of any of these facilities (Banerjee, 1992). The state in all its programmes has maintained a 'woman within the family approach'. The women in India perform within the family many of the functions that have long been, at least partially, the responsibility of the state; alternative ways of fulfilling these functions would be extremely costly for the state. More importantly under modern rationalisations of 'cultural legitimacy', women have been kept within the family, rights for women outside the family would pose a threat to the caste system and thereby to the hegemony of the upper castes. The very fundamental rights and freedom granted by the Indian Constitution to all citizens; the right against forced labour, the freedom of movement, freedom of speech and expression have been denied to women by their families. Paradoxically, there is a strong tradition of according forms of responsibility and veneration to women as 'mothers'. Women can gain access to power in the family only as agents of domination and oppression of the younger women in the family, (Kishwar, 1991).

In case of the lower caste women the fact that their labour outside the family is crucial for the survival of the family, leads to the lack of stringent controls on their labour, mobility and sexuality and this renders them 'impure' or 'lacking in virtue'. In several instances the rape of Dalit women may not be considered as rape at all because of the customary access that the upper caste men have had to Dalit women's sexuality. In almost all regional languages in India the word for 'rape' is equivalent to the phrase 'stealing the honour of' and since lower caste women by the virtue of their double oppression have no 'honour' to speak of the right to redressal is often denied. In a recent incident at Birati in West Bengal, the police argued that since the women 'crying rape' were prostitutes the matter could be overlooked. (Sarkar, 1992). The legal courts too, operate along this ideology became apparent in the two cases of rape; one of a lower caste beggar woman (Laxmi) and the other of a tribal landless labourer (Mathura), in both the cases the courts acquitted the rapists who were policemen. Questions about the 'virtue' of these women were raised and it had been argued that their character was questionable. These cases were taken up by the women's movement in India and the supreme court pushed into reopening the cases and finally into amending the law against rape, to recognise custodial rape and to put the onus of proof on the rapist and not the woman. Dalit women suffer rape as a part of the ongoing caste confrontations. In rural India, defiance of caste restrictions by the Dalits have most often resulted in arson and gang rapes of women of the lower castes. If rape is at one end of the continuum of violent practices against lower caste women, there are the less obvious and also normalised practices such as the successive marginalisation of the lower caste performers and the attempts to reform them and their creative expressions; thereby pushing the majority of these artistes into hidden forms of prostitution. (Rege, 1992). The percentage of female headed households among the lower castes is as high as 70% to 75%; since the incidence of desertion is very high and even in cases where the husband is present, (often just his presence is seen as necessary by the women to ward off the sexual threat of the men from their community), it is the women's income that goes towards the survival of the family since the husbands income is spent on arrack or bigamy being common; the income goes towards the maintenance of the 'preferred' wife. Lower caste women in Andhra Pradesh have at the local level organised anti-arrack movements, in a way that threatens the state; since most of the state revenue comes from arrack. In Maharashtra, the 'deserted' women went on a march through the state in an attempt to draw the state's attention to the gravity of the problems and the issue of maintenance. (Samata Andolan, 1990). The situation of the Dalit women who are at the receiving end of both the upper caste and lower caste patriarchies, has been portrayed by Tersamma, a lower caste activist in a poem:

> "We go to work for we are poor,
> But the same silken beds mock us,
> While we are ravished in broad daylight,
> Ill-starred our horoscopes are,
> Even our tottering husbands hiss and shout for revenge;
> If we cannot stand their touch".
>
> (Quoted by Dietrich, 1990).

In rural India, the participation of Dalit women in the different local struggles for water, land or forests, has been on the increase. (Omvedt, 1992). These struggles have to a large extent regained from taking up the issue of violence against women. The women's movement which addresses the issues of sexuality and violence has been limited to the urban centres. In recent times, there have been at least three, widely reported cases of violence against the lower castes; (Chunduru in Andhra Pradesh, Gothala and Pimpri Deshmukh in Maharashtra) in which the lower caste men had been hacked to death, because of their alleged indecent behaviour towards upper caste women. The upper caste women in all the three cases had, it was reported, not only incited their menfolk into the violent acts but also participated in them. These cases present a problem for the feminist movement (Bhagwat and Rege, 1993) in that the alleged sexual harassment of the upper caste women by the lower caste males could be a 'cover up' for caste confrontations; in that the agency of upper caste women had been invoked in caste confrontations. (Prof. Gopal Guru's field reports support such an argument, Guru, 1991). Even if one grants that the upper caste women were being sexually harassed by the lower caste males, the issue has to be seen in the light of the years of sexual abuse of the Dalit women by the upper caste males and the customary sanctions that legitimised such violence. The cases pointed to the urgent need of coalitions between the women's movement and the Dalit movement; such coalitions require a historical analysis of the links between caste and gender, the next section attempts to contribute to such analysis.

A castewise analysis of the violent practices against women would reveal that the incidence of dowry murders, controls on mobility and sexuality by the family, widow burning are more frequent among the upper castes while Dalit women are more likely to face the collective threat of rape, sexual harassment and phy-sical violence. (Dietrich, 1990). This has implications for the sociological analysis of caste; volumes of which have overlooked the essential links between caste and gender; thereby rendering a partial understanding of the caste system. Castes and patriarchies have been maintained and reproduced through the 'textually mediated practices' (Smith, 1990) of sociology.

Sociologists, (under the influence of structure-functionalism), with varying emphasis, delineated the following characteristics of the caste system in India:

(i) Each linguistic division in India shows a wide variation of castes, about two hundred groups with distinct names, birth in one of which determines the status of an individual in society. These groups are further divided into sub-castes, which fix the limits for marriage and effective social life. Each caste had its own governing body, the 'caste and panchayat'; to this day several of the interfamilial and intrafamilial grievances are referred to these bodies. (Ghurye, 1956).

(ii) The caste system operates on a principle of hierarchy and difference. (Gupta, 1990). There is a scheme of social precedence amongst the castes, though this varies with the regions, in most cases it is the 'brahmins' who are at the top of the ritual scale and the 'untouchable' or the 'scavenger' castes at the bottom. Elevation in economic and political status for a caste can lead to a collective change in its position within the caste hierarchy. (Such changes, as mentioned earlier, have been accompanied by withdrawal of women from work outside the household).

(iii) The caste system outlined the religious and civil disabilities and privileges of the different castes, these ranged from the denial of use of public resources like wells, roads, temples, the denial to use certain kinds of clothing, housing and differential punishments by caste and definite restrictions on feeding and social intercourse. (Ghurye, 1956). (Such privileges of the upper castes also included the sexual rights of upper caste men over lower caste men). Though the Indian law marks discrimination by caste and the practise of untouchability a crime, such practices continue, especially in rural India.

(iv) The caste system restricted the choice of occupation; in a land based economy, the callings were based on heredity. This factor has undergone considerable change and there is no one to one correspondence between castes and occupations.

(v) The essence of the caste system according to most sociologists is the practise of endogamy or marriage within the sub-caste. Though there are exceptions to this rule in that some castes practised hypergamy, wherein to give ones daughter in marriage to a man of higher caste was a preferred form of marriage; the reverse - the marriage of a lower caste man with a woman of a higher caste was severely punished. (What sociologists have concealed under the rubrics of endogamy is the fact that women were and are the 'gateways' (Das, 1988) to the caste system).

The principles of caste and the rule of conduct for the different castes were codified in the 'shastras' or the instructional treatises of the Hindus which date back to the third century B.C. These were written by the 'Brahmins' or the priestly castes who legitimised the rule of the 'kshatriya' castes or the warrior castes. These rules were popularised through the 'Puranas' or mythological stories. In these treatises women have been equated to the lower castes and definite restrictions have been placed on both. Both have been defined as impure, of sinful birth and as having a polluting presence. Both the lower castes and women had to observe practices of verbal difference, temporal distance and dress codes as a index of their subordinate status. (Guha, 1983). Around 800 B.C. These treatises begin to make a definite division between the upper case women and those of the lower castes. In the 'Manusmriti', the most influential treatise, the realignment of castes and patriarchies is apparent in the 'ideology of the pativrata (one who worships the husband and his kin without any grievances)'. Becoming a 'pativrata' was posed as an alternative for upper caste women to rise above their sinful birth and an access to salvation. It was posited that an upper caste woman must always be under the control of her father, husband or son. (Kane, 1974). This ideology secured the compliance of the upper caste women and rendered them 'pure' as against the lower caste women. While strict controls over the sexuality and labour of upper caste women came to be legitimised; the social and sexual labour of the lower caste women was made available to the patrilineal land economy. Paradoxically, the very 'failure' of the lower caste men to control the sexuality of their women was projected as a major root of their impurity. In a patrilineal society, the caste determined not only the right to property but also the right to occupation. The upper two sections, the 'brahmins' and the 'kshatriyas' were not related directly to the land and monopoly was developed through clearcut ideas of purity and pollution. These ideas were linked to heredity and it became essential to prove that the women of the upper castes could not have sexual relations outside of their caste. However, there were no physical characteristics that could prove caste purity and the women of the upper castes in their daily routines did come in contact with the males of the potter, bangleseller and other artisan and lower castes. Hence severe restrictions came to be placed on women and 'chastity' of women assumed unwarranted importance, (Karandikar, 1988). This argument is further strengthened by the fact that the severe controls in the form of pre-puberty marriages and widow burning became most pronounced in those periods when 'brahminism' faced a threat whether from Buddhism or the 'Bhakti' and 'tantra' movements. Feminist writings on caste have argued that gender ideology that was constructed in these texts not only legitimised the structures of patriarchy but also the very organisation of caste. (Chakravarti 1992; Liddle and Joshi; 1986, Kannibaran and Kannibaran 1991). Vaid and Sangari have argued that the lives of women exist at their interface of caste and class inequalities and that the description and management of female sexuality is crucial to the reproduction of these inequalities. (Vaid and Sangari, 1990). The counterfactual to this argument may be seen in the challenges posed by the 'tantric' and 'bhakti' movement. The 'tantric' movement is seen in the form of different cults based on the folkways and worship of the mother goddesses. These cults focused on the release and celebration of sexual energies as against controls over sexuality. The ritual practices of thes cults involved the sexual intermingling of castes. These cults were brutally curbed or in some regions their revolutionary potential lost by their integration into mainstream Hinduism. The 'bhakti' movement on the other hand was a movement led by the poet saints who stressed the direct relationship of human beings, men and women alike, to God; thereby challenging the hegemony of the upper castes, mainly the 'brahmins' in their self proclaimed role of mediators between the divine and the human. However, this movement did not directly address this issue of sexuality and therefore of the caste based division of labour and this perhaps, partly explains, the relatively tolerant attitude of the 'brahmins' towards this movement. The medieval ages have been labelled as the 'dark ages' by the colonial historians and their 'brahmin' colluders; we suspect that the stories of the dark ages could well be the stories of rebellion.

To conclude, the issue of violence against women, cannot be seen as either a 'caste' issue or a 'gender' issue, but that it must be located in the links between the two. In a political system where dominant factions lobby, organise and mobilise along caste alliances of the rich and middle peasantry; effective action requires coalitions between the 'Dalit' and women's movements. In fact, delineating the 'real interest' of women requires the analysis of the complex interlinkages of gender and other structural inequalities or else the demands of the women's movement could well lead to the consolidation of some of these inequalities.

References

1. Agarwal, B. (ed): *Structures of Patriarchy; State, Community and Household in Modernising Asia*, Kali for Women, New Delhi, 1988.
2. Agarwal, B.: Women, Poverty and Agricultural Growth in India, *Journal of Peasant Studies*, Vol. 13, No. 4, July 1986.
3. Ambedkar, B.: *The Untouchables, who were they?*; Writings and Speeches, Vol. 7, Govt. of Maharashtra Publication.
4. Banerjee, N.: *Patriarchy and Work*, (under publication), IIAS, Shimla, 1992.
5. Banerjee, S.: 'Marginalisation of Women's Popular Culture in Nineteenth Century Bengal' in Vaid, S and K, Sangari (eds): *Recasting Women*, Kali for Women, 1990.

6. Balgopal, K.: Post-Chunduru and other Chundurus. *Economic and Political Weekly*, XXVI, 1991.
7. Bhagwat, V. and S. Rege: *Towards a Gender-Sensitive Sociology*, Paper presented at the UGC National Seminar, March, 1993.
8. Burton, A: The White Woman's Burden, *Women's Studies International Forum*, Vol. 13, No. 4, 1990.
9. Chatterjee, P.: 'The Nationalist Resolution of the Woman's Question' in Vaid and Sangari, 1990.
10. Choudhary, P.: 'Customs in a Peasant Society'. In Vaid and Sangari, 1990.
11. Dietrich, G.: *The Relationship between Dalit Movements and Women's Movement, Cases and Conceptual Analysis*, Paper for the IAWS, Calcutta, 1990.
12. Dietrich, G.: *Women, Ecology and Culture*, Paper for the IV National Conference on Women's studies, Andhra University, 1988.
13. Gandhi, N. and N. Shah.: *Issues at Stake*, Kali for Women, New Delhi, 1991.
14. Ghurye, G.: *Caste and Race in India*, Allied, Bombay, 1956.
15. Guha, R.: *Elementary Forms of Peasant Insurgency in India*, OUP, New Delhi, 1983.
16. Gupta, D.: *Stratification*, OUP, New Delhi, 1991.
17. Guru, Gopal Dalit killings in Marathwada, Economic and Political Weekly, Vol. xxvi, No. 51, Dec. 21, 1991.
18. Harding, S.: *Subjectivity, Experience and Knowledge; An Epistemology for/of Rainbow Coalition Politics*, Development and Change, Vol. 23, No. 3, Sage, 1992.
19. Joshi, R. and J. Liddle: *Daughters of Independence*, Kali, New Delhi, 1986.
20. Kannibaran, V. and Kannibaran, K., Caste and Gender: Understanding Dynamics of Power and Violence, *Economic and Political Weekly*, Sept. 14, 1991.
21. Kishwar, M. and R. Vanita: *In Search of Answers*; Horizon India Books, New Delhi, 1991.
22. Lukes, S.: *Essays in Social Theory*, MacMillan, London, 1974.
23. Lukes, S.: *Power: A Radical View*, MacMillan, London, 1974.
24. Mani, L.: Multiple Mediations, *Inscriptions*, No. 5, University of California, 1989.
25. Omvedt, G.: *Theories of Violence*, Kali for Women, New Delhi, 1991.
26. Parton, N.: Feminism Under the Raj, *Women's Studies International Forum*, Vol. 13, No. 4, 1990.
27. Ramusack, B.: Cultural Missionaries, Maternal Imperialists, Feminist Allis, *Women's Studies International Forum*, Vol. 13, No. 4, 1990.
28. Rege, S.: Sati: *A Critical Analysis*; Monograph, WSC, Department of Sociology, Univ. of Poona, 1989.
29. Sarkar, T.: Reflections on the Birati Rape Cases, *Economic and Political Weekly*, Feb. 2, 1981.
30. Tharu, S. and T. Niranjana: *Problems for a Contemporary Theory of Gender*, Investing Hyderabad, 1992.
31. *Towards Equality*, Report of the Committee on Status of Women in India, Ministry of India Publication, New Delhi, 1975.
32. Trikha, S.: *A study of Women's Employment in Kandla Free Trade Zone*, Mimeo, ICRIER, New Delhi, 1985.
33. Vaid, S. & K., Sangari: *Recasting Women*, Kali for Women, New Delhi, 1990.
34. Vaid, S. & K., Sangari: Sati in Modern India: A Report, *Economic and Political Weekly*, Vol. 16, No. 31, August 1987.
35. Wolf, G.: *Re-inventing Tradition*, (Under Publication) IIAS, Shimla, 1992.

4

"PEOPLE OF INDIA" : SOME PRIMA FACIE INFERENCES WITH REFERENCE TO SCHEDULED CASTES AND SCHEDULED TRIBES

C.K. Purandare

"There is nothing deep down inside us except what we have put there ourselves, no criterion that we have not created in the course of creating a practice, no standard of rationality, that is not our appeal to such a criterion, no rigorous argumentation that is not obedience to our own conventions."[1]

— *Richard Rorty in "The Consequences of Pragmatism"*

Introduction

This exploratory article is based on the massive survey by Anthropological Survey of India carried over 8 years from 1985 to 1992 on a nationwide scale. This has been one of the most ambitious and comprehensive efforts in documentation of human surface of India. A profile of Scheduled Castes (SCs) and Schedule Tribes (STs) with special emphasis on women among these as emerges from the 'National Consolidated Tables'[2] and statistical tables (Referred to as 'Survey' henceforth) is given in this article.

The Survey took 'community' as a unit of analysis "(M)embers of an endogamous caste group... tend to share cultural traits, so that between - group variation in cultural traits is significantly larger than the within-group variations. India's cultural diversity is therefore best investigated in terms of such endogamous caste groups. Presently however, this is an impossible task given the very large numbers of groups involved. These endogamous caste groups, however, form a small number of culturally homogeneous clusters. These correspond to the 'communities' investigated by the People of India project." (Joshi N.V. et al : 1993).

Information about communities was gathered through interviews "with a large number of people out of whom there were 26,463 key informants which works out to about six informed informants per community (. .). Of the informants, about 21% (i.e. 5661) were women. Interviews were conducted in connection with the study of the communities in 4513 villages, mostly multi community ones, and in 941 towns, spread over 438 districts of India and in 89 cultural regions. On an average, a community was studied at about two places." (Singh, K.S. : 1993)

Information on 776 individual items of information (called *Traits*) ranging over identity, ecology, food habits, occupation etc. was gathered on "2753 such communities making up 4635 elements when a community population in each State/Union territory is counted as a separate element." (Joshi N.V. et al Op cit).

The number of communities are analysed by the Survey along four categories: Constitutional, Religious, Occupational and Locational.

The Constitutional Category is sub-divided in four subcategories: All, Scheduled Castes (SCs), Scheduled Tribes (STs) and General. The sub-category 'All' gives total for the other three subcategories, which are mutually exclusive.

The Religious Category is divided in main religious subcategories viz. Hindu, Muslim, Christian, Sikh, Jain, Buddhist and Other - a residual/sub-category.

Occupational Category covers various sub-categories like Hunting and Gathering; Shifting Cultivation; Fishing; Animal Husbandry; Agriculture, Unskilled labour; Artisans; Unorganised services; Business, Trade and Industry; and Organised Services.

Locational Category comprises of Rural, Urban, Rural/Urban, Pastoral Nomad and Non-pastoral Nomad.

The arrangement of this paper is as below: A note on Methodology follows Introduction. A section (Section I) on Population based mainly on the data from Census-91[3] comes next. This section is expected to situate SCs and STs with respect to geographical distribution and demographic concentration at the State and District levels. A Table giving the main four categories and their sub-categories vis-a-vis number of communities in the country as per the Survey and a Table giving distribution of SCs and STs in different religions succeed the section on Population. Subsequent section (Section II) analyses select social, economic, etc. characteristics of SCs and STs as emerge from the Survey. The order of the characteristics - each dealing with a number of related traits, is kept roughly the same as that followed in the Survey.

In the absence of detailed back-up data, the inferences derived are to be treated as indicative than definitive. The numbers in paranthеses following each Trait refer to the relevant numbers in the Survey.

Methodology

For the section on 'Population' the state-level break-up of SCs and STs is supplemented by a district-level analysis for most of the states.

Number of districts in each state have been classified in two ways. Firstly, classification is done according to whether they fall above or below the National Average for the population for SCs and STs put together (National Average: 24.34%).

However, considering SCs and STs together does not denote their relative numerical strength within a District. E.g. in UP, of the 63 districts, 58 have STs at less than 1% of the population of the district and 50 have SCs more than the national average for SCs (16.33%). 17 districts of the state are above the national average—SCs and STs put together. This higher percentage is due to percentage of SC population *alone* being higher than 24.33%. Therefore, ratio of SC population to ST population (*P-value*) was taken for each district. This second classification gives districts falling in different ranges of P-values.

These ranges have been fixed arbitrarily, aim being to give an idea of composition of a district in SC and ST populations and as it is felt that the logic of numbers i.e. the relative numerical strength of SCs and STs would be one of the important factors in the process of evolution of Dalit Consciousness at the micro-level. This section is included to redress to some extent the lack of numerical back-up of the Survey.

For the section on findings of the Survey, mainly Constitutional Category is considered. This is so firstly because it lists SCs and STs specifically. Secondly, in other categories, the sub-categories are not necessarily always mutually exclusive. e.g. under Religious Category, 35 communities reported to be following *both* Hindu and Muslim religions or 116 as *both* Hindu and Christian religions. Instance like 1 community reporting to be *both* Jain and Sikh or 7 reporting to be Christian and Buddhist are there. Likewise there is an overlap when a community is engaged in more than one occupations, in the Occupational Category.

Comparisons are made with other sub-categories mainly 'Hindu'. The comparisons are NOT strictly correct as 'Hindu' includes a very large number of SC and a large number of ST communities. As can be seen from 'Distribution of SCs and STs among Religions' given below, there are 31.3% of communities belonging to SCs and STs put together among Hindus. A comparison is still made to locate SCs and STs vis-a-vis majority Hindus despite this overlap. Comparisons are therefore to be taken only as indicative and tentative.

It is important to note that the Survey gives the number of communities and *not* the population within a community. The number or percentage of communities within a particular sub-category for a particular item of information i.e. a *Trait*, therefore, does *not* correspond to actual number of people fulfilling that item of information. To illustrate, a few communities from sub-category Hindu may have a population of 5 lacs each and a few communities from a sub-category of Buddhist may have a population of 50,000 each. A particular item of information, say worshipping a village deity, may be practised by 1 community of Hindus and 2 communities of Buddhists. This would give 5 lac Hindu and 1 lac Buddhist worshippers. Now, if the total number of communities in Hindu is 100 and that in Buddhist is 20, in percentages, 1 percent of Hindu communities (1 in 100) and 10% of Buddhist communities (2 in 20) follow worship of a village deity. The percentage of commu-nities, which the Survey gives, may be 10 times more for Buddhists than for Hindus but the number of Hindus worshipping is 5 times that of Buddhists. This caveat applies for all the traits and jumping to absolute numerical correspondence from the number of communities or their percentages will be grossly misleading.

The occurrence of a trait in a community has also been checked to see if it is significantly higher or significantly lower than the National Proportion. This check is based on tables computed for each trait and each sub-category with standard deviation as a unit. The range of plus 4 to minus 4 (Z-value) virtually rules out any chance observation and gives a very high reliability of significance. This range is called National Proportion for the sake of this paper.

Total number of traits for which both - information regarding National Proportion and number of communities displaying a trait, are available is 699. SCs and STs have been classified for individual traits against National Proportion so that each trait fits in only one type given below:

Type 1 : Both SCs and STs above the National Proportion.
Type 2 : Both SCs and STs below the National Proportion.
Type 3 : Both SCs and STs within the National Proportion.
Type 4 : SCs above the National Proportion, STs within the National Proportion.
Type 5 : SCs above the National Proportion, STs below the National Proportion.
Type 6 : STs above the National Proportion, SCs within the National Proportion.
Type 7 : STs above the National Proportion, SCs below the National Proportion.

Type 8 : SCs within the National Proportion, STs below the National Proportion.

Type 9 : STs within the National Proportions, SCs below the National Proportion.

As can be seen, the first three types give the *traits shared* by SCs and STs.

The types from No. 4 to 9 give the traits in which *SCs and STs differ from each other.*

The same can be put in a tabular form:

SCs

STs		Above National Proportion	Within National Proportion	Below National Proportion
	Above National Proportion	Type 1	Type 6	Type 7
STs	Within National Proportion	Type 4	Type 3	Type 9
	Below National Proportion	Type 5	Type 8	Type 2

All the traits have also been classified in one more way. Demography, Class, Caste and Gender are the main axes along which this classification has been done. Traits associated with each of these have been classified accordingly.

'Demography' mainly covers traits dealing with size, number, natural environment of the communities. It also covers such food habits where apparently no ideology is involved. To illustrate: a trait like population below 5000 (Trait No. 43) (of a community) comes under 'Demography'. So too traits like: 'Natural Environment: Coast' (Trait No. 26) or 'Food Habits: Oil seeds: Mustard' (Trait No. 114), etc. 'Class' mainly covers the economic aspects like occupation, employment and resource access of a community. Thus 'Land holding community' (Trait No. 406) or 'Non-skilled labour

(Newly Acquired)' (Trait No. 533) or 'Employment through IRDP' (Trait No. 729) or 'Dependent on Money-lenders' (Trait No. 776), etc. come under 'Class'.

'Caste' mainly covers traits dealing with social norms and values, cultural practices, religious beliefs, purity - pollution observances, food-habits and change in food-habits invested with ideology. Thus 'Self Perception (of the community): Low (Trait No. 176); 'Varna: Aware' (Trait No. 177); 'Social Divisions exist' (Trait No. 153); 'Festivals: Socio-Political Significance' (Trait No. 615); 'Vegetarian: Pure' (Trait No. 77), etc. come under 'Caste'.

'Gender' covers such traits as are enlisted exclusively under women's role (whether in economic or non-economic spheres), status of women, almost all traits related with marriage, remarriage and divorce practices and those in which Gender is a prime consideration. Thus 'Women's Role: Bring Water' (Trait No. 344), 'Women's Role: Political Sphere' (Trait No. 349), Status of Women: Equal' (Trait No. 351) 'Dowry in Cash' (Trait No. 249) 'Remarriage: Widower' (Allowed) (Trait No. 290), 'Reason for Divorce: Impotency' (Trait No. 272), 'Polygyny: Sororal' (Trait No. 229), etc. are taken under 'Gender'. There are however a number of traits where boundaries between Gender and other two axes viz. Class and Caste are blurred. This is so mainly in case of Caste, to some extent in case of Class.

Caste - Traits like Method of Disposal of the dead - whether by burial or by cremation have a much remoter bearing on Gender than a trait like a community's treating Elopement to be an offence (Trait No. 572) or a trait like 'Circumcision (Male)' under Life-cycle Rituals (Trait No. 366).

While the burial or cremation practice is classified as a Caste Trait, the latter type traits are classified as 'Caste-Gender'.

Like-wise for a trait like 'Child labour' (Trait No. 551), both Class and Gender are found to be strong influencing axes. Dreze's[4] study of rural widows brings out an association between a widow's pauperisation due to lack of community support and incidence of child labour. Or a trait regarding succession rules prevailing in a community viz. 'Succession: Eldest Son' (Trait No. 327) perpetuates both Class and Gender systems.[5] Traits like these are classified as Class-Gender traits.

This classification along **Demography, Class, Caste, Gender, Class-Gender** and **Caste Gender** axes is purely arbitrary. A few traits can arguably be classified differently.

The point to be stressed is, however, that, the main thrust of the paper is to elaborate similarities and differences within SCs and STs. This thrust is in no way affected by how the traits themselves are classified. Similarities and differences are analysed along National Proportion. Therefore, if SCs are found to be above the National Proportion in a trait, say, 'Divorce Permissible', they remain above the National Proportion whether the trait is called a Gender trait or a Caste-Gender trait. And if SCs are above the National Proportion for a number of such traits, say 100, the total remains 100 howsoever the traits are classified.

Nevertheless, this value-judgemental classification is attempted so that the similarities and differences within SCs and STs and vis-a-vis Non-SCs-STs are 'coloured' and sharpened.

As it is not possible to cover an analysis of all the traits individually, the same have been clustered together for a particular characteristic. Still, it leaves a large number of traits unanalyzed. The selection of the traits has been arbitrary. This article also does not analyse whether any bias exists in the framing of the trait itself.

Section I

Population

Statewise population of SCs and STs as per Census 1991 is as follows:

India: Total population	: 84.63 crores
SCs	: 13.82 crores (16.33%)
STs	: 6.78 crores (8.01%)
Total of SCs & STs	: 20.60 crores (24.34%)

Table I.1 (Major States)

State	Total Population (in crores)	SCs Population	SCs Percentage	STs Population	STs Percentage
1. Andhra Pradesh	6.65	1.06	15.94	0.42	6.32
2. Assam	2.24	0.17	7.59	0.29	12.95
3. Bihar	8.64	1.26	14.58	0.66	7.64
4. Gujarat	4.13	0.31	7.51	0.62	15.01
5. Haryana	1.65	0.33	20	–	–
6. Himachal Pradesh	0.52	0.13	25	0.02	3.85
7. Karnataka	4.05	0.74	16.44	0.19	4.22
8. Kerala	2.91	0.29	9.93	0.03	1.03
9. Madhya Pradesh	6.62	0.96	14.50	1.54	23.26
10. Maharashtra	7.89	0.88	11.15	0.73	9.25
11. Orissa	3.17	0.51	16.01	0.07	22.08
12. Punjab	2.03	0.57	28.08	–	–
13. Rajasthan	4.40	0.76	17.27	0.55	12.05
14. Tamil Nadu	5.59	1.07	19.14	0.06	1.07
15. Uttar Pradesh	13.91	2.93	21.06	0.03	0.22
16. West Bengal	6.81	1.61	23.64	0.38	5.58
Total		13.58 crores		6.22 crores	

The smaller States and Union Territories show the following figures:

Table I.2

State/U.T.	Total Population (in lacs)	SC Population	SC Percentage	ST Population	ST Percentage
Arunachal Pradesh	8.65	0.04	0.46	5.5	63.58
Manipur	18.37	0.37	2.01	6.32	34.40
Meghalaya	17.75	0.09	0.51	15.18	85.52
Mizoram	6.90	0.01	0.01	6.54	94.78
Nagaland	12.10	–	–	10.61	87.69
Sikkim	4.06	0.24	5.91	0.91	22.41
Tripura	27.57	4.51	16.35	8.53	30.94
Andaman Nicobar	2.81	–	–	0.27	9.61
Chandigarh	6.42	1.06	16.51	–	–
Dadra and N.H.	1.38	0.03	2.17	1.09	78.99
Daman and Diu	1.02	0.04	3.92	0.12	11.76
Delhi	94.21	17.95	19.05	–	–
Goa	11.70	0.24	2.05	0.04	–
Pondicherry	8.08	1.31	16.21	–	–
Lakshadweep	0.52	–	–	0.48	92.31
Total		25.89 lacs		55.55 lacs	

There are two ways to look at the above tables.

One is to go by absolute numbers of SCs and STs which may indicate the impact-potential of a state in directing the course of policies affecting SCs or STs at the National level. Second way is to go by percentages of SCs and STs within the population of a State which may indicate intra-state heterogeneity and impact-potential of the groups within the State with the State population as 100. The percentage figure would also indicate extent of marginalisation or otherwise of SCs/STs and likely states where a potential for conflict with the 'mainstream' may be there.

SCs

Seen in absolute numbers, for major states and Delhi, UP at 2.93 crores has the largest concentration. 4 other States have populations of SCs above 1 crore. West Bengal 1.61, Bihar 1.26, Tamil Nadu 1.07 and Andhra Pradesh 1.06. Karnataka, Rajasthan, Maharashtra and M.P. have them from 74 to 96 lacs.

In percentage terms, Punjab has the maximum percentage at 28.08%, then West Bengal - 23.64%, U.P. - 21.06%, Delhi - 19.15%, Tamil Nadu - 19.14% and Rajasthan - 17.27% - all higher than the National average.

The total number of SCs in smaller States and U.Ts is 7.94 lacs, excl. Delhi. Of these Tripura accounts for 4.51 lacs, Pondicherry 1.31 lacs and Chandigarh 1.06 lacs leaving 1.06 lac of SCs among the rest. Chandigarh 16.51% and Tripura 16.35% are above the national average. There are no SCs in Nagaland, Andaman-Nicobar and Lakshadweep.

The extent of marginalization can be guessed by a look at the states at the lower than - national average. These, from the bottom for major states are:

Gujarat - 7.51%, Assam - 7.59%, Kerala - 9.93%, Maharashtra -11.15%

STs

In absolute numbers for major states, Madhya Pradesh has a population of STs at 1.54 crores followed by Maharashtra 73 lacs,

Orissa 70 lacs, Bihar 66 lacs, Gujarat 62 lacs and Rajasthan 55 lacs. There are none in Punjab and Haryana. In percentage terms, Madhya Pradesh 23.26%, Orissa 22.08%, Gujarat 15.01%, Assam 12.95%, Rajasthan 12.5% and Maharashtra 9.25% are above the national average.

The total number of STs in smaller states and UTs is 55.55 lacs, comparable with Rajasthan, ranking *6th* among the major States. Pondicherry, Delhi and Chandigarh have no STs.

Among the major States, STs are much below or below national average in UP - 0.22%, Kerala - 1.03%, Tamil Nadu - 1.07%, Himachal Pradesh - 3.85% and Karnataka - 4.22%.

SCs and STs

Next we consider the States/UTs above national average in percentage terms with both SCs and STs put together. The national average, it may be recalled, is 24.34%. There are 6 major States above the average. They are : Orissa - 38.18%, Madhya Pradesh - 37.76%, Rajasthan - 29.72%, West Bengal - 29.24%, Himachal Pradesh - 28.85% and Punjab - 28.08%. Among other States, except Kerala which is the lowest (10.96%) this percentage ranges between 19 to 22.22. For smaller/states and UTs, 3 groups may be considered. From the North-East-Meghalaya, Nagaland and Mizoram; and Dadra and Nagar Haveli and Lakshadweep have percentages from 80-95 all way above the national average. Middle range is topped by Arunachal at around 64% followed by Tripura, Manipur and Sikkim between 28-47% all above the national average. At lower range are Delhi, Pondicherry Chandigarh, Daman and Diu, Andaman and Nicobar - between 9 to 18%, all below the national average.

The State-level statistics, however, conceal more than they reveal. Particularly for STs, their pockets of concentration get reflected as the state level figure. The spread of SCs comparatively is more even.

The States of Arunachal, Meghalaya, Mizoram and Union Territories of Dadra & Nagar Haveli and Daman and Diu have less than

10,000 each of SC population. Nagaland and Union Territories of Andaman and Nicobar and Lakshadweep have no SCs.

State of Haryana, Union Territories of Delhi (as it was for Census - 91), Chandigarh and Pondicherry have no STs, Goa has only 376. These States are therefore left out of the analysis. 1991 Census was not conducted in Jammu & Kashmir which too is not covered. The States covered have a total population of SCs 12.73 crores and of STs 6.38 crores out of a total national population of 13.82 crores - SCs and 6.78 crores - STs.

The following table gives the number of districts having SC + ST population more than the national average against each state. It may be recalled that the national average is 24.34% (SCs – 16.33% + STs –8.01%).

Table I.3

State	Total number of Districts	Districts above National Average		
		SCs	STs	SCs+STs
Andhra Pradesh	23	14	7	6
Assam	23	Nil	14	8
Bihar	42	11	13	14
Gujarat	19	Nil	7	7
Himachal Pradesh	12	11	3	9
Karnataka	20	13	4	7
Kerala	14	Nil	1	Nil
Madhya Pradesh	45	22	32	39
Maharashtra	30	7	13	10
Manipur	8	Nil	5	5
Orissa	13	7	10	11
Rajasthan	27	17	14	16
Sikkim	4	Nil	4	3
Tamil Nadu	21	16	Nil	5
Tripura	3	1	3	3
Uttar Pradesh	63	50	1	17
West Bengal	17	13	6	13
Total	384	182	137	173

(The extreme cases where SCs or STs are in a very small minority are: Out of 384, 138 districts with ST population less than 1% of the district population; 1 district in Gujarat and 5 in Manipur with SC population less than 1% the district population.)

For comparing SC and ST populations with respect to each other, a ratio of SC population to ST population is computed for each district. (P-Value). The districts have been classified in different ranges of P-value. When P-value is in the range of 0.67 to 1.5, SC and ST populations are comparable i.e. either is 1 to 1.5 times the other. Figures less than 0.67 mean that in that particular district STs out-number SCs beyond this proportion i.e. they are more than 1.5 times SCs. Vice versa applies for figures more than 1.5 when SCs are more than 1.5 times STs. The ranges are as follows :

$p < 0.1$: STs more than 10 times SCs.
$0.1 < p < 0.67$: STs between 1.5 times to 10 times SCs.
$0.67 < p < 1.5$: SCs or STs within 1.5 times the other.
$5 > p > 1.5$: SCs 1.5 to 5 times STs.
$10 > p > 5$: SCs 5 to 10 times STs.
$100 > p > 10$: SCs 10 to 100 times STs.
$p > 100$: SCs more than 100 times STs.

The following table gives state-wise break-up of districts in these ranges. The figures in parantheses denote the number of districts above national average for SCs + STs falling in relevant range of P-value.

State	p<0.1	0.1<p<0.67	0.67<p<1.5	5>p>1.5	10>p>5	100>p>10	p>100
Andhra Pr.	Nil	2(1)	3(2)	10(3)	8	Nil	Nil
Assam	3(3)	11(4)	4(1)	2	Nil	3	Nil
Bihar	2(2)	4(4)	3(3)	6(1)	2(1)	9(1)	16(2)
Gujarat	1(1)	1(1)	Nil	3	4(3)	10(2)	Nil
Himachal Pr.	1(1)	1(1)	1(1)	Nil	Nil	Nil	9(6)
Karnataka	Nil	Nil	2(1)	9(5)	5(1)	4	Nil
Kerala	Nil	1	Nil	2	2	9	Nil
Madhya Pr.	4(4)	12(12)	11(11)	10(7)	5(3)	3(2)	Nil
Maharashtra	Nil	6(3)	5(5)	8(1)	4	7(1)	Nil
Manipur	4(4)	2(1)	1	1	Nil	Nil	Nil
Orissa	Nil	7(7)	2(2)	3(2)	1	Nil	Nil
Rajasthan	2(2)	1(1)	7(7)	8(5)	5	4(1)	Nil
Sikkim	1(1)	3(2)	Nil	Nil	Nil	Nil	Nil
Tamil Nadu	Nil	Nil	Nil	1	3(2)	13(2)	4(1)
Tripura	Nil	2(2)	1(1)	Nil	Nil	Nil	Nil
U.P.	Nil	Nil	Nil	2	2	6(1)	53(16)
W. Bengal	Nil	Nil	2(2)	7(7)	2(1)	6(3)	Nil
Total:	18(18)	53(39)	42(36)	72(31)	43(11)	74(13)	82(25)

At extreme end are 53 districts in UP, 16 in Bihar and 9 in Himachal where SCs are more than 100 or even 1000 times STs. The population of STs in such districts is in tens and hundreds in some cases, and a few thousand in many cases. In 74 districts SCs are more than 10 times STs and in 18 districts reverse is the case.

It is to be noted that for p < 0.1, > 10 and > 100 there are 56 districts having SC + ST population *above the national average.*

The national average can be considered as a threshold figure as, at 24.33%, the group may be in a position to make its presence felt and subvert attempts to ignore its interests on its own numerical strength. But, in these 56 districts, it is difficult to foresee how either SC or ST, depending upon who is smaller, can have enough leverage to affect the political agenda.

In that case, the pursuit of social, economic, gender and resultant political interests (which are different for SCs and STs as the following analysis of the Survey shows) can be backed up by respective numerical strength in districts where the ratio is in the neighbourhood of 0.67 to 1.5. Beyond this, divergence of interests does not have this back-up and unequal partnership may result.

This gives 42 districts of which 36 are above national average. Going only by the logic of numbers, convergence of interests of SCs and STs under a single banner may be more meaningful in these 36 districts. These districts are as follows:

Andhra Pradesh	: Adilabad and Warangal.
Assam	: Marigaon.
Bihar	: Palamu, Deoghar and Giridih.
Himachal	: Chamba.
Karnataka	: Chitradurga.
Madhya Pradesh	: Dewas, Hoshangabad, Raisen, Narsimhpur, Jabalpur, Panna, Satna, Rewa, Durg, Bilaspur and Raipur.
Maharashtra	: Amravati, Nagpur, Bhandara, Chandrapur and Wardha.
Orissa	: Dhenkanal and Balangir.
Rajasthan	: Jaipur, Sawai-Madhopur, Kota, Jhalawar, Bundi, Chittorgarh and Sirohi.
Tripura	: West Tripura.
West Bengal	: Darjiling, Purulia.

Geographically three major and one smaller clusters of districts among these are seen to be contiguous. In Rajasthan from Jaipur to Chittorgarh in the order mentioned above all the districts are contiguous in Southern part of the State leaving only Sirohi in the west.

(The intervening district Udaipur sharing boundaries with Sirohi in the West and Chittorgarh in the East is above the National Average but has P-value of 0.23).

In Madhya Pradesh from Dewas eastward, upto Jabalpur and then northward upto Rewa 8 districts in the order mentioned above form a belt. Durg, Bilaspur and Raipur in the Southeastern part of the State are one more cluster. In Maharashtra the 5 districts are again contiguous. Adilabad in Andhra shares boundary on the North with Chandrapur.

Rest of the districts are more or less isolated.

Further analysis at Block level may show to what extent Class, Caste and Gender interests of SCs and STs match or otherwise. Ecologically, however, they seem to be in a uniform system in the clusters mentioned above.

Following two tables are from the Survey :

Table 1. All-India distribution of communities in various categories.

Category	Sub-category	Number of communities
1. Constitutional	1.1 All	4635
	1.2 SC	751
	1.3 ST	636
	1.4 General	3248
2. Religious	2.1 Hindu	3539
	2.2 Muslim	584
	2.3 Christian	339
	2.4 Sikh	130
	2.5 Jain	100
	2.6 Buddhist	93
	2.7 Other	427
3. Occupational	3.1 Hunting & Gathering	484
	3.2 Shifting cultivation	262
	3.3 Fishing	454

Category	Sub-category	Number of communities
	3.4 Animal Husbandry	1152
	3.5 Agriculture	2943
	3.6 Unskilled labourers	2922
	3.7 Artisans	1621
	3.8 Unorganised services	1487
	3.9 Business & Trade & Industry	2653
	3.10 Organised services	3690
4. Locational	4.1 Rural	2779
	4.2 Urban	393
	4.3 Rural & Urban	1336
	4.4 Pastoral Nomads	37
	4.5 Non-pastoral Nomads	276

Note:- Following occupational sub-categories cover:

3.5 Agriculture: Agriculture labour, Tenant share cultivation, Plantation labour, cultivation etc.

3.6 Unskilled Labour: Bamboo work, Begging, Rickshawpulling, Cart-pulling, Forest Labour, Sweepers, Earth Digging etc.

3.7 Artisans: Agricultural implement making, Blacksmithy, Cloth & leather embroidery, Goldsmithy, Coir making, Carving, Mat-weaving, Metal work, various Cloth-weavings etc.

3.8 Unorganized services: Dancers, Combmaking, Brick-making, Astrologers, Bow & arrow making, exorcists, Wig making, Snake charming, Washerman, Thieving etc.

3.9 Business, Trade & Industry: Bakery, Butchery, Grocery, Jute, Coir, Fruit, Vegetables, selling, Money lending, Private shops etc.

3.10 Organised Services: Teachers, Village messengers, Police, Temple management, Land-lords, Contractors, Village accountants, Professionals like doctors, lawyers etc. in the Survey.

Table 2. Distribution of SCs and STs among religions

Religious	Sub-category	SCs		STs	
Religion	Total No. of communities	No. of communities	% (3) to (2)	No. of communities	% (5) to (2)
(1)	(2)	(3)	(4)	(5)	(6)
Hindu	3539	728	20.6	378	10.7
Muslim	584	5	0.9	19	3.3
Christians	339	21	6.2	149	44.0
Sikh	130	38	29.2	0	0
Jain	100	0	0	0	0
Buddhist	93	12	12.9	44	47.3
Other	427	24	5.6	300	70.3

Section II

Type 1: Traits for which both SCs and STs are above the National Proportion

1.1 Demography:

1.1.1 Population (Trait Nos. 43 to 47)

Of the total 751 SC communities, the Survey gives a break-up for 631. Of them, 268 have a population of 5,000 or below. 62 are between 5-10,000; 84 between 10-20,000, 115 between 20-100,000; 65 between 1-500,000 and 37 above 5 lacs. Thus a major number of communities (414) are less than 20,000 strong each. If the 115 upto 1 lac each are added, it leaves only 102 communities with a population of 1 lac and above.

For STs, of the 636 communities, the Survey gives break up of 481 communities. Of these, 176 are below 5,000 and only 71 are above 1 lac. STs fall within the National Proportion for communities with population 5 lac & above. Thus both SCs & STs tend to have a large number of communities with smaller populations.

We may recall that the definition of a community entails a distinct socio-cultural system. These two factors - smaller population and larger number of such communities are likely to portend internecine tension during a process of bringing SCs & STs on a single platform.

There is also room to infer that the smaller communities are located in different ecological zones, as wide apart as Kerala to Himachal Pradesh to Arunachal Pradesh. (These states show higher than the national proportion for ranges of population above.) However, the data does not point to a definite correspondence of State - SCs or STs - Size of the community. If so, i.e. if the smaller of SC or ST communities are indeed so widely spaced it would be an additional factor contributing to divergence of interests within SCs and STs.

1.2 Class

The Class characteristics of SCs & STs can be judged by considering following traits. To reiterate, for all these traits SCs & STs are significantly higher than the National Proportion.

For 50% of SC & ST communities each 'Labour' is a 'newly acquired' means of livelihood. (Trait No. 501). While increase of Agricultural labour among STs is more than that in SCs (Trait No. 547), reverse is the case for increase in wage labour (Trait No. 546). Within 'Labour', Non-skilled Labour (Current, as against Traditional or Newly Acquired) (Trait No. 449) obtains in 32.9% communities each in SCs & STs. Both have a large number of communities who seek employment through IRDP (Trait No. 729) (475 out of 751 - SCs i.e. 63.2% & 499 out of 636 - STs i.e. 78.5%). The economy is also not fully monetised, it is 'Barter & Cash' (Trait No. 544) for 145 SC & 166 ST communities.

Basket Making (Current & Traditional) (Trait Nos. 444 & 486), Mat-weaving (Current & Traditional) (Trait No. 445 & 487) and Piggery (Trait No. 735) are the occupations where SCs & STs come under Type 1 i.e. are above the National Proportion. Dependence on Firewood as a fuel resource (Trait No. 756) is also higher for SCs & STs. This trait has a bearing on Gender and it is commented on under 'Women's Role: Collect Fuel', under Gender.

Considering the process of SCs & STs joining the unskilled labour market, one may say that they are pauperizing selectively over the others, and in a big way.

1.3 Caste

1.3.1 Food habits:

Women non-vegetarian (Trait No. 90), Non-vegetarian - Pork (Trait No. 94) Eat-Carrion (Trait No. 95) Alcoholic Drinks: Occasional: women (Trait No. 126) and Alcoholic Drinks: Regular: Men (Trait No. 127). These traits may be seen to be likely impediment in intermarriages with vegetarian communities, vegetarianism being vested with ideology. For comparison, women are non-vegetarian in 81.9% of SC & 86.8% of ST communities. In Hindus they are non-vegetarian in 70.5% in Sikhs 67.7%, in Buddhists in 78.5% and in Muslims, Christians & Other religion-followers, more than 83% each. Jains at 1% are the lowest.

1.4 Gender

1.4.1 Divorce

Divorce is permissible (Trait No. 264) in more than 91% of SC & ST communities each. It has social approval (Trait No. 266) in more than 76% of communities each. Either Party can seek divorce in more than 86% of communities each. (Trait No. 284).

The Survey lists 9 reasons for divorce. The number of communities citing a particular reason follows a pattern not only among SCs & STs but roughly also across religious, occupational and locational categories. For SCs & STs the reasons in the descending order of number of communities citing that reason are: Maladjustment, Adultery, Cruelty, Barrenness, Impotency, Insanity, Chronic sickness, Sorcery and No Male Issue. Thus Maladjustment and Adultery occur in maximum number of communities and No Male Issue in the least, or near the least. Only Adultery falls in Type 1. Other reasons have been enumerated under various Types depending upon SCs' & STs' proportion vis-a-vis National Proportion. Still, these are covered here to give an overall idea about 'Divorce'.

'No Male Issue' (Trait No. 270) is a reason in 28 (4.4%) ST communities, the lowest figure among causes of divorce, and in 57 (7.6%) SCs - Second-lowest figure (lowest being 'sorcery' Trait No. 276). The figures across the 3 categories are comparable in percentages. Only among Sikhs at 17.7% and in Other (i.e. followers of other than the listed religions) at 11.9% it is more than 9%.

The number of communities seeking divorce due to Barrenness (Trait No. 269) is almost equal to those seeking it due to Impotency (Trait No. 272). One would expect Impotency to be a cause in much *less* number of communities if only woman is held responsible for lack of a child. e.g. number of communities citing barrenness and impotency as causes respectively are: Hindus - 970 (27.4%) and 862 (24.4%), Christians - 50 (38.5%) and 46 (35.4%). The differential in percentage is more than 10% only in muslims.

Patriarchy, however, may be operating at subterranean level. Maladjustment (Trait No. 271) is a cause in more than 70% of almost all subcategories under other 3 categories. For SCs it is in 594 (79.1%) and in STs in 515 (81%) communities. What constitutes maladjustment and who decides it? Adultery (Trait No. 268), the only Trait under Type 1, to reiterate, is a cause in 518 (69%) SC & 502 (78.9%) ST communities. Across other subcategories it is mostly in more than 50% communities. Is it alleged adultery by wife or by husband and who corroborates the allegation? These two causes are likely to be more man-friendly than woman-friendly. The third major cause, again across all categories, is cruelty (Trait No. 274), more likely by the husband than otherwise. Insanity (Trait No. 275) is a cause in 126 (16.8%) SC and 148 (23.3%) ST communities. The percentage is comparable across most of the other subcategories. If insanity is genuine, this is an alarmingly high figure. Domestic violence in conjunction with other forms of harassment, if it rebounds more on women than on men, is likely to be one of the major causes of insanity. If it is alleged so as to foreclose any possibility of a rapproachment, again more likely that man is in a stronger position to allege so.

Violence against women seems to be a more weightier cause than preference to a child or a male child. This inference seems closer to radical feminist position as far as material explanation for women's oppression is sought in violence. But it also seems to undermine a premise of radical feminism that "... the whole weight of culture makes clear that having sex and having children (sons in particular) are things wives owe to their husbands...." (Delphy & Leonard: 1992) Reproductivity does *not* come out as a priority to an extent that lack of it would lead to divorce.

Another inference that can be drawn is that if cruelty or maladjustment leads to divorce is such a high proportion of all the communities, the incidence must be much more wide-spread in the families where it does not come upto divorce. The incidence of bigamy or desertion of wife is also reported to be quite high without recourse to divorce.[6]

1.4.2 Bride-Price/Dowry

Bride-Price (Cash, as against Kind or Cash & Kind) (Trait No. 245) exists in 153 communities in SC (20.4%) and 146 in STs (23%).

It may be mentioned that prevalence of bride price does not preclude dowry, as a few communities from both SCs & STs are reported to be having both the practices.

1.4.3 *Remarriage*

In allowing remarriage of widows (Trait No. 289) SCs & STs are more liberal than Hindus. 711 (94.7%) SC and 609 (95.8%) ST communities allow this. For Hindus the percentage is 76.6% and for Jains it is the lowest among all categories at 28.0%. For female divorcee (Trait No. 292) 658 (87.5%) SC & 573 (90.1%) ST communities allow remarriage. For Hindus and Jains the figures are 73.4% & 29% respectively. Remarriage of male divorcee (Trait No. 291) is allowed in about 91% of SC & ST communities each; in 80.3% Hindu and 36% Jain.

Though remarriage of widower (Trait No. 290) does not fall in this Type - SCs & STs being within National Proportion - the figures are worth mentioning for comparison. Among Hindus, 96.4% communities allow it, in SCs - 98.9 % and in STs 93.7%. For Jains it is 97% of communities. The differential between widower's & widow's remarriage, if taken as an index of *lack* of autonomy of women for remarriage on the loss of husband, it is much higher in Hindus (17.8%) than in SCs & STs. In fact, for STs, less number of communities (596) have widower remarrying than widow remarrying (609). For Jains, of course, the differential is huge at 69%.

Levirate: Junior (Trait No. 210) (widow marrying late husband's younger brother) is a practice in almost 40% of SC & ST communities each. It is interesting to note that among other religious sub-categories, Muslims also come above the National Proportion in all the above traits related to remarriage alongwith SCs & STs.

Regarding Divorce traits, SCs & STs appear to be more egalitarian than other communities with respect to women.

The practice of Levirate however needs some comment. It is reported,[7] particularly from some landholding communities in North India, that Levirate being 'permissible' means a widow is compelled to remarry her brother-in-law so that land is not partitioned and is kept within the family. If the widow does not have support of the community or natal family, alternative to her is destitution and starvation.

1.4.4 *Women's Role*

Women's role in Animal Husbandry and other economic activities contributing to income is quite high in SCs & STs (Trait Nos. 342, 345, 356, 357) *Additionally,* they are also responsible for collection of fuel and water. (Trait Nos. 343, 344 resp.). Fuel & fodder collection is reported to be increasingly difficult. The dependence for these is mainly on Communal Property Resources. (CPR) Fire wood remains the main source of fuel. In the hills and desert areas of the north,[8] CPR provides 67.69% of the domestic energy. It provides 91-100% of firewood, 66.84% of all domestic fuel and 69.89% of the grazing needs of the landless and the land poor in semi-arid areas. With shrinkage in CPRs the survival systems become increasingly fragile. The dependence on firewood and it being almost exclusively women's job; coupled with the landless or landpoor nature of SCs particularly, as seen below, contribute more to women's hardships.

1.5 Class-Gender

1.5.1 *Perception of Developmental Programmes and their Impact: Formal Education*

Boys' and girls' education upto primary level (Trait Nos. 686 and 694) seems to be acceptable to both SCs & STs above the National Proportion. However, as mentioned in the next section this is not to be construed as an attitude favourable to education in general. Rather, response to these two traits seems specifically connected with the level of education i.e. primary education.

1.6 Caste - Gender

1.6.1 In forms of Punishment by the community (Table 26.1), Adultery (Trait No. 570), Rape (Trait No. 571) and Elopement (Trait No. 572) are treated as offence, presumably meritting punishment.

In all these offences, though both SCs & STs are above the National Proportion, between them, STs are still higher. Within the offences, more number of communities consider Adultery as an offence (62.3 % - SCs & 75.8% STs) than Rape (35% SC and 39.3% ST) Elopement is closer in No. of communities to Rape as an offence on a higher side for both. It is not clear whether Adultery by either husband or wife is considered an offence i.e. who defines Adultery - whether either spouse and community or husband and the community.

Type 2: Traits for which both SCs & STs are below the National Proportion

2.1 Class

2.1.1 Middle Class

The proportion of formally educated persons is lower among SCs & STs. For the traits - Professionals: Entrepreneurs/Businessmen (Trait No. 671), Scholars (Trait No. 672), White-Collar Employees (Trait No. 674), Administrators (Trait No. 676), Engineers/Doctors (Trait No. 677) both SCs & STs lag behind. If formation of Middle-Class is a yardstick of upward social mobility, both come out quite weak, and SCs come weaker than STs. Among religious sub-categories, Jains and Christians are above the National Proportion in all these traits.

Relatedly, both SCs & STs trail in Business (Current and Traditional) (Trait Nos. 422 and 464 resp.), Industry (Current) (Trait No. 424), Employment through Small-Scale Industry (Trait No. 737) and Employment through General Merchandise (Trait No. 739).

2.1.2 Consumption

On the consumption side this is reflected in less SCs and STs watching television (Trait No. 746), using electricity (Trait No. 755) and using kerosene as fuel (Trait No. 760).

2.1.3 Savings

The trait 'Savings Favoured' (Trait No. 775) also features negatively for both.

2.2 Caste

2.2.1 Food Habits

Pure vegetarianism (Trait No. 77), proportion of vegetable being high (Trait No. 86), Women: Vegetarian (Trait No. 89) and consumption of non-alcoholic drinks (Trait No. 124) are the traits under type 2, i.e. less proportion of SC & ST communities are pure vegetarian and so on, than the National Proportion.

2.3 Class - Gender

2.3.1 Education

Here, both SCs & STs fall significantly below National Proportion in their attitude towards either Boys' or Girls' Education (Trait Nos. 682 & 683 resp.) Muslims share this negative attitude towards Girls' Education with SCs & STs, Jains & Christians are above the National Proportion for both boys and girls which finds a corroboration in these two communities being over-represented in 'Middle Class'.

Boys' education upto college level (Trait No. 688), upto Post graduate level (Trait No. 689) and Girls' education upto college level (Trait No. 696) are also perceived as a developmental activity in less number of SC & ST communities than the National Proportion.

2.3.2 Number of Children

SCs & STs prefer more than two children. They score negatively on the Trait 'Prefer one/two children'. (Trait No. 709) Decision regarding number of children to have, if does not vest with the wife equally, implications to woman's reproductive autonomy are obvious. Spacing of children and family planning methods adopted are related issues, the latter being covered separately.

Type 3: SCs & STs both within the National Proportion

3.1.1 Identification

In whether a community identifies itself regionally (Trait No. 2), nationally (Trait No. 3), internationally (Trait No. 4), SCs & STs are within the National Proportion. Hindus are below the National Proportion in Identification: Transnational and Buddhists and Muslims above it. Jains & Sikhs are above the National Proportion in Identification: National.

3.1.2 Distribution

In the Distribution of a community whether Regional (Trait No. 15) or National (Trait No. 17) SCs & STs are under Type 3.

3.1.3 Other traits: Those related to Natural Environment

Desert of Valley; High humidity; Medium or scanty rainfull etc. find SCs & STs within the said proportion. So too are traits regarding food habits like staple foods, oil seeds and pulses. These have not been gone into details.

3.1.4 Migration to present habitat

This has been in recent years (Trait No. 13) for 79 (10.5%) SC & 47 (7.4%) ST communities.

Though this is a small number, if migration is more out of lack of choice than by choice it entails trauma. For some SC migrant communities in Maharashtra like Kanjarbhat, Dangat, Vaidu, Joshi, Gondhali, Vanjara etc. migration has been found to be hitting women harder than men. A dependency syndrome arising out of continuing insecurity, lack of social network, lack of community and legal support, detrimental neglect of own & children's health and children's education are some of the problems reported, by field activists. Other traits related to migration are covered under relevant types. It may however be mentioned that migration in historical account (Trait No. 12) or that in oral tradition (Trait No. 11) are qualitatively different from migration in recent years. The former may be more a community signifier than due to economic reasons as the latter is. The Survey, however, does not touch upon cause of migration; the same has to be inferred from other traits like change in occupation etc.

3.2 Class

The class traits shared by SCs & STs with the rest of the communities in the country are mostly dealing with the nature of occupations. These cover various trades like textile dyeing, masonry, pottery, self-employment (Newly Acquired), skilled labour (Traditional) woodwork etc. Agricultural land relations like Landlord Tenant Relationship (Trait No. 668), Cultivator - Labour Relationship (Trait No. 669) also fall under this type. In avenues of employment, employment through Employment Guarantee Scheme (Trait No. 730) is sought by 86 communities each.

3.3 Caste

3.3.1 Social Division (Table No. 7.0 & 7.1)

Social divisions exist (Trait No. 153) within SCs & STs. The National Proportion itself being quite high, SCs & STs being within it means that they are *equally divided* among themselves. Across the 4 categories the percentage of communities in which social divisions exist ranges from 74 to 93 (except Muslims - 52.6%). For SCs - 87.1% STs - 83% are the figures. Hindus are above the National Proportion and Muslims below it.

However nature of Social Divisions seems more horizontal than vertical as Hierarchy with Social Divisions (Trait No. 162) exists in much less number of communities across all the 4 categories. This trait is observed in 189 (25.2%) SC and 160 (25.2%) ST communities.

The difference among social groups is reported by the Survey at various levels: Social (Trait No. 163), Economic (Trait No. 164), Religious (Trait No. 165), Territorial (Trait No. 166), Occupational (Trait No. 167) and Educational (Trait No. 168). Of these the major level is social level where more than 54% each SC & ST communities are reported but this trait is covered under Type 4. For the rest of the traits coming under Type 3, the maximum figure is 125 (16.5%) SC communities where difference is at occupational level.

3.3.2 Festivals and their significnace (Table No. 30.0)

Not only among SCs & STs but across all religious sub-categories festivals retain mainly socio-religious significance (Trait No. 613).

559 (74.4%) SC and 437 (68.7%) ST communities show this trait. Next comes religious significance (Trait No. 611) 172 (22.9%) SC and 212 (33.3%) ST communities. Christians and Muslims are above the National Proportion in ascribing religious significance to festivals while Hindus are below it. Socio-political significance (Trait No. 615) to festivals obtains only in 9 communities each. Only Buddhists are above the National Proportion for this trait. In Sikhs no community and in muslims only 2 communities are found for this trait.

3.4 Gender

3.4.1 Marriage & Remarriage

Community endogamy (Trait No. 187) is the norm among SCs and STs as it is among religious, occupational and locational categories. The least figure is 94.6% for Pastoral Nomads in the last category. 723 (96.3%) SC and 615 (96.7%) ST communities follow the practice. Surname exogamy (Trait No. 198) and village exogamy (Trait No. 195) are followed by less than 15% of SC or ST communities each.

Child Marriage is allowed (Trait No. 212) in 61 (8.1%) SC and 67 (10.5%) ST communities. For religious sub-categories following are the figures: Hindu - 7.4%, Muslim - 7.7%, Christians - 1.8%, Sikhs - 1.5%, Jains - 2.0%, Buddhists - 3.2% and Other 9.4%. Hunting and Non-pastoral communities are above the National Proportion.

Adult Marriage (Trait No. 214) is followed by more than 86% of SCs and STs. Monogamy (Trait No. 226) is a norm among 99.1% SCs and 97.5% STs. Muslims are below National Proportion in this Trait.

Remarriage is liberalized (Trait No. 303) in 130 (17.3%) SC and 105 (16.5%) ST communities. The increase in divorce rate of Sikhs as seen below, seems to be set off by an increase in liberalization of remarriage as at 39.2% they top the religious sub-categories.

Sororate is permissible (Trait No. 293) in a large number of communities. SC: 622 (82.8%) and ST: 494 (77.7%). As for levirate, 'permissibility' may mean it to be a widower's *right* to marry the deceased wife's sister with little choice to the sister. (Relatedly, sororal polygyny (Trait No. 229) is prevalent in 12.8% SC & 24.1% ST communities while polyandry - fraternal or nonfraternal (Trait Nos. 227, 228) prevails in zero to 2.4% only communities - SCs or STs. These traits, however, do not come under Type 3).

Within sororate, Junior sororate (Trait No. 208) - marrying deceased wife's younger sister is quite prevalent - 474 (63.1%) SC and 390 (61.3%) ST communities report this. Senior sororate (Trait No. 209) is rare - in 5 to 7% of communities each.

3.4.2 Divorce

Divorce due to Chronic Sickness (Trait No. 273) - 88 (11.7%) SC & 115 (18.1%) ST communities; that due to Insanity (Trait No. 275) - 126 (16.8%) SC & 148 (23.3%) ST communities; and due to No Male Issue (Trait No. 270) fall under this type.

The rate of Divorce, whatever be the cause, is declining (Trait No. 300) in 175 (23.3%) SC and 147 (23.1%) ST communities. It is increasing (Trait No. 301) in 78 (10.4%) SC and 54 (8.5%) ST communities. Marriage as an institution seems to be stabilizing going by the difference between increase and decrease figures. Internalization of marriage as an ideology and confining marital discord to 'private sphere' or recourse to non-divorce means as stated earlier may be the off-shoots. This pattern is observed in all the religious sub-categories except in Jains where decline and increase are matched in terms of number of communities, and in Sikhs where increase is in more number of communities than decrease.

3.4.3 Liability of Children

After divorce, children become a liability of father (Tr. No. 285) in 42.1% SC & 45.6% ST communities. Next comes their becoming a liability of either father or mother (Trait No. 287) 34.2% SC and 28.8% ST communities. But they become a liability of mother (Trait No. 286) only in a small number of communities. 7.9% in SC and 8.6% in STs. This finding gives more than one interpretations. Firstly, 'mother-only' is relegated. It may be that she prefers to have custody of children but has no wherewithal to provide for them vis-a-vis father - particularly if support from the natal family or community is not forthcoming. Then it may be in the material (only) interest of the children to be a liability of the father though it deprives mother and children of each other. On the other hand, the father may not want this liability though has wherewithal to look after them and he may not de facto look after them. Community seems to be playing a decisive role which may not always be in the interests of the mother.

3.4.4 Status & Role of Women

Though SCs and STs are within the National Proportion for Status of Women: Equal (Trait No. 351) and Status of Women: Low (Trait No. 353), the difference between the number of communities corresponding to each trait is considerable. Status is equal in 160 (21.3%) SC and 180 (28.3%) ST communities; Low in 548 (73%) SC and 436 (68.6%) ST communities.

Traits regarding women's economic role and spaces of autonomy they enjoy in various communities give an unclear picture with respect to association between the two.

For SCs & STs, women have a role in economic activity in more than 88% communities each and they contribute to income in more than 90% communities each as noted in Type 1.

For SCs & STs, 5 traits fall under Type 3 which may be taken to some extent as indices of autonomy. These are; in the descending order of number of communities involved:

Women's Role in Social Function (Trait No. 346) - More than 88% each, Women: Control Expenditure (Trait No. 358): more than 43% each; Women in Decision Making (Trait No. 354): about 20% each; Women's Role: Political Sphere: (Trait No. 349) about 13% each and a role in Social Control (Trait No. 350): about 5 to 9% each.

Similar pattern is observed for Hindus with comparable figures, for Muslims with smaller figures. For Christians, Sikhs and Jain, however, each seems to follow a different pattern altogether. Jains, for example have only 39% communities in which women contribute to income but in 62% communities they control expenditure. Women's role in political sphere (27.7%) is the highest among all sub-categories in Sikhs but they show a relatively smaller figure for economic participation. In the absence of any back up data it is difficult to interpret such findings within the extant frameworks of feminism viz. Liberal, Marxist, Socialist or Radical.

3.4.5 Family Planning

Sterilization: Generally Men (Trait No. 714) is followed by only 60 SC & 55 ST communities as against in 288 SC and 196 ST communities it is generally women who are sterilized (Trait No. 715).

3.5 Class - Gender

3.5.1 Inheritance

The system of inheritance/succession shows the same gender bias operating in the society at large, within SCs and STs also. Thus male equigeniture, i.e. property to be divided equally among the sons (Trait No. 323) is the norm followed by 619 out of 751 SC & 479 out of 636 ST communities. Only Muslims and Christians show a less-than-the National Proportion for this trait. Equigeniture, i.e. both male & female children inheriting equally (Trait No. 322) is followed by 92 SC & 56 ST communities 12.3% & 8.8% resp. For this trait too, they are within the National Proportion. Succession by Adopted Son (Trait No. 331) or Succession by Nephew (Trait No. 333) are marginal cases (Less than 4% each in the Type 3.)

3.5.2 Drop-out of Formal Education

Boys drop-out of school as they are required to earn to support the family (Trait No. 692) in 437 SC and 386 ST communities-more than 58% each.

3.6 Caste-Gender

3.6.1 Family

More than 89 % SC & ST communities each report to be nuclear

(Trait No. 304). Vertically extended family (Trait No. 305) is reported in more than 49% each of SCs & STs.

3 reasons for familial conflicts are covered by the Survey. Of these, conflict due to check on freedom (Trait No. 316) and due to challenge to Authority (Trait No. 317), both presumably having implications on generational and gender relations, fall under this Type. Between 25 to 33% SC and ST communities each have such conflicts. The family conflict however arises mainly on account of property (Trait No. 315) in more than 77% of communities each. For this trait, SCs are below National Proportion and STs within it. Hence it is enumerated under Type 9.

Type 4: SCs above the National Proportion, STs within the National Proportion

4.1 Demography

Population of a community : 5 Lac & above (Trait No. 48) falls under this type. As elaborated in Section I, this factor is important in deciding mutual positions between SCs & STs.

4.2 Class

Leather related occupations like tanning and embroidery on leather (Trait Nos. 438, 480) are more in SCs than in STs. More light on class character of SCs is thrown by traits of Non-skilled Labour (Traditional) (Trait No. 491) and Labour (Traditional) (Trait No. 459) occurring in this Type.

4.3 Caste

4.3.1 Food Habits

101 SC & 67 ST communities have turned from non-vegetarian to vegetarian (Trait No. 144) as against 29 SC and 4 ST communities from vegetarian to non-vegetarian. (Trait No. 143 - not under Type 4). In the absence of further data it is difficult to infer if the transition to vegetarianism is due to paucity of fuel (if non-vegetarian

cooking consumes more energy), pauperisation (if vegetables are cheaper) or Sanskritisation.

4.3.2 *Social Division*

Social Division is along social level (Trait No. 163) in 428 (57.0%) SC and 347 (54.6%) ST communities. That along other levels like religious etc. is covered under Type 3.

4.3.3 *Self-esteem*

Self - Perception of SCs is low (Trait No. 176) and Other's perception about them (Trait No. 186) is also low. These seem to be mutually reinforcing factors. More than 72% communities have low self-perception and about more than 91% other's perception is low. For STs the picture is better as 25.3% of communities have a low self-perception and about 49.4% communities others perceive them to be low.

Seen locationally, for these two traits, urban communities (incl. SCs & STs) have the lowest figures for both the traits. Urban dwelling may be helping a community raise in its own eyes and reduce being looked down upon by others. May be this applies to half-a-crore STs and more than two and half crore SCs in urban areas.

4.4 Class-Gender

4.4.1 *Child-labour*

Child-labour (Trait No. 551) exists in 441 (58.7%) of SC communities. Dreze's study (already referred to above) shows a strong association between child labour and widowhood. Rural widows' disability to earn livelihood due to structural factors like lack of family and community support forces many of them to push children into labour maket. Among STs too, though they are within the National Proportion, this trait is observed in 293 (46.1%) of communities indicating a high National Proportion. The least figure obtains for Jains at 14% among all sub-categories.

4.4.2 *Drop-out from education*

For boys, drop-out is due to Economic reasons (Trait No. 691) for

539 (71.8%) SC and 414 (65.1%) ST communities. Drop-out of Girls due to poverty (Trait No. 699) is reported for 424 (56.5%) SC and 323 (50.8%) ST communities.

Except Jain (9%) all other religious sub-categories show more than 32% girls dropping out of education due to poverty, in occupational sub-categories the minimum figure is 42% for Business & Trade & Industry.

4.5 Caste-Gender

4.5.1: Social Division regulates marriage (Trait No. 169) in 668 (88.9%) SC and 553 (86.9%) ST communities. Seen with the trait of community endogamy (Trait No. 187 under Type 3) in more than 96% of SC & ST communities each, it means that the *rigidity of a community's boundary is perpetuated.* There seems little chance of intercommunity marriages within SCs or STs, much less between SCs and STs or across with non-SCs/STs.

Social Division regulates marriage also across religious, occupational and locational categories ranging from 70% to 93% of communities. Only for Muslims the figure is low at 37% in keeping with a low figure of 52.6% to start with, for Social divisions: Exist.

Type 5: SCs above the National Proportion, STs below the National Proportion

5.1 Class

The Nature of community: Landless (Trait No. 407) is observed in 523 (69.6%) of SC communities. STs are significantly below the National Proportion 181 (28.5%) communities. A related trait Nature of community: Landholding (Trait No. 406) comes under Type 6.

5.2 Caste

5.2.1 Varna

The trait Varna: Aware (Trait No. 177) is found in 602 (80.2%) SC communities and 201 (31.6%) ST communities. For SCs & STs, related traits, their no. of communities and percentages are: Varna: Recognize (Trait No. 178) - 511 (68%) SC & 101 (15.9%) ST; Varna: Recognize Place (Trait No. 179) - 527 (70.2%) SC and 75 (11.8%) ST; and recognize their plaçe as Sudra (Trait No. 183) - 527 (70.2%) SC and 48 (7.5%) ST communities.

5.2.2 Religion

The trait Hindu (No. 580) falls under this Type with 728 (96.9%) SC and 378 (54.4%) ST communities showing adherence to it. It is noteworthy that even if 378 ST communities profess themselves to be Hindus, only 201 show Varna awareness a central tenet of the 'Great Tradition' of Hinduism, pointing to a different understanding of it among the rest 177 communities.

Though other religions do not fall in Type 5, the break-up of SCs and STs among them as mentioned in Table 2 at the beginning of this Section is considered here.

Most of the SC communities are Hindu followed by 38 in Sikhism, 24 in 'other', 21 in christianity and only 12 in Buddhism. 5 are Muslims.

STs are split in 300 - 'Other' (presumably 292 of these - animists), 149 in Christianity, 44 Buddhists and 19 Muslims.

This break-up points to a wide variation of knowledge systems. It also spells structurally different religious exploitation (if and when it is there) from religion to religion and also within the same religion - like Hindu where the sheer number of SC & ST communities put together is more than 1100. Going by number again, agenda for Dalit consciousness may be decided by Hindu SCs & STs. If we look at the number of communities as percentage of communities in a religious sub-category, while 20.6% of Hindu communities (Total No. of Hindu communities 3539) are SCs, 29.2% of Sikhs communities (Total No. of Sikh communities - 130) are SCs. For STs, 44% of Christian communities (Total No. of Christian communities - 339) are STs and 47.3% of Buddhist communities (Total No. of Buddhist communities - 93) are STs. In such a

Hindu dominated agenda, Sikh SCs, Christian and Buddhist STs are likely to be relegated. Their geographical location - Punjab & North East mainly, also may not be helpful in forging a common platform. Even with considerably high percentages they may not be 'represented' qualitatively. The SCs among Christians or 'Other' and STs among Muslims who do not number more than 6% in each of religious sub-category may have virtually no political participation *even within Dalits.*

5.2.3 Pollution

Death Pollution (Trait No. 380) is observed in 715 (95.2%) SC and 491 (77.2%) ST communities. Hindus are also above the National Proportion with SCs.

5.3 Gender

5.3.1 Symbols of Marriage

Vermillion (Trait No. 236), Bangles (Trait No. 237) and Nose -Ring (Trait No. 243) all pertaining to women, are found in SCs and much less in STs. Observance of symbols is strict (Trait No. 297) in more than 76% of SC communities compared to 46.9% ST.

5.3.2 Pollution

Post-Delivery Pollution (Trait No. 361) is observed by 724 (96.4%) SC communities and 522 (82.1%) ST.

5.3.3 No. of Children

Communities of SCs preferring 3 children (Trait No. 710) is higher than the National Proportion alongwith Hindus & Jains. STs and Muslims are below National Proportion for this trait but are much above it for preferring 4 children (Trait No. 111 under Type 6).

5.3.4 Dowry

Transition from Bride Price to Dowry (Trait No. 298) is found in 247 SC communities (32.9%). Hindus are also above the National Proportion. 86 (13.5%) ST communities report this transition.

5.4 Class-Gender

Fuel Resource - cowdung cakes (Trait No. 757) for 482 (68.2%) SC communities puts them above National Proportion with Hindus.

Type 6: STs above the National Proportion, SCs within the National Proportion

6.1 Demography

6.1.1 Identification

SCs have a wider identification than STs. 309 (48.6%) ST communities identify themselves locally (Trait No. 1) i.e. over one or two districts, as against 233 (31%) SC communities.

6.1.2 Natural Environment

Environment-Extremely cold (Trait No. 22), Hilly Terrain (Trait No. 23), High Altitude (Trait No. 29), Thin Forest (Trait No. 36), Dense Forest (Trait No. 35) and High Rainfall (Trait No. 37) all point to STs' distinct living system than SCs.

6.1.3 Food Habits

Roots & Tubers (Trait No. 123), Animal Fat (Trait No. 122), Nagli (Trait No. 100) etc. also distinguish STs from SCs.

6.2 Class

6.2.1 Economy

As mentioned earlier, the Nature of Community is mainly land holding (Trait No. 406) in 253 (39.8%) ST communities. Also a related trait is Economy: Forest based (Trait No. 394) for 310 (48.7%) ST against 101 (13.4%) SC communities.

6.2.2 Occupations

Hunting and Gathering (Traditional & Current) (Trait Nos. 450, 408); Fishing (Traditional, Current and Newly Acquired) (Trait

Nos. 451, 409 & 493); Horticulture (Traditional and Current) (Trait Nos. 452, 410); Trapping Birds and Animals (Traditional & Current) (Trait Nos. 453 & 411); Shifting Cultivation (Traditional & Current) (Trait Nos. 456 & 414); Terrace Cultivation (Traditional, Current & Newly Acquired) (Trait Nos. 457, 415, 499), Animal Husbandry (Traditional, Current and Newly acquired) (Trait Nos. 460, 418, 502), Bee keeping (Current & Newly Acquired) (Trait Nos. 421 & 505) etc. All these occupations come under Type 6 - indicating different relations of production for STs than SCs.

6.2.3 Control of Resources

An important clue to access and control over means of production of STs can be had from these set of traits. In the descending order of number of communities involved, controlling agencies are as follows : Resource Control : Individual (Trait Nos. 398) -457 (71.9%) (under Type 9); Government (Trait No. 399) 227 (35.7%); Community (Trait No. 395) - 103 (16.2%). Clan & Headman are between 5 to 7.5%. The latter three forms of resource control are taken under 'Caste'.

6.2.4 Link with Market

This is through Middlemen (Trait No. 535) in 20% ST communities, a figure almost double in percentage terms than SCs. This point is further discussed under Type 8.

6.2.5 Non-Skilled Labour

This is a Newly Acquired activity (Trait No. 533) in 189 (29.7%) ST communities already commented upon. STs may be coming in the labour-market faster than SCs.

6.3 Caste

6.3.1 Social Divisions

Existence of division along clan (Trait No. 156) is in more than 80% of ST communities. Those along Phratry (Trait No. 154) Moity (Trait No. 155) and Sub Tribe (Trait No. 161) also exist in a much smaller proportion between 2 to 13%. For division along Clan, Hindus are also above the National Proportion with STs.

(Clan : Believers in a common mythical ancestor - animate or inanimate; Phratry - Cluster of exogamous clans; Moity - Division of society in two halves).

6.3.2 Food Habits

Regular non-vegetarian (Trait No. 88) and Beef eating (Trait Nos. 92 & 93) occur in this Type with bearing on intermarriage. Muslims & Christians share these traits above the National Proportion with STs.

6.3.3 Village Council

Village Council exists (Trait No. 556) in 271 (42.6%) ST communities it has a chief (Trait No. 559), its functions include Social Control (Trait No. 563), Punishment & Award (Trait No. 565) & insult to it is taken as an offence (Trait No. 575). Considered with marriage rules below, this set of traits seem to self-insulate a community.

6.4 Gender

6.4.1 Marriage

Clan Exogamy (Trait No. 194) is observed by 72% of ST communities.

For STs, Sororal & Non Sororal Polygyny (Trait Nos. 229 & 230) are followed by 153 (24.1%) & 239 (37.6%) communities though monogamy is the norm as mentioned earlier. Forms of marriage for STs are mainly: that by Elopement (Trait No. 221) 310 communities; by Mutual Consent (Trait No. 220) - 297communities, etc. Thus though modes of acquiring mates seem to be gender egalitarian, wide prevalence of levirate & sororate may have to be further investigated. As mentioned earlier, they mean a less than equal treatment to women as in some North Indian communities.

6.4.2 Bride-Price

Prevalence of Bride-price in Cash & Kind (Trait No. 247) is in 307 ST communities and in 82, in kind only. Other traits like Divorce: Maladjustment, Barrenness under this Type have already been covered.

6.5 Class - Gender

6.6.1: Locational disadvantage with respect to formal education is shown in Dropout of boys and girls due to there being no school near by (Trait Nos. 690 & 698) in 93 & 92 ST communities respectively. In 210 communities girls dropout as are required to earn to support the family (Trait No. 700).

Though the trait Girls' dropout: due to social reason (Trait No. 701) does not come under Type 6, it is worth comparing with Boys' dropout: due to social reason (Trait No. 693) (which comes under this Type). Boys dropout because of social reasons in 60 (9.4%) ST communities and girls in 357 (56.1%). For SCs the difference in percentage is almost 59%. Across the 3 categories the difference ranges from 45% to 79% showing a clear relegation of girls' education.

6.6 Caste-Gender

6.6.1 Residence

This is neo-local (Trait No. 258) for the newly-wed in 153 communities in STs and 58 in SCs. It is matrilocal (Trait No. 260) only in 21 ST and 4 SC communities.

Type 7: STs above the National Proportion, SCs below the National Proportion

7.1 Class

Economy is land based (Trait No. 393) for ST as mentioned earlier. It is interesting to note that Individual proprietorship (Trait No.

401) obtains for STs in a highly significant proportion - 379 communities (59.6%). Settled Cultivation (Current) (Trait No. 416) is in 438 communities (68.9%). Taken together alongwith class traits mentioned under Type 6, *STs are more owners of means of production than 'free' sellers of labour power*, though pauperization is also simultaneously taking place. Actual Population involved in either class would reveal the extent of labour-component, the data not gone into.

Type 8: SCs within the National Proportion STs below the National Proportion

8.1 Demography

Traits dealing with Natural Environment & food habits are not gone into.

8.1.1 Linkages

SCs are more exposed to media and 'Mainstream' as in all the following traits they are above STs: Listening to Radio (Trait No. 745), Visiting Cinema (Trait No. 746); Agent of Dissemination: Political Parties (Trait No. 749), Roads Exist (Trait No. 751), Railway Exists (Trait No. 752) and Post office is near-by (Trait No. 753).

8.2 Class

8.2.1 Exposure to Markets

From the class-traits under this Type inference can be drawn that SCs are more exposed to market forces. Link with market: Direct (Trait No. 534) - 706 (94%) SC against 562 (88.4%) ST communities; Local Market Regulated (Trait No. 540) 398 (53%) SC as against 228 (35.8%) ST communities; Daily Market (Trait No. 536) 573 (76.3%) SC as against 318 (50%) ST communities; economy more monetised as 546 (72.7%) SC communities transact business in Cash (Trait No. 543) as against 403 (63.4%) ST communities.

8.2.2 Employment

Government seems to be the single biggest employer for SCs.

Government Service (Current & Newly Acquired) Trait Nos. 426 and 510) employs members of more than 58% communities. The Trait Government Service (Traditional) (Trait No. 468) features only 1.6% communities. (This trait not under Type 8). STs are closer in percentage on a lower side, and below the National Proportion.

Industry also is a major new employer for SCs with around 20% communities having industrial workers (Trait Nos. 425, 509) STs around 9% lag by more than 10% behind SCs for this trait. Industrial labour has increased (Trait No. 549) in 17.3% SC communities as against 7.7% ST.

8.2.3 Land Relations

Patron - client relationship obtains (Trait No. 667) for 364 (48.5%) SC communities as against 223 (35.1%) ST.

8.3 Gender & Caste-Gender

8.3.1 Marriage

Marriage by negotiation (Trait No. 224) - 739 (98.4%) SC and 597 (93.9%) ST communities seems to be the national norm as whether marriage is by mutual consent or courtship, it also takes place by negotiation in more than 90% of all communities.

Dowry in cash or kind or both (Trait Nos. 249, 250 & 251) exists for between 5.5% to 37.5% of SC communities, a shared trait with the 'mainstream'. For STs the range is between 1.6% to 8.3% communities.

Residence is patrilocal (Trait No. 259) in 98% SC and 91.7% ST communities. (Enumerated under 'Caste-Gender')

Marriage taking place at Bride's residence (Trait No. 373), Feast by Bride's Parents (Trait No. 375), Nuptials at Groom's Residence (Trait No. 379) are other related traits in SCs over STs showing expense on girl's side. This is corroborated by transition from Bride-price to Dowry, mentioned earlier.

8.3.2 Family

Nuclear family is rising (Trait No. 334) in 82.7% and extended family is declining (Trait No. 336) in 76.0% of SC communities. STs are less by 9 and 15.2 percent for these figures respectively. (Enumerated under Caste-Gender).

8.3.3 Family Planning

The set of traits - Family Planning Favoured (Trait No. 708), Modern Family Planning Methods used (Trait No. 713), Family Planning done by other than sterilization (Trait No. 717) shows a *differential* of SCs with STs between 7 to 24% of number of communities.

Type 9: STs within the National Proportion, SCs below the National Proportion

9.1 Class

9.1.1: Control of Resource remains primarily with individual (Trait No. 398) for STs as mentioned earlier - 71.9% communities as against 54.2% in SCs.

9.1.2 Entrepreneurship

If the traits Business (Newly Acquired) (Trait No. 506) and Industry (Newly Acquired) (Trait No. 508) are taken as signs of entrepreneurship and upward mobility, SCs & STs are quite comparable with each other with STs leading slightly. There are between 23% to 29% communities of each reporting each activity.

9.2 Caste

9.2.1 Self Esteem

In self-Perception: High (Trait No. 174) and Self-Perception Middle (Trait No. 175) STs are much above SCs. 26.9% and 46.9% ST communities have high & middle self-perception respectively as against 4.4% & 23.2% SC communities. Other's perception: Medium (Trait No. 185) applies to 39.2% ST and 7.9% SC communities.

9.2.2 Inter Community Linkages

Exchange of Water across communities (Trait No. 652) takes place in 73.3% ST and 64% SC communities, that of Kachcha food (Trait No. 654) in 67.1% and 65.8% communities respectively and sharing of water resources (Trait No. 661) in 86.8% and 79.8% communities respectively.

Following two tables summarise the findings of the foregoing discussion in Section II. (Figures show the number of traits in each Axis and Type)

Table 2.1

Type	Demography	Class	Caste	Gender	Class-Gender	Caste Gender
1	6	16	17	19	-	3
2	3	15	5	7	-	4
3	35	56	53	48	7	20
4	10	5	16	5	3	5
5	1	-	14	7	1	-
6	22	47	51	39	2	7
7	1	8	4	-	-	1
8	30	18	15	26	4	5
9	4	10	15	7	1	1

Sub-total: Similarity Traits (Types 1, 2 & 3) : 314
Sub-total: Difference Traits (Types 4 to 9) : 385
Total No. of Traits analysed : 699

Table 2.2

SCs

		Above National Proportion	*Within National Proportion*	*Below National Proportion*
STs	Above National Proportion	Type 1 61	Type 6 168	Type 7 14
	Within National Proportion	Type 4 44	Type 3 219	Type 9 38
	Below National Proportion	Type 5 23	Type 8 98	Type 2 34

It may be noted that the maximum no. of traits come under Type 3, in 'Similarity Traits', *and* Within the National Proportion i.e. with the 'mainstream'.

Conclusion

1. *If* equal weightage is ascribed to each trait, then there are more difference traits than similarity traits between SCs & STs. Further, if the traits they also share with 'mainstream' are discounted, the traits they share *as Dalits* are less than a hundred. Weightage, however, need not be equal as it would depend upon the action orientation of the interventionist group. Traders in edible oil may ascribe more weightage to a trait like whether a community consumes ground-nut oil or not, than a political party may.

2. Class, Caste and Gender - the three categories premised on dilectical approach, corrollarily, may be inadequate to subsume SCs and STs under Dalit - a category that is tending to be inclusive (as the on-going debate regarding OBCs indicates). Defining Dalit may be a longer-drawn process, a situation akin to problematisation of category woman in feminism.

3. *If* the traits of the Survey are taken as defining living system of a community, consisting of survival system and knowledge system, a localised and contextual approach may be more useful than resort to metanarratives.

[*Note:* If all the traits unanalysed (due to lack of definite information about National Proportion/No. of communities) are Similarity Traits, their total would go up to 391 as against that of Difference Traits - 385. The question of weightage, however remains.]

—X—

[Thanks are due to Dr. Anil Gore, Dr. A.P. Kulkarni for clarifications regarding statistics; to Dr. Gopal Guru, Dr. P.G. Jogdand for comments on the findings.]

Bibliography

1. Joshi N.V. et al 'Exploring Cultural Diversity of The People Of India', *'Current Science'*, Volume 64, Jan. 10, 1993. p. 10.
2. Singh K.S. 'People Of India: The Profile Of A National Project', *'Current Science'*, op. cit. p. 6.
3. Delphy, Christine and Leonard, Diana cited below. p. 22.

References

1. As quoted in Hekman, Susan J. *'Gender and Knowledge: Elements of a Postmodern Feminism'*, Polity Press, 1990. pp. 12.
2. *'People Of India' - A Quantitative Profile* (National Consolidated Tables based on Constitutional, Religious, Occupational and Locational Categories), Anthropological Survey Of India, New Delhi, 1992.
3. *'Final Population Totals' - Census Of India 1991*, Series - 1, Paper - 1 of 1992, Volume II, Government Of India, New Delhi, 1992.
4. Dreze, Jean *'Widows In Rural India'*, The Development Economics Research Programme, London School Of Economics, Paper No. 26, August 1990, pp. 3-4.
5. Delphy, Christine and Leonard, Diana *'Familiar Exploitation: A new Analysis of Marriage in Contemporary Western Societies'*, Polity Press, 1992, pp. 151-8.
6. Datar, Chhaya (ed.) *'The Struggle Against Violence'*, Stree, Calcutta, 1993.
7. Dreze, Jean op. cit. p. 20.
8. Agarwal, Bina 'Social Security And The Family' in *'Social Security In Developing Countries'*, Ahmad E. et al (eds.), Clarendon Press, Oxford, 1991, p. 184.

5

DALIT WOMEN IN CONTEMPORARY INDIAN SITUATION

M. Prabhavathi

Caste is an important element in India and it is still the foundation of Indian Society, and it is the best guide to the changes in the various social strata in the Indian society.

The attainment of equality of status for women was one of the specific objectives which is implicit in the preamble, Fundamental rights and Directive Principle of the state policy of constitution of India. But the examination of this constitutional guarantee reveals the heterogenous nature of the Indian society such as inequalities in the social structure based on sex, caste and community. The social change is a complex process which has not affected the different sections of women in an uniform manner, therefore, the status of women cannot be defined simply. A detailed and careful study is necessary to understand the nature of constraints and disabilities that affect the women in their performance and multiple roles in the society, economy and polity as members of different sections of the population and with their level of social status.

The political power in this country has too long been the monopoly of a few dominated uppercaste men, which merely deprived the downtrodden the changes for betterment, in which the condition of dalit women is insignificant. No doubt that some of the women have taken participation during freedom struggle and were also able to enter in the formation of Government in power sharing. But these representatives are all mostly from the uppercaste and class women, which clearly reflects the degree of inequalities of the society. The women leaders who enjoyed the power have not worked for the betterment of downtrodden women, in order to improve their social, economic and political status. But they must have played an important role in forming the social programmes, legislation for the welfare of women. It is regrettable and unfortunate for dalit women who have neglected in considering their share in the active politics and their potential in the national deve-lopment process.

There are various barriers for dalit women not to take participation in the active politics, such as Social, Economic and Political inequality in the Indian society.

The social barriers such as practice of untouchability, casteism, illiteracy, socio-cultural variation, religious exploitation and superstitions and class variation in the society.

Education

The progress of literacy among dalit women still presents a dismal picture. The 1981 census of Karnataka state reveals only one percent of dalit women are literate against 11% of upper caste women which is highly negligible. The education is the means of realising the life desires which helps to develop the personality and qualifies in improving the status of person in all respect and which directly relates to the socio-economic and political status of women.

99 percent of dalit women are illiterates, the school going girls discontinue their education and sacrifice to contribute to running of the houses as well as the family economy. Therefore,

it is necessary to start the vocational courses and training along with the general education for the dalit women.

The image of the Indian women created by a few uppercaste women holding high position or academic qualification conceal rather than reveal the low status and educational level of the dalit women.

Socio-Cultural Variation

Because of the secondary role and unequal situation in society, the women have suffered the effects of violence to a greater degree than men.

The social and cultural behaviour of men and women influences the social expectation in determining the position of women in the society.

The exploitation of dalit women under the name of religion such as "Nude Worship", practice of Devdasi system and many other similar type of superstitions make dalit women more submissive.

The atrocities on dalits by uppercastes is also directly affecting the normal life of dalit women, the murders of dalits, stabbing, social boycot, loss of property, preventing them using the public well, tanks, entry to public places such as temples, cinema hall, denial of employment to the dalit women and many such types of inci-dents distress the dalit women. The social security and protection of dalit women are low.

Illustrations

1. The incident reported, that on 6.9.1988 in Dongargaon village 40 Km. away from the Gulbarge district in Karnataka State the powerful caste Hindus allegedly descended on dalit Basavantaraya's house, beat-up his son, looted the house and dragged out his teenaged daughter Geeta, outraged her modesty in front of Babasaheb Ambedkar Statue. The simple reason

is that the uppercaste Hindus do not tolerate the prosperity of dalits, (Indian Express 14.9.88).

2. In Sindanur Taluka of Raichur district in Karnataka four dalit women were beaten and stripped and paraded on August 30, 1988, because of small dispute between families.

3. April 17, 1988 the SC/ST colony at Amrutur village in Tumkur district Karnataka were subjected to harassment allegedly by caste Hindus. The incident relates to the difference that arose between the caste Hindus and dalits over the celebration of the annual Jatra in which dalits were not allowed to enter the temple and take participation in the procession during the jatra. This practice of untouchability has been protested by dalit youths. But previous to jatra day, by the intervening of Tahsildar the dalits entered the temple and performed the pooja, and the very next day the caste Hindus surrounded the scheduled caste colony threw stones at the houses and allegdly molested the women, again with a mob of 1000 people attacked the dalits with sickle, cycle chain and other lethal weapons and finally declared the social boycott.

A small village called Chandraguthi in Shimoga district, there was a temple of Renuka for which the women use to go to temple naked, after taking the holy bath in a river, 3 km. away from the temple. This nude parade or worship is watched by several thousands of people both in and out of India. It is unfortunate to note that these women who were participating in this nude worship belong to scheduled caste/tribe and other backward classes.

Kustogi a village in Raichur district of Karnataka, Sharanavva the dalit anganawadi worker and the daughter of Kariyavva a Devdasi allegedly summoned to the local travellers bungalow and gang raped by Taluka Tahsildar, Assistant Engineer of Zilla Parishad, a P.W.D. Junior Engineer and a Lawyer on February 10, 1993. When the victim fell unconscious, bleeding profusely the accused put her in a car to take her to Hubli Hospital, where she died on way to hospital.

The early marriage and child rearing and their type of hard work in the fields make them more malnutritious and become unhealthy and unhygienic. The physical distress makes them to lose interest in their life.

Lack of awareness about socio-economy and polity is another barrier for dalit women.

The Judiciary system in India is also not seriously concerned about the crimes against dalit women. The law enforcing agencies and our judicial processes have not reflected in their effective commitment in implementation of law to protect and safegaurd the interest of dalit women. There should be sensitive and strict administration necessary to enforce the law and also certain changes in the existing laws for the benefit of dalit women.

Economic status

The economic oppression of dalit women has made them live below the poverty line. The dalit women often descend below the subsistance line with the disappearance of their means of earning and livelihood.

The women's economic dependency leads to exploitation and is a denial of social justice and human rights. The declining role of women in Indian economy is mainly because of increase in unemployment, poverty and the cost of living, and importantly development of modern industries with its increasing advanced technology.

The Industrial societies are experiencing one of the worst economic crisis in history, with the result that women are the first to become unemployed, representing the largest group of unemployed people. Unemployment is a severe problem that effects both men and women. The women must have equal opportunity of employment with equal pay, training, promotion, pension, security and other benefits.

Women work both in organised and in unorganised sector. The

dalit women employed mainly in unorganised sector, and work as labourers in agriculture, construction work, landless labourers, factory work and other house-hold and marginal works, as daily wage workers.

The basic problem that affects the dalit women's role and opportunities for employment in this sector spring from their helpless dependence caused by lack of adequate employment apportunities, limited skills, illiteracy, restricted mobility and lack of autonomous status. The lack of control over productive resources and a persistent gap between consumption and expenditure leading to perpetual indebtedness, deprive them of all bargaining power and occupational mobility. The proportion of dalit women below the poverty line is comparatively higher than upper caste women. The components of this vast group are unskilled workers, landless agricultural labourers, factory workers, members of households with uneconomic holdings and those in traditional menial jobs. These women have been deprived from wage discrimination, physical harassment, maternity benefit, pension, promotion, leave facility and other job security.

The opposition to increasing women's economic activities is mainly from the conservative view that women's role must be confined within rigidity defined limit and a fear of chronic unemployment may result if women enter the labour market on a large scale.

About 90% of women working in unorganized sector are mainly from the lower castes.

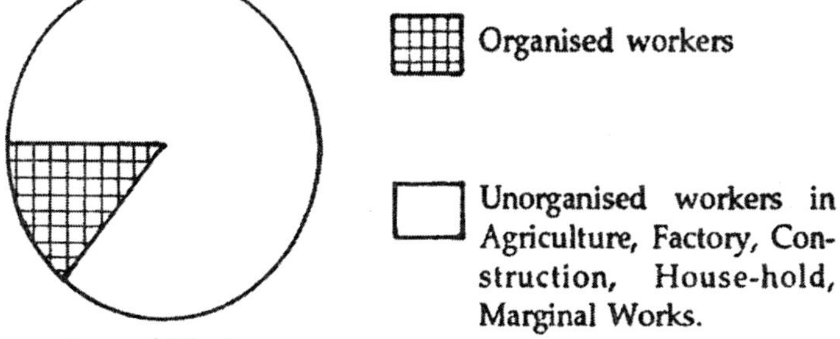

Percentage of Workers

The structural adjustment in the new economic policy lists women, which leads to decline in employment and income by the introduction of imported technology.

The policies totally ignore women's role in Indian economy, and specially rural untouchable women, so far none of the political parties brought any useful policies for the betterment of economic status of women and also right to work, and not even allowed the single dalit woman to take participation in policy and decision making.

The women working as agricultural labourers are discriminated in the new economic policy proposed by Government of India by not considering the output of the labour in the developmental process of the nation. The participation of women in both organized and unorganised sector will be reduced, they suffer from competition from foreign technicals. This reduced employment will affect women both directly and indirectly. In many industries women are employed in the relatively low skill area. The import of modern technology will lead to a cut back in such jobs and secondly many men will also be without jobs become potential competitors with women for the low skills and low paid jobs or even the women who do not lose the jobs having to accept lower wages or undertake more straneous jobs for the same pay.

The loss of agricultural land due to industrialisation results in the unemployment of agricultural labourers. The replacement of human labour at agriculture by mechanisation, the patent rights in the name of modernisation replaces the agricultural workers. The tradition knowledge of women about land, soil, seeds, livestock management, water, agriculture will be destroyed. The natural resources like soil, water, forest will be exploited.

There is necessity to plan for the certain jobs in a massive scale, particularly in the agrarian sector through Agro-based industries, special vocational training for self employment and with proper funding.

It is important to generate the alternate schemes which can increase the employment opportunity to women both in organised and unorganised sector with their effective participation. The areas which needs an advanced technology, the women working under such areas can be trained. The technical experts should be more conscious of their social responsibilities in identifying or organising the training facilities. The new economic policy should clarify more on agricultural problems like land based activities as such illiterate dalit women in rural area have got scope only in land based activities such as social and commercial forestry, dairy, poultry, sericulture etc., but her potential is totally neglected in considering the developmental project and economic success.

The economic oppression of women leads to social and cultural oppression, because these factors go hand in hand with the thinking of one person is superior to another. Therefore the economic liberation is a very important factor for the betterment of women in overcoming the class discrimination apart from casteism.

Political Status

Women constitute half of the total population, but are unable to get equal share in active politics of the country. In politics the organisational structure, leadership and sharing of power in government are dominated by men. The money and caste are an important factors which play the main role in Indian Politics. Women participation in the political process is centered to their struggle against oppression. The social, economic status of women directly depends on their participation in the decision making.

Unfortunately all the political parties in India speak much about equality of women, and have totally ignored the dalit women, where their political status and participation is insignificant. It is regrettable that the dalit women have not been given the representation in all the political parties which reflects the social difference. The women involved in politics and power sha.ing are mainly from the upper caste women with political, high financial background of the family. It may be surprising to know that till

1932 the representation in legislature was only by uppercaste Hindus and untouchable were totally neglected.

And if special representation is not given to the women of weaker sections, they will be politically suppressed by the minority of high caste women.

By recognising the seriousness of women's participation in politics, in the year 1987 the Janata Government in Karnataka announced 25 percent reservation for women in Zilla Parishad and Mandal Panchayat, as per Zilla Parishad Act 1932, with a special provision of 5:1 ratio reservation to dalit women in 25% women reservation, which is a very important and significant aspect. Due to this reservation a number of dalit women had an opportunity to take part in active politics, 19 dalit women against 211 upper caste women in Zilla Parishad and 2469 dalit women against 14025 upper caste women in Mandal Panchayats were elected. The Participation of these representatives in active politics varies. A few women have really showed good performance in the participation. But with their social and economic background and the level of education they need proper guidance and time to reveal their responsibilities in power sharing and decision making.

The representation of dalit women in Zilla Parishad and Mandal Panchayat does not widen the reality of women's political visibility. Therefore efforts should be made to increase the scope and percentage of reservation in legislatures and in Parliament.

All the political parties should strictly implement the reservation specifically for dalit women. And it is the responsibilities of voluntary social organisations, dalit organisations and women organisations to pressurise the political parties for the implementation of reservation and also to create the political awareness and its importance among women.

The dalit organisations and women organisations have to play a very important and serious role in establishing the equal status of dalit women with other section of people in the class and caste dominated society. The women organisations or dalit organisations have not taken the dalit women's problem to the fore.

The status of dalit women is in such a pathetic condition, the uppercaste men exploit the women, and the lower caste men and women, again the upper caste women exploit the lower caste women. The dalit women exploited by dalit men, and the upper-caste men and women.*

Therefore it is very urgent and important to give an attention and policies to be planned for the betterment of dalit women and to establish their equal status and personality as human being.

The National women Commission of Government of India formed in 1992 is also not having any specific programme for the upliftment of dalit women. The dalit women herself is not in a position to identify her own personality.

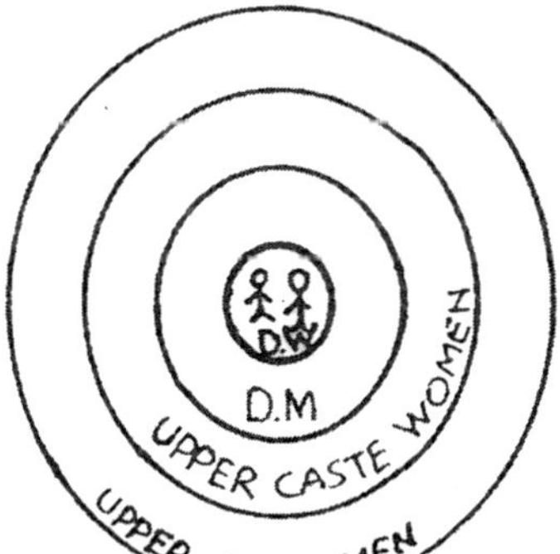

D.W. - Dalit women
D.M. - Dalit men

* CONCENTRIC CIRCLE SHOWING EXPLOITATION OF DALIT WOMEN

Dr. B.R. Ambedkar in his writings on 'The Riddle of Women' has explained that how Manu has deprived the status of women by curbing the liberty and equal rights of women. And Babasaheb also expressed his concern for the improvement of women's status. He wanted to bring certain changes in the Hindu law for the betterment of women. In 1951 when he was a law minister in Jawaharlal Nehru's Cabinet, he wanted to bring an amendment in Hindu Law such as adoption, guardianship, divorce, Hindu Marriage, Widow Re-Marriage and property rights to women. But because of the strong opposition by the traditional caste Hindus the bill was not accepted in the parliament and because of this Dr. Ambedkar had to resign from Nehru's Ministry.

It is important to note that under Dr. Ambedkar's leadership the Dalit women participated in Dalit protest movements on a number of occasions.

Until and unless there is an improvement in the status of dalit women and their equal participation in the society there is no meaning in speaking of nations' progress and development.

6

HINDU EPICS : PORTRAYAL OF DALIT WOMEN

Vizia Bharati

The society always treated women as an object of sex and sexual exploitation. It was an established fact that woman was looked down in all aspects of life. Discrimination is shown towards her in all spheres, in the disguise of tradition and culture.

I wish to state a few points about the status and portrayal of Dalit women in the traditional literature.

According to reports issued by the present Ministry of Welfare, over half of the rape cases officially registered in India concern women belonging to the scheduled castes and tribes. On average one thousand such cases of rape are reported each year; and they are often not investigated and difficult to prove. The use of torture and other forms of cruel behaviour towards poorer and oppressed sections is not new in Indian Society. There are many examples in our literature to show that.

The Indian literature gives controversial statements regarding the status of woman in the society. At some point it says that the mother should be respected highly more than the father and guru (teacher). And elsewhere it advises not to trust woman.

One of the ancient scriptures say that if father is bad, the son can abandon him. If Guru is bad the disciple can leave him but one should not leave one's mother though she is of bad character. It says one should respect one's mother. The son should obey the mother. But later Manudharma Shastra says woman should not be given freedom. She should be kept under the control of man at every stage of life.

In the earlier days of civilization, women enjoyed a superior status. The matriarchal system of society placed the control in the hands of woman. They were the owners of wealth, and enjoyed power and freedom. This is in prevedic and vedic period. In the prehistoric society people lived in groups. Group marriages were common system of society. Women because of their productive functions enjoyed superior status. Children were identified with the names of their mothers. The family was known after the mothers. This is the symptom of matriarchal society. Mahabharata depicts this type of system.

In later days the structure of the society has undergone several changes and it slowly moved towards patriarchal system. Mother's right was overthrown and property came into the hands of men. This overthrow of the mothers' right was the time where caste evolved. Transition from group marriage to single marriage is for private property. This system gave way to class and caste structure in the society. One can see this transition in Ramayana. 'Mahabharata' and 'Ramayana' the great epics of Indian literature reveal this truth.

Dalit women were portrayed in both these epics. Nowadays 'Dalit' word is used commonly for oppressed and depressed classes. It has much historical context which took present shape. Let us examine some oppressed women characters from Ramayana and Mahabharata. Among them some are not specifically from lower castes; but they are from oppressed classes. I am illustrating five characters mainly from the literature. 1. Matanga Kanyas, 2. Tataka, 3. Surpanakha, 4. Aayomukhi, 5. Mandodari. There is much to say about the genealogy of these people. They come under 'Shudra' category. There are many other characters which come under Shudra category but are not dealt with in this paper.

In Telugu we have different divisions of literature. Some are identified with the trends of literature and some with the names of the poets purana, kavya and prabhanda periods are known for the rich contributions of classics. They are full of flowery language. Poets maintained to have certain number of descriptions in their works as a rule, so as to show their talents. Telugu prabhandas usually had Ashtadasa varnanas, i.e. eighteen types of descriptions : description of the city or town (Nagara) and description of the four varnas are part of it. They indirectly show the social structure. Through the attitude of the poet towards a character one can guess the status of the character in the prevailing society.

Kavya is that which touches the inner most chords of the human mind and diffuses itself into the recesses of the heart, working up a lasting sense of delight. Social and religious emotions are also part of it. All Kavyas express this attitude directly or indirectly to some extent. In puranas we can find out this ethical and classical expression. In describing the three aims of life dharma (duty), artha (profit) and karma (enjoyment) one can see the social, economical and political structure of the world. In primitive societies women were generally robust muscular strong and capable of carrying heavy burdens and responsibilities.

Much of the ancient history of India has been made mythology. It was done deliberately. The "Deva, Danava, Yaksha, Gandharva, Kinnara kimpurusha..." etc. are the words used for different races of human family. But puranas and epics explain them differently. They say that "Deva means 'God', 'Sura' is used as equivalent to 'Deva' i.e. 'Gods'. This is not correct. The words 'Sura' and 'Deva' are intended to indicate the names of different races.

Our holy scriptures say 'Asura'means Rakshasa. They are opposed to 'Sura' race. Mahabharata and Ramayana speak highly of 'Deva' race and degrade 'Asura' race.

One can notice Arya and Anarya differences in both the epics. On the whole the Puranas say that Asura, Rakshasa, Desyu races are opposed to Aryan culture. They are aboriginal and wicked people. In that sense one can come to a conclusion that these above mentioned races were oppressed races; i.e. Dalits of that time. Ramayana tells as clearly how Rama killed Rakshasas to protect sages (priests) and Yajnas. And the most important point I wish to state is that, how the Rakshasa women were insulted by Rama who belonged to higher caste.

Tradition tells us that the Ramayana came into being prior to Mahabharata. But when examined critically this convention was proved wrong. Mr. C.V. Vaidya after a careful examination of both the epics concludes that the. Mahabharat as it exists today is no doubt more ancient than the Ramayana as it is today. The language of Mahabharata is very near to the language of Atharve Veda. We find clear references of polyandry in Mahabharat. In Ramayana the polygyny is in practice. According to sociologists polyandry preceded polygyny.

Dr. B.R. Ambedkar says that the present Ramayana is not the Ramayana originally written by 'Valmiki'.

'Arya' means 'man of a noble birth'. Dictionaries give many other meaning also. 1. Aryan an inhabitant of Aryaverta, Name of the race migrated into India in vedic times. 2. Worthy of an Arya. 3. Respectable, noble, high - etc. 4. A Buddha - a man who has thought on the four chief principles of Buddhism and lives according to them....

Like this there are fourteen meanings in the dictionary. On the whole they say Arya is one who lives by Truth and Law. For Dasyu they say lawless, inhuman and riteless i.e. opposed to rituals.

The power of wickedness is called Dasyu in vedas. They praised 'Indra' as destroyer of Dasyus in Rigveda. Tribes and professional groups were converted into 'Jatis'. There they were given varna status. This is seen in Mahabharata. The tribes were of hunting and pastoral communities.

Matanga Kanya

Mahabharata speaks of pastoral communities as well as hunting tribes. The story of 'Satya Harishchandra' is very famous in Mahabharata. Matanga Kanyas (Girls from an untouchable family) play important role in this story. The story of Harischandra became famous in almost all regional languages in India. It was propagated as Sravya Kavya and Drisya Kavya i.e. Drama. It became popular as cinema too.

King Harishchandra was a famous king of Tretayuga. He is one among the six famous kings. He is praised for his Satyavach (i.e. Truthfulness). Let us examine some facts of the story. Once King Harishchandra went to the forest for hunting. He was much tired. Two matanga girls approached him and entertained the King with their dance and music. The King was much pleased to give them something in praise of their talent. On his request, they asked for an 'umbrella'. 'Umbrella' in those days is a symbol of royal honor. Only higher caste people were eligible for that honor. The lower castes, how much talented they may be, cannot ask for such an honor. It was a sin on their part to wish for such an honor. The poet describes the two girls as very pretty and talented. Poets whenever they describe a woman they describe her from top to toe with much enthusiasm. They give importance to their physical beauty, color, complexion, etc. They describe their lips, nose, ears, etc. with much lust. They give less importance for their ladies feelings. 'Matanga' Kanyas are no exception to this. All the time nobody suspects their caste. Even the King Harishchandra could not make out their caste. But after listening to their wish for an 'Umbrella', i.e. for the honor which is strictly restricted to upper caste people; the King got angry and rejected their wish. The King gave them another chance to ask for a wish. The girls express their wish to marry the King. The King was stunned. He rejected their wish this time also saying that the girls are untouchables - as such, he cannot marry them. In the beginning of the story the girls were described as very beautiful and well mannered. But later much discrimination is shown towards them. As untouchables they were insulted and sent off. They were abused in the name of the caste. Later Sage Viswamitra comes to the King and declares them as his pet daughters; and ask the King to marry them. He assured the King that it will not be counted as sin. But the King rejects the proposal saying that the girls wer untouchables. Pandits and scholars say that people get respect only through behaviour and merit but not through birth. But in practice they do not show that. Caste through birth dominates every thing. This is a clear evidence for their outlook.

King Harischandra rejected the plea of the sage and is ready to do anything to avoid the marriage. He expresses his aversion towards lower castes repeatedly. He says that he cannot disgrace his pious caste by marrying the Matanga girls. This is the story given in Mahabharata vana parva, Chapter 77.

People say that the wager between two sages "Vasista" and "Viswamitra" cost Harischandra much undesired suffering. But that is not true Harischandra suffered because he observed caste. He denied that Matanga girls their due right, their share of honour and recognition - i.e. honor of getting the unbrella. Their scholarship in dance and music was not recognised because of their caste. Harischandra was the observer of caste system. Probably he is one of the foremost Kings propagating Vamasrama Dharma system.

Puranas depict Harischandra as an ideal king, because they want to establish vamasrama Dharma. This story was given wide publicity in the disguise of "truth". King Harischandra rejected to marry lower caste girls. He stood adamant for caste and was ready to undergo anything instead of such marriage. He lost his kingdom, son, wife and everything for the sake of the caste. He was asked to pay the promised money to Viswamitra within the time limit. He could not raise the money from higher castes. As a last resort he sells himself to a Chandala. Strictly speaking he did not like the idea of being sold to a Chandala because it is strongly condemned by the holy scriptures. He offers to be the slave of sage Viswamitra rather. But somehow he was made to agree to the proposal.

There is much to say about the chandala who was so rich as to buy a king when nobody in that city could afford it. 'Matanga' was a powerful tribe of those days. Mahakavi Kalidasa prayed Matanga Kanya,... "Matanga Kanyam Manasam Smangami..." etc.

There were many slokas praising 'Matanga Kanya'. Even Shankarcharya prayed her. The Matangas are suppressed by the society in the name of Varnasrama dharma. Dr. Ambedkar in his book on "Riddles in Hinduism" discusses many points on these tribes and races which were insulted by "Manu". Dr. Ambedkar says that varna-dharma which formed so fundamental part of the Hindu Dharma is very much peculiar and nobody could give a consistant explanation of its origin. We see Dalit women as mature individuals and good representatives of primitive society. They have potentiality and powerful past. It is no surprise to note that the realities were wrongly recorded and were focussed in negative way.

Puranas and other scriptures sometimes give contradictory statements regarding such stories. Manu restricted women, particularly Dalit women and made unfair codes and comments against them. These codes are visible in Ramayana.

Tataka

The greed of upper castes i.e. of Kshatariyas (rulers) and Sages led the Journey of Rama in Dandakaranya. Ramayana is a story of upper and lower class conflicts; Aryan and non Aryan conflicts for power.

Killing of Tataka is the consequence of domination of Sages over the land of Tataka in Dandakaranya. This was done for, "Gobrahmana Hithardhaya..." (for the welfare of cows and Brahmins) and "caturvarna hitardhaya" [for the welfare of the (four) caste system says] Ramayana. This caste system decides the status of the people by virtue of the birth.

Tataka is a dignified and powerful ruler of "Malada" and "Karusha" lands. According to the Dictionary of Hinduism "She is a female vegeted godling (Yakshini) who was changed into a malevolent spirit (Rakshasi) for having disturbed the Rishi Agastya".

The story of Tataka is mentioned in two places in Ramayana. She is a Yakshini: Yakshas are of "Tamasa" guna. "Manudharma Sastra" identifies some races as higher and some as lower depending on their births. He also says that the births are in accordance to the 'guna'. Manu says, "Births as dancers, arrogant men, Rakshasas and pishachas are the effects of the refined kind of Tamasa guna (Manu 12-44).

Births as shudras etc. are the middle kind of Tamasa guna. Births as gandharva, guhyaka, Yaksha, attendants of Gods and Apsaras are the superior kind of Rajasa guna" (Manu-12-46).

So Manu is equating shudra, rakshasa and pishachas births more or less with 'Tamas guna'. Tataka being a Yakshini by birth is of Rajasa guna which is superior to Shudra. But she became a Rakshasi by the curse of Agestya and became the victim of domination of higher castes. They killed her husband and gave curse to her son to become a rakshasa and made her also a rakshasi. In that way she was oppressed and was degraded. She can be equated to a Dalit woman.

Tataka by birth was a beautiful and strong lady, a peace loving ruler. She opposed "yajnas", which involved killings i.e. Himsa (violence). The Sages were not allowed to do sacrifices (Yajnas) in her territory. So the Sages were not happy about her Ahimsa. They went to King Dasharatha and brought his sons Rama and Lakshmana along with them for help and attacked Tataka, they got her killed, and occupied her territory.

The realities of the story were not focussed properly in Ramayana. Tataka was neither cruel nor of aggressive nature. Vishwamitra brought Rama to her land "Tatakayaamvanam" purposefully, and caught her unaware; and got her killed. Tataka was not given a chance to fight or protect herself. Tataka, when she heard the sound of Rama's bow became frightened and fell unconscious ("Krodha Moorchita") says Valmiki. They attacked her mercilessly, defamed her by cutting her nose and ears and killed her in a most cruel way. Now-a-days we often come across incidents of sexual exploitation. When a girl rejects to fulfil the desire of higher caste man or landlord they punish her by way of making her ugly. They cut her nose and ears. In some cased strip her naked. It is interesting to note that such type of punishments were in vogue in Ramayana and Mahabharata.

According to Mahabharata Draupadi was insulted in a full court. They tried to strip her naked. The reason may be different. But that is the attempt made on a woman.

In Ramayana the lower caste women like Shurpanakha, Aayomukhi and Mandodari (belonging to Rakshasa community) were punished and insulted.

Shurpanakha

"Shurpanakha" is Ravana's sister. She is a Rakshasi. When she sees Rama, Lakshmana and Sita in Dandakaaranya forest she asks Rama why he has come there to her land, with wife and brother. She enquires in a friendly manner. (Aaagata Stav mimam Desam...) She wants to know the matters out of curiosity. Rama replies her and in turn asks about her. He continues his dialogue without waiting for the girl's answer. He says "because you are not having nice features I think you are a Rakshasi". One can see the pride of Rama and the degrading attitude. This is the attitude of upper caste people towards lower caste women. Ramayana says, that Shurpanakha wanted to marry Rama; and Rama did not agree for the proposal. Instead he recommended Lakshmana for marriage. Both the brothers made a fool of Shurpanakha when she realised it, she tried to hurt Sita. Then the two brothers caught hold of her, and cut her nose and ears. They knew that it is sin to attack woman; but did it.

This story needs critical study. It is to be clarified whether they have cut her nose and ears as a punishment for not obliging them, or because of her aggressive behaviour. As per Valmiki's Ramayana that land is owned by Rakshasas. (Rakshasa Sevitam...") Rakshasas never followed Aryadharma. They have their own Dharma. Ram tells Shurpanakha that he came for fulfilling his Dharma. (Dharmartha Dhayma Kamksheecha vanam vastu mihagatam).

This Dharma of Rama must be the 'Chaturvarna Dharma' which is not followed by Rakshasas. Ramayana i.e. Rams's journey was made with a purpose. The purpose is to suppress the Rakshasa i.e. observers of Matriarchy and to spread Arya Dharma i.e. Patriarchy.

Aayomukhi

There is one more woman 'Aayomukhi'. According to Ramayana, she comes to Lakashmana and asks him to marry her. She too is of Rakshasa background. She too gets the same punishment and a bit more cruel. The two brothers Rama and Lakshamana cut her nose, ears and breasts. This is a barbaric, inhuman punishment indeed.

These two Rakshasa women Shurpanakha and Aayomukhi were given cruel punishments so as to frighten the society and there on to establish a firm trend in the observance of Varnasrama Dharma. Shurpanakha is described as a powerful and independent natured woman. She tells Rama that she is, "Prabhava Sampanna ... Swachanda bala gamini..." i.e. having much power and freedom as to go anywhere according to her will. She introduces herself to Rama".. Aham Surpanakha naam Rakshasi kama rupini... Aranyan Vicharami Idam Eka Sarva bhayankara...' She is very frank. She says she is "Kamrupini", capable of changing her appearance at will. When she is having that power of changing the appearance, she must have approached Rama with a pleasant and good looking features. Any woman naturally desires to approach people with good looks. But here it is not so. She did not intend to impress Rama. That is evident through Rama's words. (These incidents of Ramayana need critical Study).

Hence the cutting of ears, nose and breasts done towards the above characters depict the attitude of upper castes. One has to doubt the character of Rama in this regard. Ramayana Uttara Kanda speaks of Rama as lustrous man enjoying with beautiful women, indulged in singing, dancing and drinking. According to Hemachandra's 'Jaina Ramayana' Rama had four wives. Another Ramayana speaks of Rama having 3000 queens and Lakshmana 16000 queens. So it is a thing to be studied carefully. Usually men when they come across any lady behave politely. They do not hurt the feelings particularly with regard to their beauty. Because Surpanakha is a Rakshasi, she was not shown that minimum courtesy. This 'Rakshasa' race is not original race. It was a cursed race driven to forests on punishment by Aryans not observing 'Aryadharma'.

The initial attack on tribal culture and identity can be seen in Ramayana. The Aryan domination over lower castes and tribes can be seen in the killing of 'Tataka' the tribal queen; and in the insults inflicted on Surpanakha and Aayomukhi. The so called tribals and outcastes were pushed into the forests and mountains and there they maintained separate identity of their own. Some got submerged into the Aryan society in varying degrees.

There are evidences of Aryanization in Rigveda (ix 63.4-5)

> "May the libations of soma joice active in streams of righteousness (Rita) be glorifying God Aryanising all the driving out the foes"

(It is prayed that the ritual of offering "Soma juice" may glorify God as Indra champion of Rita or eternal Moral Law, making righteousness (Rita) prevail, turn all (people) into Aryans (men of noble conduct) and drive away enemies engaged in aggressive acts.)

To make people Aryans is to persuade them to live by Rita or moral law. This moral law is the law framed by Aryas consisting of varnadharma propagating inequality. Those who do not agree to that Dharma were driven out to forests or were punished and finally killed.

This is the transition period of the society changing from Matriarchal system to Patriarchal. This Puranic age is the time when the caste system came into existence.

Mandodari

There is one more character 'Mandodari' in Ramayana. She is wife of 'Ravana'; and daughter of 'Maya' (the architect of Asuras). She used to play chess with Ravana and is the founder of the game. Valmiki port-rayed her character with much care. In Yuddha Kanda - when the war between Rama and Ravana was going on, Ravana started a puja to gain more strength. At that time the vanaras (Ramas army) wanted to divert Ravana's attention. They brought Ravana's queen Mandodari to the place of puja, dragged her by her hair and ill treated her. She was insulted in front of her husband. After much humiliation she requested Ravana to save her and his concentration was thus disturbed. Ramayana describes this incident in detail.

Though 'Sita' was kidnapped and kept in 'Lanka' in Ravana's 'Ashoka garden' for such a long time, there was no illtreatment towards her. She was looked after with great respect. But Mandodari was ill treated by Rama's soldiers. Surpanakha and Aayomukhi were ill treated by Rama and Lakshmana. It clearly shows the outlook of society towards lower caste Dalit women.

These are the few characters chosen to show the trend of Hindu caste based society towards Dalits. Even in modern literatures Dalit characters are not given proper treatment.

It is time the writers to imbibe the spirit of Mahatma Jotirao Phule and Dr. B.R. Ambedkar who fought for human values and Women Liberation through their writings, specially of oppressed classes.

References

1. The Call of the Vedas - Bose A.C., 1970.
2. A Dictionary of Hinduism - Margaret & James Stutley, 1977.
3. Hindu Epics: Historic or Imaginary by Prof. Surindera Ajnat.

7

THEORETICAL UNDERPINNING OF EMANCIPATION OF DALIT WOMEN*

Surendra Jondhale

[1]

The project of emancipation of Dalit women derives inspiration from two major theoretical sources. The first is philosophy of Mahatma Phule and Dr. Ambedkar. The second is a total rejection of Hindu religion. Dr. Ambedkar's position is spelt out in his analysis of castes in 'Castes in India': Their Mechanism, Genesis and Development: 1977; The Rise and Fall of Hindu Women (Mahabodhi monthly, Calcutta); his speeches in Bombay and Nagpur in All India Dalit Women's Conferences and finally in his insistence in passing of the Hindu Code Bill in Indian parliament. Throughout his career he emphasised the need of awakening Dalit woman regarding her dignity, self-respect and self-perception.

Hinduism has degraded women. Patriarchal social system manifested in Manusmriti, Hindu festivals, Hindu pantheon of gods victimised and preyed upon women. *Chaturvanya* treated

* Translated by C.K. Purandare

woman as born Dalit. She led a life of deprivation and subjugation. As a woman she was also in a slave like positon vis-a-vis Dalit man. Psychological, social and cultural proscriptions unleashed by Manu restricted her autonomy. The entire Dalit society including men and women[1] did not have equal economic rights. *Sudras* were slaves and *Sudra* women were doubly enslaved, were slaves of their slave-husbands. Manu upheld this slavery.[2]

[2]

Is the issue of Dalit women different from that of other women? Is it possible to separate the two? There are two opinions in proponents of emancipation of Dalit women to look at this problem. They have different priorities to address the problem. As inequality in India has arisen due to religious, social and economic-factors, Sudra and women have been treated at par. Then in analysing women, a classification will have to be done as Dalit women, other-than-Brahmin women and Brahmin women. One school of thought[3] proposes treating Dalit women not in isolation but treat all women subjugated by Manu's dicta as on an equal footing for the twin projects of emancipation of Dalits and emancipation of women. Need is to combine Dalits and women as both are the victims of the same system.

Religion has ascribed both the groups same status and both share similar disabilities. Dalits were deprived of education. They did not have religious rights, neither social status. Likewise women in India did not have equal openings in educational, religious or social spheres. Therefore it is imperative that both join hands.[4] Commensurate with this logic, struggle for emancipation of Dalit women is a struggle for emancipation of all women. There is no need to distinguish between Dalits and women as women from uppermost to lowermost classes i.e. all women fall under the same category. Upper class woman does not realize the subjugation she is subjected to and suffers from the same predicament as Dalits do. Even *Sita,* an empress was abandoned. *Draupadi,* another empress was dragged in a full royal court for disrobing her. Whether *Ahilya* or *Savitri* or *Sita*, all great women were treated as next to nothing. They faced the same misfortunes and thus irrespective of Varna or Caste, any woman qualifies to be called Dalit. Hence, efforts for Dalit woman's emancipation mean efforts for emancipation of entire womanhood.[5]

The other strand of thinking does not treat all women as one category. Social conditions prevailing in the country point to different nature of disabilities of upper caste women and Dalit women, the latter being at a still lower rung. Upper caste woman is an adjunct to a man, a dependent and a slave in the household. Dalit woman has additionally to face outside world necessitated by economic deprivation and an urgent need to earn for livelihood. Her subjugation is more acute. Being Dalit she is treated with contempt by uppercaste women. There is a qualitative difference between the plights of non-Dalit and Dalit women.[6] Dr. Ambedkar realised this double bind of Dalit woman and tried to restore human dignity to her. As per this positon emancipation of Dalit women originates in the agitation launched by Dr. Ambedkar. A major reason of differentiation between an upper caste woman and a Dalit woman is that the upper caste woman has been ahead of Dalit woman in education and other social spheres for last many decades. It is a fact that Dalit woman lags behind her.[7] The emancipatory movement for women has so far been a prerogative of uppercaste women. These women never took Dalit women along with them in the movement.

Dalit women are never included in agitations launched by these women, nor in their programmes. Upper caste women have never reached upto Dalit women to empathise with them. They have neglected Dalit women. This line of thinking, therefore, proposes a separate movement for emancipation of Dalit Women.[8] If all women are Dalit, why do upper caste women not get perturbed and came out against atrocities committed on Dalit Women. Then what is the point in calling all women Dalit?[9]

These two view points show the spectrum of Dalit women's movement.

[3]

The context of these two streams will be clearer once we look at the intellectual climate of each. Dalit woman's life is a mosaic of many interconnected parts. Political awareness due to Dr. Ambedkar's movement, a new cultural self-perception arisen out of conversion, the mind-set still rooted in Hinduism, a yearning for middle-class white collar way of life, overwhelming poverty, a burning desire to have formal education fostered by the modern environment around coupled with the reality of illiteracy, grinds of daily life to make two ends meet worsened by a husband who does not contribute as much as he should, hardships and innumerable slights - all these make up a Dalit woman's life. Lack of education, an additional factor, makes Dalit woman look down upon herself as dependent and weak vis-a-vis society-at-large. But in political or religious sphere she does not consider herself inferior to others. At the same time, her caste and environment try to further restrict her autonomy.[10] Therefore, attempts of emancipation of women have to be more down to earth. As Dalits rejected a religion, a culture and a god that treated them as sub-human; the women have to reject the religion if they aspire to be liberated. They will have to have courage to reject a god who declared them to be *'Papyoni'* (Evil born) in Bhagavadgita.[11] Dalit woman has got a permanent sanction to reject religion and god on conversion to Buddhism. Her political awareness has arisen out of trials and tribulations of dalit political movement around her.

Priorities of emancipatory movement of Dalit women have also to be listed. Dalit woman today is inspired by Dr. Ambedkar. Her way is paved with difficulties. Dalit woman's social struggle will first of all be a familial struggle. Even an educated Dalit man's mind-set is not necessarily progressive. Only if a Dalit woman has support in her family can she take part in social sphere. As long as she does not have wherewithal for self-actualization, she cannot be considered as liberated. This entails a change in the value system of the society. This would mean a treatment of pathology in human beings and a change in attitude of man towards woman. Till then, Dalit woman cannot forge ahead.[12]

As Dalit social life is full of inner contradictions, dalit woman's emancipatory movement will invariably be dalit man's emancipatory movement. The Dalit man is equally in bondage. He cannot accept a girl more educated or taller or older than himself as a wife. He just wants a woman more good looking than himself because he wants a woman to sleep with. If a man wants a woman inferior to him just to satisfy his lust, then women's liberation movement loses all its meaning. Women's liberation means men's liberation. Once men start treating women as equal, a woman will be automatically free.[13]

The movement for emancipation of women is a movement to end the cultural subjugation.[14] Dalit woman is still oppressed by the Hindu tradition. Ignorance and poverty enslaved Dalit woman socially, culturally, psychologically and in religious sphere. Dr. Ambedkar's movement for women's liberation started with an attack on Manusmruti which fostered blind faith and insulted womanhood. Decision of conversion had many reasons but Dr. Ambedkar also had Buddhism as a religion of choice which treated women as equal and which ennobled them. Conversion has changed Dalit woman very rapidly. She has rid herself of religion imposed restrictions. A woman who was till recently burdened by 33 crore gods and was blaming her fate, has now started living with self-respect. This change is due to conversion.[15] But the psychological and intellectual change in a Dalit woman is still confined to personal and familiar circles. It has yet to spill over to social sphere. It is contended by some observers that the world view of literate Dalit women of today is in transition. Material well-being and to a large extent economic independence have come about. But legacy of Dr. Ambedkar arising out of social commitment has still not effected a change in the consciousness of Dalit women. This is a matter of regret.[16] The only way that Dalit woman could be free of ignorance and superstition was to educate her. This is the cornerstone of the emancipatory impulse coming from Dr. Ambedkar. To change the mind-set, education is a must. Value change would come about through education of Dalit women. Superstition and religious blind faiths will be corrected through education. Those who are supposed to fight for liberation are required themselves to be free to start with. If women remain mental slaves no struggle for women's liberation will succeed. Such freedom through shaping up of the personality can come about only through learning. A person's mental ability should be the key of attraction to him/her. Unfortunately most of the women in women's liberation movement do not follow this course and the movement receives setbacks.[17] There are many difficulties in the Dalit women's movement. Dalit family life is male-centred. The biggest hurdle is man. A woman is restricted even from stepping out of the house by a husband or a brother or a father. The constant hammering of correct norms of behaviour, of dress, of speech make her feel unequal from childhood onwards. These husbands, brothers and fathers have to be freed first if Dalit woman is to be freed. Even an educated Dalit woman cannot take decisions on her own as per her conscience, character assassination being always a hanging sword. Dalit woman is hardly seen in the Dalit political movement today. She is always worried about how her husband would react if she is held up in a meeting or comes home late. Educated Dalit men have not given psycholo-gical space to women in the house, nor freedom of opinion and expression. Hence she is not to the fore in conscientization programmes.[18] Men do not differentiate between an educated Dalit woman and uneducated Dalit women, both are treated at par.[19] The atmosphere in Dalit movement is also not conducive for Dalit woman to trust Dalit male activist. This hampers their full participation.[20]

[4]

The project of Dalit woman's emancipation threatens the existing social order. For millenia Hindu tradition and patriarchy have weakened the Dalit life system. Dalit woman is attempting to seek her identity now.

So far the Dalit woman's movement has prioritised issues of atrocities on Dalit women, their economic problems, their health problems and their legal and constitutional rights. Violence, exploitation through relations of production and sexuality are very much interlinked in Indian society. Sexual division of labour and patriarchy can be major targets to be attacked for women's libe-ration. Sati, ban on widow remarriage, child marriage, tonsure, education of girls were the main areas of protest in preindepen-dence days. Post-independence period has seen ban on dowry, rape, violence and atrocities on women to be main issues of Dalit women's movement. Was the social reform movement prior to independence a women's movement in the real sense?[21] Are the post-independence movements of women's organisations move-ments of *all* women? As the pre-independence social reform kept on insisting on Hindu revivalism, post-independence women's movement have had a preponderence of upper-caste, upper-class, highly educated urban women. They have a limited space to oper-ate in society. The movement has still not reached the lowest strata. Even Dalit and left movements have not reached dalit and unor-ganised labourer women.[22] Why did women's problems and not caste-system become the central issue of preindependence social reform? As there is a need to raise this question, so too is it nec-essary to apportion blame to inadequate understanding of post-independence women's movement about the structure of Indian society and about violence against women.[23]

Dalit women's emancipatory project has a distinct identity because it envisages an alternative value system. If the class inte-rests within the movement are analysed, as against a restrictive view only of social, political and economic peculiarities of a soci-ety, Dalit women's liberation movement shows different charac-teristics from other women's movement. Women do not constitute a single class but are members of different economic classes. There-fore, besides superficial commonalities, demands of one class of women will not coincide with demands of another class of women.

This is reflected in different demands for women put forth by different political parties. Political parties chalk out programmes and analyse women's problems as per the political philosophy they profess. Hence there are a number of currents in women's movement. A uniform autonomomous women's movement cannot sustain because a common material base to launch such a movement is just not there.[24]

Not only is there no common material base but there is neither a common philosophy to combine Dalit women's movement with other women's movement. Dalit women' emancipation entails a dual struggle as Dalit and as woman. Compared with other women, dalit woman is a borne feminist and militant as she has to fight the caste oppression continuously. Caste and women's problems cannot be separated in Indian context.[25] Religion, rituals, texts and the organisation of caste system have intensified and aggravated women's problems. The caste system and women's problems are inseparable. If intermarriages take place on a mammoth scale, then only will caste system disappear. Women's exploitation will also disappear simultaneously. Dr. Ambedkar combined the caste problem and women's problem treating both as fundamental. His paper on Castes in India is important not only as a critic of the caste system but also in the context of women's issues.[26]

Hindu revivalists are aggressive today. It is important to attack caste, the backbone of *Hindutva* philosophy. The attempt of *Rashtra Sevika Samiti* women members from Sangh Parivar in glorifying *Ramlalla* is an attempt to restrict the dialogue within Hindu religion and propose a unitary concept of Hinduism.

Dalit woman's life is difficult because patriarchal social norms are in control among Dalits. Equally true is a fact that Dalit woman's attempt at self-actualization is not restricted to her family. Different experiential world obtains for urban Dalit women and rural Dalit women. There are innumerable instances of Dalit rural labourer women falling prey to atrocities by rich, upper-caste landlords. The dual exploitation is more severe for Dalit women in rural areas. Urban Dalit woman is more conscientized because of the educational environment. New cultural ethos is attractive to her but she lacks the confidence to imbibe these values. One reason for this lack of confidence is patriarchal ideology being quite strong within the household. This results in Dalit woman becoming more self-centred. Middle class/ white collar dalit woman tries to imitate upper castes. To quote a Dalit scholar, "Dalit woman is confused today. She cannot rid herself of the old values neither can absorb new values. She cannot adjust to new values but she has to change". The very inner drive for Dalit woman to change is a ray of hope.

References

1. Ladhake, Nalini "Udhayachi Dalit Stri Sanskratik Gulamgiri Todil" *Ashamitadarsh*, special issue on Dalit Women, quarterly, in Marathi, published from Aurangabad, 1981.
2. Gokhale Pradeep "Stri Purash Vishamata Ani Manusmuriti" *Ibid.*
3. Somkuwar, Nalini *Ashamitadarsh*, May-June, 1984.
4. Ibid.
5. Muthal, Prabha *Ashamitadarsh*, May-June, 1984.
6. Mool, Sushila and Thorat Asha, *Ashamitadarsh*, *Ibid.*
7. Lokhande, Aruna "Aajchaya Dalit Strine Dalitatva Nakarle Aahe" *Ashamitadarsh*, April-May, 1981.
8. Thorat, Asha *Ashamitadarsh*, May-June, 1984.
9. Nandshawar, Kaushalya, *Ashamitadarsh*, April-June, 1984.
10. Bhave, Sumitra *Tawa Chulayawar* Shriwani Prakashan, Pune, 1987.
11. Somkuwar, Nalini - *op.cit.*
12. Lanjewar, Jyoti *Ashamitadarsh*, 1981.
13. Muthal, Prabha, *op.cit.*
14. Ladhake, Nalini, *op.cit.*
15. Mool, Sushila, *op.cit.*
16. Ladhake, Nalini, *op.cit.*
17. Muthal, Prabha, *op.cit.*
18. Lanjewar, Jyoti, *op.cit.*
19. Madhav, Asha, *Ashamitadarsh*, April-June, 1987.
20. Pawar Daya, *Ashamitadarsh*, April-June, 1987.
21. Omvedt, Gail "Ekonisawa Shatkat Udya Pavleiya Bhartiya Stri Chalwali", *Paramarsh* May, 1989. This Quarterly is being published from the Department of Philosophy, University of Poona, Pune; see also *Violence Against Women:*

New Movements and New Theories in India, Kali For Women, New Delhi, 1990.

22. Bhagwat, Vidyut "Maharashtratil Striyanchya Chalwalicha Adhawa" *Paramarsh,* May, 1989, op.cit.
23. Omvedt, Gail *op.cit.*
24. Desai Rajni, Brahme Sulbha and Purohit Sharau "Stri Mukti Andholancha Bhutik Adhar" Research Unit for Political Economy, Bombay, 1989.
25. Somkuwar, Nalini *Ashamitadarsh,* (Special issue on Dalit Women), 1981.
26. Pawar Daya, *Ashamitadarsh,* April-June, 1984.

8

DALIT WOMEN AND THE WOMEN'S MOVEMENT IN INDIA*

Avinash Dolas

One of the striking features of the Ambedkar movement is the participation of women in the movement. Except for the Gandhian movement (nationalist period) probably no other social movement in India shows such widespread participation by women from 1927, dalit women have been in the forefront of the social, cultural and political programmes of the dalit movement. Separate 'parishadas' of women is a case in point. The important issue to note is that dalit women have been active as a group for the last sixty to seventy years. Whether it was the Mahad Satyagrahs, thè Kalaram or Mukhed of Ambadevi Satyagraha; the dalit women have since then been in the forefront just as they were in the satyagraha of the landless in 1960-1965 which was a 'jail Bharo' Satyagraha. Women have been more active than men in popularising the 'Dhamma' of Ambedkar. That education could be the first step in emancipation and hence education for the entire family has been the constant struggle of dalit women. The texture of the dalit family life changed considerably as the neo-Buddhist women consciously

* Translated by Sharmila Rege

brought about changes in the family by transgressing traditional religious norms and rituals and hereditary occupations. In fact even today it is these women who constitute the backbone of the movement. Be it the installation of Dr. Ambedkar's portrait in Parliament, the 'Namantar' issue or land rights issue, dalit women are in the forefront in all local struggles.

The sense of 'community' is strong in this movement of dalit women. It is in this sense a movement of the masses. The Ambedkar movement had always conscientised women to look upon atrocities committed upon them in a broader perspective.

The atrocities on dalit women are not to be seen merely in the light of their being women but must be analysed within the broader framework of societal structure. Hence the struggles of the dalit women are not individualistic; inspired by the teachings of Buddha, Mahatma Phule and Dr. Babasaheb Ambedker, their struggles are in the long run, struggles for human emancipation. Emancipation from religious and caste bondage and creation of a new society are the push factors of this movement.

Feminist activists have often been dismayed by the relatively low participation of dalit activists in the women's movement in India. They complain that despite the movement having taken up issues of dalit women, dalit women have not really joined in their struggles. They see this as a critical issue, viewing at the level of ideas such a complain seems just. Feminists have struggled for change in legal provisions and on issues of importance. But why is it that dalit women, by and large have not felt drawn to this movement? Answers to this question would get revealed if we undertake a caste-class analysis of the women's movement. In a caste ridden society such as ours-which castes constitute and lead the movement-becomes a crucial issue. Such an analysis would reveal why the women's movement could not become a broad based movement.

The women's movement in India gathered momentum after 1975 the declaration of International women's year and the publication of the Report of the committee of status of women in India were crucial happenings. The Women's question assumed importance.

Women from the upper castes gained an opportunity to be conscientised and therefore the issues earmarked by the movement were issues-affecting the women of the upper caste and middle classes. The decade from 1975 - 85 saw the movement centring around the following issues.

(1) Domestic violence
(2) Sexual atrocities
(3) Dowry
(4) Conscientisation and amendment in law.

The very nature of these issues reveal that their protagonists were upper caste, middle class women who had reaped the benefits of education and had felt therefore the need to organize as women. This is not to deny the crucial importance of these issues but to note that these issues did not focus on changing the social structure and therefore could not become mass-based issues.

The women's movement has close historical links with the social reform movement. The social reform movement had focussed on urban, educated, brahmin women and had not brought to the forefront issues of caste discrimination. The reform movement of the 19th century did not have a vision of restructuring rather its major aim was to keep up with changing times. The Western educated Indians sought to fit their wives into the standards and models set by the 'British madames'. This led to proliferation of British etiquette and manners among the women of this class. This period also saw the struggle launched by Mahatma Phule but there was no attempt by Ranade, Agarkar and others to establish links with this struggle. Women's issues therefore could not emerge as broad based and this problem remains to this day.

Social reform movement brought to the fore issues of tonsure, widow remarriage, issues that concerned brahmin women. 90% of the society could not relate to these issues. The women's movement emerged in 1975 in its second phase and here too leadership remained with the upper castes. The movement remained elite. The issues taken up did not appeal to the majority of women and this has been a lacuna of the women's movement.

The women's movement will have to grasp the pulse of the Indian reality in order to become broad based. The differences of region, caste, literacy, class are important in the analysis of women's question. If these issues are not considered as crucial finding a common ground between rural and urban women is almost impossible and no dialogue between the two can possibly emerge. Sexual harassment and exploitation cannot be the only major issues or else the women's movement will find that they cannot reach out to the pulse of the common woman.

For the rural women finding employment, drinking water, fuel and fodder are the pressing needs. In times of drought, the rural women came to be preoccupied with acquisition of drinking water. In the light of the new forest policies and shortage of kerosene, fuel is becoming a major problem. 'Fodder for the cattle has also become a major problem. How has the women's movement looked at these issues? Even if the movement has made mention of these, these issues do not become central and to that extent 'tap for every home' has never been a major demand of women's organisations.

'Rape' bas been a major tool of subordination against women and the dalit movement has reacted strongly against this. The dalit movement analyses 'rape' as an out come of the complex relationship between caste and women's subordination. The dalit women can therefore have the confidence that the entire movement would stand in support of her against such oppression. She does not have to oppose these atrocities as a 'woman'. The women's movement however does not adopt such a broad analysis. The dalit women, therefore do not feel the need for a woman's movement.

Dalit women see their liberation as linked to the abolition of caste oppression. Such a conception of liberation is based on the 'community' and not individual since the dalit women feel a part of the community. She does not feel personally/individually insecure. Since they are as much breadwinners as the males, the artificial, subordinating relations that develop between men and women in the upper classes, do not emerge among in the working-class dalit families. Dalit women do not look upon their husbands as 'protectors' and 'providers'. In this sense, the dalit woman is a part of the larger movement and the 'struggle' an every day practice from which will emerge a new society.

In analysing why the dalit-tribal nomadic-Bahujan communities do not become a part of the women's movement, we will have to give due notice to the very difference in the Brahmin and Bahujan conception of liberation. Mahatma Phule's satyashodhak movement was a contemporary of the social reform movement of Ranade and Agarkar, yet this movement opposed brahmanism, which subordinated the shudras and women and rebelled against it. Tarabai Shinde and Pandita Ramabai carried forth this tradition. Later Dr. Babasahed Ambedkar continued this trend through his 'Dharmantar' and rebelling against the established Hindu order and caste system. Women were in the forefront in large numbers in this 'Ambedkari' movement. These women faced the struggle not as only 'women' but for democratic values and change in relations of production. Women participated in struggles for water, grazing pastines and against caste oppression. At Kannad in Aurangabad District, in 1987, Chandrasena Shejwal led one of the largest 'Rasta Roko' andolan. The participation of large numbers of women pointed to the consciousness of dalit women at the grass root level. From Shantabai Daani, Zadabai, Ishwarabai, Dongrebai to every dalit woman who participates in the Ambedkari movement at the village level, the tradition lives on.

The women's movement has rarely explicated its relationship with this movement. Though the name of 'Mahatama Phule' is often mouthed, the women's movement is probably not yet ready to denounce brahmanism and the Hindu order. Though the women's movement does not really uphold Hindu religion or the caste order there have not been deliberate attempts to denounce these either. Each liberatory struggle begins by denouncing Manu. for e.g. the struggles led by Ramaswamy Naykar, Dr. Ambedkar have symbolically brunt the Manusmuriti. The women's movement has expressed that religion has led to the subordination of women, time and again such views have been expressed in 'Baija' and 'Miluni Saryajani' but not much effort seems to be made to make a public statement or action on the same. Dalit women therefore come to feel alienated from this movement.

Inter-caste marriages as one means of annihilating castes, has been suggested by Dr. Ambedkar in the 'Annihilation of caste', 'Exchange in marriage' is closely linked to inequality. But the women's movement has not paid much attention to this. There seems to be no effort on the part of activists to socialise atleast their own children towards such values. It is such an ambiguous stand that leads the women's movement not to make clear statements against the demolition of the Babri Masjid of 6th December, 1992, or Balasaheb Thakare's anti-women statements at Parbhani in 1989. In a sense with dismay, one notes that the women's movement has not been able to transcend the identities of caste and religion.

The women's movement is almost non-existent. Mangal Khinsara a feminist activist had also expressed the same view about the women's movement. The demands made during the 1975 - 85 decade have been met. Family courts, dowry prohibition, women's representatives on issues concerning women's atrocities, setting up of Mahila Ayog, 30% reservations on local bodies have all been met. Women's activists have little to do except give speeches and clamour for establishing their identity.

Women's movement has always struggled for women's right to property. In 1986-87 when the 'Mahila Aghadi' of the Shetkari Sanghatana took up the 'Laxmi Mukti' programme, it was proposed that the man transfer the land title on his wife's name. Women activists were carried away by this move and established links with Joshi's Movement. On the contrary 'Hakk Savrakshan Samiti' (Samiti for Protection of Rights) had given a call since 1987 for a common title of landholding. A Morcha was organised for the same at Bombay, a Paani Parishad at Ambejogai and 'Draught Parishad' at Aurangabad. Several women's organisations had been invited but none came. It was a historical happening, in Maharashtra when Land was distributed to the landless and a GR was issued to have common title to distribute the land in the name of both men and women in the family. When in Sillod Taluka, land was distributed only in the name of men, one thousand families returned the land. Why did the women's movement ignore this consciousness? Why could not links be established with Prakash Ambedkar if they could have been established with Sharad Joshi? Does the women's movement want to remain with the masses or wants to pamper its own image and establish links only with the upper castes and repeat the rhetorics of equality?

In order to establish links between dalit women and the women's movement these issues need to be considered. It has been assumed that the activists will conscientise the masses. But the masses have the wisdom which activists and leaders must be ready to take. The activists of the women's movement are no exception to this. Such a dialogue is crucial for the relationship between the masses and the women's movement.

9

HUMAN RESPONSE TO DALIT WOMEN TODAY

Fr. Leo Sequeira

Strictly speaking, a non-Dalit male in India, however, sincere in his attempts, cannot do justice to his representation of the life of the Dalit women. I am privileged to share my reflections with you since I had been working and living with the dalits for the last 12 years, in one of the remote areas of U.P./Bihar border. I had the privilege to share in their humanity, joys and pains, celebrations and conflicts, struggles and humiliations, torture and harassments. The best way of knowing what the life of a dalit woman is to experience it, to be a dalit woman. Second best is to step into her *chappals,* or her bare feet, identify with her and live through her experiences.

I admit that it is not going to be a scientific paper, giving the scientific socio-economic analysis of the dalit women today. However I do accept that scientific approach to the whole issue is vital for an effective and integral response. But one has to be aware that the scientific-rational-analytical intellectual approach might satisfy our intellectual curiosity, stir our brains and add to our information. To read about dalit women and their oppression is one thing. It might move you to shed a tear or two at the most and perhaps in seldom cases move you to act but in typical remedial charity. To talk about oppression, is another thing, most politicians and social workers among others are so adept at the art but remain ineffective. To be critically aware, through a concrete experience and common reflection is another thing altogether. It compels you to revolt. Let us remember that every true revolution is also an intense emotion, somehow we need to feel deeply, somehow we need to be touched deeply by the real life experience of dalit women today. It is not a matter of mere words, thoughts/ideas, reading or hearing but one of experiencing and responding.

Before I proceed, let me point out my biggest limitation in treating this issue, namely the realization that dalit women do not need any one taking up their cause, it is to trust in their own humanity, in their own potential to liberate themselves. It is enough just to be a brother, with them in their struggle for humanity.

I am dealing with the human response to dalit women today. The human response includes socio-religious political response since human beings are socio-religious political entities. But I will be touching these aspects from an ethical perspective, from human values and human rights perspective. In the ultimate analysis, it is the issue of the humanity that is being denied to our dalit mothers and sisters of this country.

Factors that Determine the Response

To be human is to respond to human suffering and pain with compassion and effective concern. It is not enough to feel with the dalit women in their pain, we need effective action, otherwise it would be mere sentimentalism. Now the effective action depends upon the real needs of dalit women in a concrete historical situation. The needs and the problems of dalit women differ with city-village, area and caste. Moreover your response to the priority of needs depends upon your anthropology and sociology. If your anthropology tells you that human person is a soul residing in a body that is passing, only extrinsically associated with it (body is like a cloak, soul is the charioteer in the chariot) your response will be purely spiritual. The entire Indian milieu appears to be a theatre or shall I say a museum of sacred places, religious persons and spiritual Gurus. But yet, this inhuman social system remains deeply entrenched and moreover, carefully left untouched by the promoters of spiritual tradition. Nothing significant has ever been attempted or reported to have been done by 'religious' India for the liberation of these impoverished dalit mothers and sisters except raising high sounding slogans. All this indicates that there is something very special about our Indian religiosity and spirituality.

On the other hand, if your anthropology tells you that human person is animated body, rooted in the cosmos and is related to other human beings, your response will be this worldly, communitarian and holistic. Perhaps one has to learn something from the *Carvakas*(Lokayata) who affirm the *dehatmavad* and this worldism.

If you understand the society as mere collection of individuals (Rousseau and company) your response will be individual action. Change the individual and you will change the society. This is exactly how people in power try to show few examples of dalits who have come to such heights. This is the problem of "tokenism". Some women have been given a status of equality and privileges. But this does not make any difference to the vast majority of our dalits living in this country. One needs to keep in mind that dalits are not mere individuals but belong to a sociological and dialectical group.

On the other hand, if you understand society as a system of structure, that is, various mechanisms that determine the distribution of goods in a society. These goods are money=economic structure, power=political structure, status=social structure, that is caste, then your response will be the change of unjust socio-economic and religio-political structures and ideologies.

If you understand that society is basically good and only the operation or implementation is faulty, then your response will be reform or relief. But if you understand that society is basically evil, then your response be towards total change, namely revolution.

Gandhiji tried to reform the caste system, while B.R. Ambedkar tried to change the system, that is, annihilation of caste.

The Dalit Issue

As result of the conflict that took place between pre-Aryan communities and the Aryan invaders (There are some who reject the historicity of the coming of the Aryans to India from outside. This can be denied mythically and mystically but not historically) a section of Indians who enjoyed the casteless and classless (Indus Valley) culture, lost the proud past, their pristine glory and their standing as human beings in their very homeland, and this inspite of their integration with Hinduism. The model of development which is capitalist in orientation, (built on the maximization of profit, and the compulsion of the market forces) built on a social structure, the main bulwark of which is caste feudalism, led to the undermining of traditional economics, the people's art and crafts and their way of life and livelihood. Their cultural heritage, if there is any, consists in their total alienation, economic degradation and sub-human living conditions. The people who are largely the victims of this developmental model and the traditional segregative *varna* ideology are dalits, women and tribals. The alienating and oppressive designs of the forces within Hindu institutions are systematized and legitimized by and through a religious ideology which I call traditional segregative *varna* ideology.

Varna ideology teaches and propagates that humans are born unequal from different parts of the divine body. This inequality and hierarchy of humans is justified by *karma-samsara* theory. If I am a dalit, I have done something wrong in my past life. Your very nature of birth is determined. You have no choice. Your *svadharma* is intrinsic to you. Your salvation lies in your faithful observance of your *varna (Jati)*. There is no mobility in this system. Stay where you are till you die.

Outside the system of *varna* are dalits, the *avarnas,* who are lower than Shudras who belong to the lowest rung of the four-fold caste hierarchy. Dalits are outcastes, too impure to belong to the caste hierarchy. The pollution-purity principle operates so strongly that their touch, and sometimes their shadows and even voices are believed to pollute the caste Hindus! *Avarnas* are not simply human beings. No need to talk about them. They have neither any rights nor is there any possibility of liberation. They exist either as objects of pleasure for the high castes or as means for their welfare and luxury. They are cast out and left out, they are dalits. Determining a person's humanity on the basis of birth is the speciality of Indian culture. This is strictly implemented in the daily life of the majority of Indians though it is rejected outright both in the Indian Constitution and the Declaration of Human Rights.

The term dalit here implies 'those who have been oppressed, broken, crushed and ground down by those above them in a deliberate and active way. To these upper sectors of society the outcastes are nameless, they have no self and no identity of their own. They do not count, except, of course, when there is work to be done to produce wealth, to create leisure and the conditions for the development of culture, and to keep the society healthy and going'.

The dalits in our country are known by many other names given to them by others, mostly to despise them or to show contempt. A name is not a mere label but a disclosure of a reality. They are *avarnas,* colourless and non-descript; or *pancamas,* those left over as it were after the four castes have been counted; or *antyajas,* lastborn, as if they were an accident, an unwelcome appendix, an unwanted tail. They were called untouchables. The unclean castes, the unclean feeders, Harijan and Scheduled castes etc. In the regional language, *Chura* in Punjabi, *Bhangi* or *Lal-Bhangi* in Hindi, *Mala* and (*Madiga*) in Telugu, *Paraiyan* in Tamil, *Pulayan* in Malayalam, *Koragas* in Tulu and Konkani. It is interesting to note even the individual names of these dalits: *Bhikari, Sukadi, Vipatia, Panpatia, Dukni, Chinta, Marni* etc, whereas the names of the upper sector are *Devender, Daya Sagar, Satyanand* etc.

So far, then, others have been giving names to the oppressed. Others have been defining their identity for them and informing them of who they are. The information was that they were untouchables, negatives, non-persons, nothings. But now these nobodies are beginning to name themselves, to show a new self-awareness, to find their own identity and to claim their due place in society. They call themselves dalits, the oppressed. That is what they are. Dalit is the mark of self-identity, self-respect and self-assertion of the ex-untouchable communities and their fighting slogan against the dehumanizing caste-oppression. Dalit acquired revolutionary content within emerging cultural and literary protest movements of Untouchables in the late '60s and early 70s, as part of the larger Dalit Movement, inspired by the late Dr. B.R. Ambedkar.

Dalits form only 16% in India, half of which are dalit women. A major part of the labour force in our country is dalit women. Dalit women go through greater oppression and violence. They are dalits among dalits, down trodden among down trodden. They are oppressed in the family as well as in the society. They are exploited socially, politically, economically and culturally. They are the victims of triple oppression. The caste, class and gender factors all join to crush her inhumanity. Our dalit mothers and sisters are the last, least and lost of our society.

Dalit women have little access to education. They are assetless, being mostly landless agricultural labourers or small artisans. They stand no chance in the battle for livelihood; the contest is unequal. There is equality only among equals. To treat unequals as equals is to perpetuate inequality. The greatest injustice is to divide equally among unequals. Most of them are underemployed. Wages are arbitrary and pitiably low. All this drives the dalits into indebtedness, the result of which is bondage to which even death brings no end. They are denied access to drinking water wells, mahila mandals and co-operatives. Sexual exploitation of the dalit women by the powerful and the upper castes is the worst form of dehumanization. They are left with no voice and face. They are the victims of violence and atrocities both at home and outside.

Reports of the Commissioner for Scheduled Castes and Scheduled Tribes, 1977-78 admit that the Scheduled Castes in many parts of the country... are humiliated, insulted, manhandled, assaulted, burnt alive, tortured and their womenfolk molested. "Their miseries are aggravated when they are boycotted socially and economically".

Dalit Movement

Dalit movement represents a search for an alternative system of values, it is primarily a counter ideology.

The earliest attempts to challenge the traditional Brahminic *varna* ideology were *Nastika* schools, namely, Buddhism, Jainism, and *Carvaka (Lokayata)*. These schools with all their limitations, they do affirm the centrality of the human person and equality of human beings. The anti-caste legacy of Buddhism is definitely a powerful weapon for the enlightenment of the Indian masses. We cannot forget our roots.

Bhakti movement represents another attempt to search for an alternative. With all its short comings, it did promote social, religious and women's liberation. But it was a reform movement within Hinduism.

Then we have the modern period which goes through three phases. 1860/70-1930: It is marked by mass conversion movements to Islam, Christianity and Sikhism. Mass conversion is a rebellion, protest against Hinduism. Both Christianity and Islam preached equality. Human dignity was the main issue.

1900-1955: The mass conversion shook the Hindu leaders. They were losing the cheapest labour force, the dalits. The upper caste in Hindus try to do something for dalits. Hence we have voluntary orgainzations.

Depressed classes mission - 1906; All India Shudhi Sabha - 1909; Gandhiji's Harijan Sevak Sangh - 1932. 1937 onwards Govt. agencies take interest in the social welfare of the dalits.

1920: Self-assertion of the dalits. Only they can redeem themselves. Dr. B.R. Ambedkar tried to solve this caste contradiction, on the one hand, by trying to obtain equality within the framework of the caste system and waging anti-caste mass struggles like Mahad lake - and - temple entry satyagrahas on the Gandhian model, and by waging class struggles like the texitle general strike of 1929 and forming the Independent Labour Party on the other.

He played a crucial role to obtain reservation for scheduled castes and tribes in the constitution itself and provision for the Other Backward Classes to be legislated by State governments. Ambedkar places the human person at the centre. One man, one value. *Dhamma* was greater than *Dharma*. *Dharma* is something private, based on rituals etc. *Dhamma* meant social relationships, religion based on morality, liberty, equality and fraternity. His famous slogan was: educate, agitate, organize.

According to Sharad Patil Marxism-Phuley-Ambedkarism, having its own and more advanced epistemology and having raised the understanding of the law of contraditions to a qualitatively new and higher level, is a new philosophy. Its multilinear methodology is the only applied philosophy in India which has been able to lay bare the laws that regulated the pre-colonial caste-society and that govern the modern caste-class society. The implications of non-Brahmin and Dalit anticaste philosophies and movements have thus become explicit in this new philosophy and its methodology and in the caste-class and women's emancipatory struggles of Maharashtra that promise to assume all India character. (Sharad Patil, "Non-Brahmin and Dalit Movements" in Philip Mathew & Ajit Murican, *Religion, Ideology and Counter Culture* (Essays in Honour of S.Kappen) Bangalore, Horizon Books, 1987)

Human Response

Today dalit women need a humanizing movement, not simply a social reform or an economic Uncle Tom. The highest achievement that humans can aspire to, is no more than to be human and do human.

To be human is to be related. To be related is to *experience* every human being as my brother and sister. Normally we don't experience people in this way. In India people spontaneously perceive fellow human beings as pact of a complex highly stratified system of caste. We see people as member of a caste. Of late, we have begun to see people as Hindus, Muslims, Sikh and Christians. We are very much caste, class and creed conscious. We seldom experience people as human beings especially our dalit mothers and sisters.

The need of the hour is to experience and treat our dalit women as human beings, human persons. They are not objects or things but human persons with beating hearts and living affections. They are not means who live for others as beasts of burden. Things are for use, persons are not for use. For things, usefulness is the chief title for value and worth, but persons have value and worth in themselves, simply because they are human persons.

To be human is to realize that human beings are sacred. Dalit women are human persons and they are sacred. When we meet a dalit woman, we are in the presence of the divine. Hence the dalit women are to be treated with utmost respect, reverence, dignity, awe and admiration.

To be human is to recognize that dalit woman is *someone*, someone who matters, who is significant, who cannot be forgotten or be absent or invisible in our society. She is the subject of history and the future of humanity lies in her hands and in her heart. When we don't recognize the dalit women, their full humanity, we are killing them, we are mutilating them. The dalit women have the basic right to life. Poverty and untouchability in the ultimate analysis is denial of life, and insignificance. It means death. To be human is to affirm life.

To be human is to affirm the radical equality of dalit women. They have the same dignity and worth like any other human being on earth. The worth and dignity of a person does not consist in what one does or what one has but simply because they are human persons.

To be human is to accept the fact that this earth is meant for all, just like water, air, sun, moon and stars. The earth, the land and goods of this earth are meant to be shared in order to have a humane existence. To recognize the real needs and rights of other human beings.

To be human is to recognize that our dalit women are lovely, beautiful loving mothers and sisters who have the potential for humanizing the upper sectors of our society who have become heartless, inhuman and empty. The world of dalit women offers community instead of individualism, simplicity instead of opulence, helpfulness instead of selfishness, creativity instead of enforced mimicry, celebration instead of mere enjoyment, openness to transcendency instead of pragmatism, wisdom instead of information, and naturalness instead of artificiality.

Our dalit women are ordinary people but real. Not the intellectual or the pseudo-intellectual type. Both of these categories of people are fakes, anyway. Our dalit mothers and sisters are genuine and simple, while the intellectuals-in-air-conditioned rooms and the pseudo-intellectuals of mega cities claim to have wisdom but I have experienced the real wisdom, not knowledge, in the dalit women-folk. Mind you, I am not talking romantic nonsense. Just talk to them, be with them, live with them and see how they relate to you from their hearts without pretension, without any show, without any artificiality. They love dramatization. Even their smiles are so genuine that you are simply attracted to them. They are oppressed and exploited but they are human, indeed very human. They are the people who have the ability to live when all means of subsistence have been removed from them, they have the ability to raise a family amidst practically nothing. They are able to celebrate life, one is simply filled with wonder. There is something that keeps these wounded dalit women going amidst acute proverty and misery.

To be human is to respond to human suffering and pain with compassion. It is to be in touch with the primordial experiences our dalit women go through in life. To get into their subconscious, one has to listen attentively to their primal scream as uttered through their inarticulate groanings for life. One of the primordial scream of these women is hunger. When her child is hungry, she suffers in her child. Hunger is a negation of life process. They have no time-table for meals, they have no menu system. Rice and dal are luxury for them, when they get these, it is a celebration. They don't have choice of clothes, no winter and summer clothes. The second primordial experience they go through is bondage. Caste, class and gender, all join to crush her freedom. Third primordial scream is one of fear. They are afraid of invisible forces like bhoots, evil spirits, malevolent gods; they are also frightened of sickness; they are frightened of land-lords, police, local Govt. officials; even afraid of any well dressed powerful looking person. It is to these primal screams that one responds with compassion, acceptance and understanding. It is to respond with gentleness for they are broken and wounded people who get enough shouting and calling of various names with lot of foul language and abusive words.

To be human is to be angry, to revolt. You discover that poor are or have become poor but they have been made poor by a process of exploitation and oppression that is systematic, methodic, structural and purposeful. Rights are never given but always taken. You get angry, you revolt against the politicians, religious leaders etc. I am angry with those who make my people suffer. Anger is the other side of the coin of compassion.

Then comes the third stage or rather the realization that the dalit women don't really need me. they will liberate themselves. I trust in their power. It is enough for me just to be a brother, nothing more or nothing less.

To be human is to reclaim one's roots. It involves the task of rediscovering and reconstructing one's historical past and heritage. This process of reconstruction has to begin from the known Indus Valley civilization in India and its ancient roots. The history of conflict, alienation,and cultural subjugation of dalit women by the dominant culture and its agents, is told in the language of myths, stories, hybrid religious symbols, and rituals. Thank God, the process is already begun.

To struggle is part of being human. There is a price that we have to pay for our freedom and dignity. Freedom is acquired only through struggle and is never given as a gift. In this process we will be opposed, persecuted, harassed, tortured and killed. But then we are glad that the dalits have been taken note of, that dalit struggle is sensed as a challenge and that is a good sign. Once the dalit women are awakened, nothing can stop them. The success of the anti-liquor movement in Andhra is a glaring example. No doubt we are progressing!

Conclusion

The struggle between caste-conscious religiosity and justice-conscious humanity is bound to get sharpened in modern Indian society. The humanizing struggle is neither totally spiritual nor exclusively material but existential in its thrust. We commit ourselves to build a society in which humanity recognizes the humanity of other, especially of our dalit mothers and sisters, is the greatest gift of humankind. I would like to conclude with a dalit poem:

Dalits:

We assist you in your birthpangs,
We bring forth your children,
We wash your linen
We clean your utensils,
Yet we remain *'achuth'*

We plough your fields,
we fill your large godowns,
but, you in turn, starve us.

We cremate your ancestors,
We do mundan for the clan
so that you can mourn
Is this why you burn us alive?

As the lamentations were going on,
I smelt the burning flesh, which echoed:
Woe to you the touchables,
You burnt us alive,
Woe to you the zamindars,
the land that you grabbed from us
will be confiscated and distributed.

Woe to you the politicians,
you sided with the upper castes;
your power will be curtailed.

Woe to you the police
you harassed us unnecessarily;
you will be buried alive.

Woe to you the dalit leaders,
you sold us for your survival;
your security will be shattered

Slowely the woes turned into blessings
Blessed are the bandua-mazdur
for you will break out
from the bondage.

Blessed the dalit women,
for you will mother the
martyrs of Dalitsthan.

Blessed are you the activists,
you shall be rewarded for
your commitment.

Blessed are the dalits,
for you will create a
Dalitsthan
from your burnt out ashes.

10

DALIT WOMEN AND COMMUNALISM

Gail Omvedt

All sections of the recent women's movement have seen the rise of religious fundamentalism, or communalism, as a major threat to women. They have been concerned about the victimization of women in riots, and they have warned that communalists are using religion to tighten patriarchal restrictions on women. According to three feminists,

> "The fate of Hindu women in a Hindu *rashtra* will be no different [from that of Muslim women on whom the veil is imposed]. All kinds of *Lakshman rekhas* will confine us and a good Hindu woman will inevitably have to be like Sita, performing *agniparikshas* every time anyone suspects her of infidelity" (Kamla Bhasin, Ritu Menon, Abha Bhaiyya, "Why Women Fear the Fundamentalists," *Times of India*, January 20, 1991).

The Shetkari Mahila Aghadi has made a similar point:

> "The atmosphere of violence and insecurity thereby generated puts further restrictions on the already crippling restrictive

> life to which most women are condemned. As social and political life becomes more violent and criminalized, women become even more peripheral in public life and are pushed further into the confines of the [home]..." (Resolution of the second conference of Shetkari Mahila Aghadi, Amraoti, Maharashtra, November 10, 1989).

And, the national women's conferences meeting at Calicut (1991) and Tirupati (1994) have made similar arguments. The Calicut conference decided to take up a "national struggle against communalism," and in a review of the "women's decade" in Bombay in January 1994, attended by leading feminist scholars and activists from around the country, nearly half of the three days of discussion were taken up with the issue of communalism.

Yet in spite of these concerns of the women's movement, the endless debates and discussions on "women and communalism" have not yielded much result. The women's movement has been singularly *unsuccessful* in combating the rising forces of Hindutva in particular. Not only that, but it has not been able to prevent these forces from attracting militant women to their cause, women who like Uma Bharati and Sadhvi Ritambhara, somehow find scope for their aspirations within the organizations of the communalists and in the processes become voices of hate against others.

Dalit/Bahujan Women: A Different Approach

Where do dalit women stand in this? Organisations that have had a strong base among dalit women have also protested against communalism, and have pointed out that the attack of Hindutva is not only against the religious minorities, but also against dalits and low-castes within the Hindu community. For instance, "Stri Mukti Sangarsh," working among rural and low-caste women in southern Maharashtra, pointed out that

> "While calling themselves 'Hindutvavadis' these organizations are undertaking a campaign to impose the old brahmanic religion upon us once again. They say that the "Dharma Sansad" is superior to the "Lok Sansad" elected by the people.

> They are undertaking to restore a regime described by the old Marathi saying, 'knowledge in the house of the Brahmans; grain in the house of the Kunbis; songs in the house of the Mahars and Mangs'. They are undertaking to reimpose slavery on women. Just as Rama abandoned Sita, without any fault of her own, on only the whisper of scandal, so many men today are abandoning their wives, making them "parityakta." According to these people, disinheriting women—making them properties—is considered to be a model" (Resolution #1, Second Conference, Islampur, February 7, 1993).

It seems that there is an important difference between the approach of the "mainstream" women's organizations and the women's organizations based on dalit-bahujan women. The mainstream organizations, based largely on upper-caste urban women, draw their theories of communalism and women either from traditional Marxism or from the neo-Hindu, neo-Gandhian thinkers of today. Traditional Marxists see the solution to communalism in an abstract "secularism" backed by what they consider "class struggle," while the neo-Hindus argue for restoring the "real" traditions of Indian communities. Both have joined hands in concentrated their political attack on the forces of "imperialism" (including cultural imperialism) and "globalization"—and in doing so, they are not only ignoring the issue of brahmanism in "Hindu" culture, they are also joining hands with the forces of Hindutva communalism even while pretending that Hindutva is their enemy.

In contrast, the dalit-bahujan traditions sees the cultural roots of communalism as being in the brahmanic versions of "Hinduism" within India, and calls for an out-and-out attack on the BSO or "brahmanic social order" as part of the fight against communalism. Instead of "secularism," they believe that the solution must bring in an Indian cultural renaissance which will defeat brahmanism and revive and develop the true culture of the people, which will stand on the side of Sita and Shambuk, Tataka and Bali Raja in opposition to Rama and his armies.

Marxist Theories of Communalism

Marxism in India has had a noble record, in many ways, of

including people of all castes and religions in its movement and of standing up against the worst of communalism and fundamentalist forces. Yet this same Marxism has been affected by the brahmanical traditions of India, and has accepted the brahmanical interpretation of Indian culture as being primarily a "Hindu" culture; it has ignored the significance of caste divisions and patriarchal controls. In taking the fight against "imperialism" to be primary, it has ignored the realities of the caste-feudalism. Originally, Marxists saw Phule and Ambedkar as simply British agents; now they do not dare to openly condemn them as such; instead they use the names of Phule and Ambedkar, in much the same way as the BJP tries to recruit Ambedkar—without any serious effort to examine their theories or to change in any way their own "class analysis." As a result, they have no real theory of caste, and their analysis of class itself—and of the contemporary nature of world capitalism—remains inadequate, and works only at the level of sloganeering. The power that a historical materialist theory should have to comprehend the world has remained undeveloped.

The version of "historical materialism" that most Indian Marxists use sees the economic roots of communalism as being in, first, "feudal remnants," and second, the economic insecurities resulting from stalled development within a "world capitalist system." But, their analysis of feudalism does not criticize the brahmanic and caste elements in it, and they have a wrong analysis of the capitalist system and imperialism.

As a result, they make several serious mistakes in analyzing communalism. For instance, looking at "feudal remnants" they tend to see the roots of communalism in the rural areas and among rich farmers (the "agrarian bourgeoisie," or "the rise of the rich peasants" are seen as behind the growth of regionalism, communalism, etc. etc.) It is of course true that many farmers and many rural people have communal ideas; it is true that it was the low castes who were dominant in the mobs that tore down the Babri Masjid. But that is no different from the fact that the armies of every country are filled with workers and peasants who kill each other! The fact remains that it has been the urban centers, not the villages, that have been the main bases of communalism. Some sections of the farmers have opposed communalism just as strongly as any section of the proletariat; while the Shiv Sena began in Bombay, and of the mass organizations linked to the BJP-Sangh Parivar, the BMS remains much stronger than their peasant organization, the BKS. It also has to be pointed out that, even though the BJP gets funding from many industrialists, the "bureaucratic" forces appear to be more communal than the "bourgeois" forces: within the Sangh parivar, it has been the brahmanic (bureaucratic) RSS element that has been the most hardline, in contrast to the bania (business) element.

Similarly, much of the left today is pointing to liberalization and "structural adjustment" as being responsible for communalism. But there is no real basis for this. Asian countries which have been the most open to the world economy (South Korea, Taiwan, Malaysia, Indonesia) and have had high rates of economic growth have included many countries which are religiously and ethnically divided; they have been countries with Buddhist, Muslim and Confucian traditions. While religious fundamentalism has existed in some of them, it has not grown to be as strong a force as Hindu and Muslim communalism have become in India and Pakistan, countries which up to now have had closed and state-dominated economies.

Neo-Hinduism and Communalism

Another major social-political trend in India today is neo-Hinduism or neo-Gandhism. However, though it draws on the name of Gandhi and on many Gandhian critiques of industrial society, it differs from Gandhi in crucial respects. Similarly, though it is often very critique of the BJP-RSS brand of communalism, it shares many themes with them. This trend is represented by theorists such as Rajni Kothari, Ashis Nandy, Vandana Shiva and by many sections of environmentalists and some feminists.

They see the basic contradiction as being not between classes, but rather as being between traditional peasant and tribal communities and the modern market and state, which is seen as dominated by "western science and technology." In contrast to marxists, they talk more of ideology and culture than of economic classes; but they have an unreal and elitist interpretation of culture.

Just as Marxists speak in the name of the proletariat and oppressed classes, these claim to speak on behalf of peasants, adivasis and local communities. But they are no more peasants and low-castes themselves than the Marxist activists are workers. In contrast to Marxists, they may praise the "traditional communities, traditional knowledge,"etc. But, just as Marxists ignore caste and patriarchal domination in the Indian social system, these theorists ignore the role of caste and brahmanism in the "traditional" society.

They sometimes claim to be also opponents of the centralized state; but their analysis basically also praises the Nehruvian state. According to Rajni Kothari, for example, the Indian state was essentially "liberatory" after independence, but failed in its goal of bringing a real development, and now the processes of imperialism, world capitalism, privatization etc. are taking over. The major enemy is thus taken to be "privatization," globalization and the market. Here they depart from Gandhi, who was opposed to centralized planning and a centralized state even more than private capitalists.

The New "Grand Alliance" Against the Congress

Today, strikingly, we find that the traditional Marxists and the neoHindus are joining together politically, in an opposition to liberalization and globalization. They are giving an over-simplified, outdated analysis that this represents a "new colonialism," a "new East India company" taking over—and they are falling in line behind the BJP in opposition to the Congress. Politically, what we see today is a new "grand alliance" grown from the opposition to the "Dunkel draft" and the "new economic policy." The claim of Marxists and neo-Hindus that they are opposing communalism is proving to be false. Instead, they are going back to their old habits of making electoral alliances with the BJP (if not openly then under the name of "seat adjustments"); they had an implicit alliance with the BJP in bringing a "no-confidence" motion against the Congress last year, even though they knew that if the motion succeeded the only opposition party capable of forming a government would have been the BJP. The Bahujan Samaj Party was criticized for abstaining on this no-confidence motion, but today we see that the real defeat of BJP in U.P. elections was brought by political forces standing for "anti-brahmanism" and based on dalits and bahujans, that is by the Bahujan Samaj Party-Socialist Party alliance. If there is to be an alternative to Congress today, it has to be an alternative that also opposes communalism effectively, and that presents a positive economic program to the people.

Dalit-Bahujan Women and the Analysis of Communalism

What can we learn from the struggles of dalit women that will help in analyzing and defeating communalism—and not only the communalism of the Sangh parivar, but also the more subtle brahmanism of the supposedly "secular" Congress?

Let us examine the following points about communalism:

- *Communalism is not a "religious" phenomenon; really it is a case of distorted nationalism.* What communal ideologies stress is not so much the defense of a religion as of a *people* which is said to have a particular religion. Elements of heritage and blood are stressed in a way that makes it a racist ideology. (Even with Christian "religious fundamentalism" this can be seen; in the U.S. for instance it has always been connected with white racism). Thus communalism is an outgrowth of nationalism in which the elites within any community are trying to maintain control by depicting the community or nation as beseiged by real or imagined oppressors who must be fought. The "religion" that communalism stresses is always a warrior religion or interpreted as such. In India the "communalism of the majority" (Hindutva) is openly nationalistic; but the "communalism of the minorities" (Muslim or Sikh communalism etc.) also tends to seek a nationalist expression.

It is here that the themes of feminism and the anti-caste movement: women are oppressed within all "national" boundaries; dalits are linked to all the oppressed peoples of the world etc.—remind us of a universalization going beyond narrow nationalism.

* *Gender or patriarchal characteristics are inherent in communalism.* Communalism is a kind of "nationalism" in which the community or "nation" is seen in family terms. Such phrases as "motherland" or "fatherland" are of course common. The militarization of the community is also expressed in gender and kinship terms. There is the patriarch (Khomeini, Bhindranwale, or the imaginary form such as Ram) and the warrior sons; the guerrila warriors defending the nation are the "boys." Mothers and sisters become symbols of the community/family which is to be defended, and the image of rape by the enemy is an all-pervasive part of propaganda. Women can play their role in the struggle, a few can even become "warriors" themselves; but they are primarily to be enclosed and protected. A few women warriors do not change the patriarchal character of communalism. And the protection of the sister from rape can easily turn into wrath when the sister becomes seen as the worst betrayor for consorting with the enemy: the sister becomes the whore, the breaker of boundaries.

As against this, the low-caste women are not only victims of rape; they assert their own rights to revenge (as in the case of Phoolan Devi) and they resist the efforts of men of their own "community" to keep them enclosed and protected in a new "Lakshman rekha."

* *Historically the rise of communalism is related to the nature of world capitalism and statism.* But the left has had an inadequate analysis of this in talking only about private property and in ignoring the role of the state. For example, in the South, the conditions that have fostered communalism include:

(1) Capital-intensive industrial growth occurring only in enclaves, capable of employing only a minority of the working class in industries that are often environmentally destructive. The biggest polarization in India has taken place not between "rich farmers" and poor and landless peasants in agriculture (here there is often great inequality, but this inequality has not increased); but between the organized sector and the unorganized sector. The organized sector, employing only about 10% of the work force, increased its share of national income from 23.5% in 1960 - 61 to

38.8% in 1984-85; organized sector incomes are three to four times Higher than the incomes of unorganized sector wage workers and farmers—and about six times as high as incomes of agricultural labourers (see Centre for Monitoring the Indian Economy, *Basic Statistics on the Indian Economy, 1989*).

This organized sector continues to be dominated by uppercastes (as the Mandal Commission has made clear, the top 15% of the population hold nearly 70% of all public sector jobs and 90% of Class I positions). Its growth has been part of an industrialization policy that has focussed on building up a public sector-dominated, heavy industrial base with discrimination against agriculture and small artisan producers (the traditional dalits and OBCs). Agriculture, it is now admitted, has not been "subsidized" but rather under the guise of giving subsidies and government "schemes" it has been *taxed* through policies of low prices etc, trade mechanisms that discriminate against exporters, etc. The same can be said for other sectors such as textiles, leather and crafts etc.

(2) The result of this exploitation of agriculture and the unbalanced developmental model followed has been to tear apart traditional communities and to bring about a massive exodus to the cities in countries like India. People have found more freedom and economic opportunities in urban slums than in the depressed villages. Ambedkar's statement, "villages are cesspools," was made into a truth by the developmental path of India! Throughout the South, urbanization rose in the last decades: from 17% in 1965 to 35% in 1988 for low-income countries (*World Development Report, 1990*, Table 10). But even the cities offered opportunities only for a few; and it has been in their festering slums and among their frustrated lower and middleclasses that communalism has found its main material base.

(3) This unbalanced development was encouraged by the "industrialization" policies of imperialist countries and by the World Bank etc. Yet the elites of the countries of the

South—such as the high-caste brahman dominated elites of India—cannot escape their responsibility for this by only pointing a finger at "imperialism." In fact a policy of industrialization, domination of the public sector, "big dams" and other huge developmental projects, an educational system that favoured the elite—all of these were part of the "Nehru model." Here V.T. Rajshekar's critique of "socialist brahmans" rings true:

"Socialism means nationalisation of industries. Nationalism means no need of work. So, occupying key positions our 'sacred threads' will get fat salaries without doing any work. It was Jawaharlal Nehru's brainwave to promote the *bhoodevatas* through nationalisation. Nehru served the *bhoodevatas* better than all you sacred brahmans put together..... Nehru led a life of supreme pleasure, wining and dining and womanising too, which is what every *bhoodevata* is expected to do. Nehru did all this and ruled India for over a decade and yet remained the darling of the idiots and the wretched...." (*Dialogue of the Bhoodevatas*, p. 37).

* *The failure of Marxism to offer a real liberatory alternative and find a true path to socialism has also aided the growth of communalism.* People in despair have turned to national and communal identities rather than building on their identities as oppressed and exploited people. Marxist illusions about industrialization, the confusion of nationalism and state control with socialism, the one-sided emphasis on economic identities without taking cultural factors into account, have all left the socialist movement in tatters.

* *As against this, the long tradition of indigenous social radicalism in India has emphasized alternatives of identity as well as alternative economic theories.* Phule, Ambedkar, Pariyar and many others have contested the idea that brahmanic Hinduism represents Indian culture, and have put forward a low-caste, peasant-based alternative that also offers much more equality for women. Women have been part of building this alternative from the beginning—from outcaste Brahman women such as Pandita Ramabai to Marathas such as Tarabai Shinde to dalit activists

such as Jayabai Chaudhuri. Now it is clear that dalit and bahujan women are again coming forward. For instance women activists in the Bombay seminar reported that girls were very active in the BSP-SP campaign in U.P.

But again there is a problem. Mayavati's role in the BSP has been central, but few feminist activists have defended her from the vicious attacks regarding statements on Gandhi. Phoolan Devi has become a symbol to women throughout the world for revenge against rape—but the Indian women's movement has ignored her. Taking up the struggles and listening to the needs of dalit and bahujan women is a crucial necessity for any women's movement in India.

11

SOCIAL DEVELOPMENT AND DALIT WOMEN

Neelam Gorhe

'The issue of not only participation but sharing the fruits.'

Mohan Kamble, brother of Adnya Satwaji Kamble-a twelve year old Dalit girl, and Satwaji Kamble, her father, were murdered on the 7th of September, 1991 in Gothala, Latur District, Maharashtra. A crisis was brewing in the village on the issue of appointment of a Dalit as a Kotwal. Till then the non-Dalit sections of the population and even the media were under the impression that casteism has not played any role in this incidence and the struggle was between 'Good' (Non-Dalits who attacked) and 'Bad' (Dalits, who were attacked). I visited the village along with a team of activists. We asked Adnya "Where do her people get water from?" The Dalits with her informed that they get it form a source within their basti. And "What if this supply runs short or you require more water, say, for ceremonies and all?" Adnya shot back, "if we go to the main village we are driven away with choicest curses and abuses".

A few members of Latur Mahila Mandal with us broke down on hearing this reply.

Only a very few are interested in understanding the intricacies of the Dalit problem. Usually there are two compelling factors behind any action directed towards the redressal of the problem. For society at-large it is pity; for the state power, it is the unavoidability of the problem. 'It would not go away' sort of attitude.

During 1991-92, Scheduled Castes and Scheduled Tribes had to face 3,351 instances of atrocities. These included 120 cases of murder and 275 cases of rape as quoted in National Statistics. The Dalit woman lags behind her upper caste counterpart or a Dalit man in all the spheres which enhance the standard of living-whether literacy, health, employment, property rights and economic status, or political participation. In education, in the State of Maharashtra, to cite only one area, following are the statistics.

Out of 100 children enrolled, 47 boys and 29 girls reach upto the 8th standard and 15 boys and 7 girls upto the 12th. Among SCs/STs, of the 100 children enrolled, 37 boys and 22 girls reach upto the 8th standard and 11 boys and only 4 girls upto the 12th.

There are a few problems which are specific to the plight of the Dalit woman. Caste is the foundation of the Hindu religion. More the power wielded by religious institutions, more the controls exercised and more the exploitation deriving out of inequality. Not only is human dignity denied to the exploited but even basic human rights are seen as favours.

Caste domination takes many forms. It may be a ban on intercaste marriage, it may be restrictions on educational or employment opportunities or on adopting better cultivation practices in farming. It may even be a resentment if Dalits wear better clothes or have better utensils in the house.

19th century saw rise of a new awareness of human rights the world over. This was about the time the British consolidated their colonial rule in India. The awareness found its expression in India. Muktabai, a girl student in Mahatma Jyotiba Phule's school expresses doubt about benevolence of a God who selectively bestows misery on 'us'. There were set of rules and norms governing behaviour of each caste and sub-caste. There have been many attempts by scholars to explain the origin and rationale, if any, behind the caste system. Among these, Dr. Ambedkar's contribution to unravel the labyrinth has been a landmark combining as it does analysis and an orientation to action. Things have not been the same after him, to use an off repeated phrase. According to him the Indian Caste system was not a division of labour in society but that of labourer class in society. Each caste has an hierarchy wherein each stratum feels it is above another stratum. Change in economic conditions does not change a caste. Such postulates went a long way in conscientization of Dalits particularly in Maharashtra. As an effect, social perceptions of Dalit women changed after conversion to Buddhism. This change in perception has given rise to two distinct sections of women among SCs and STs. One is of those conversant with and inspired by Dr. Ambedkar's thoughts while the other of those totally unaware of this conscientization. Both the groups have to be addressed differently. Alternatively we may consider three categories of women from the movement point of view : Women from the nomadic castes/tribes, Non-neo-Buddhist Dalit Women and women in the Ambedkarite movement. These categories are useful for understanding the issues of consolidation of organization and unity.

Some of the experiences from grassroot will highlight complexities and specialities of each group.

1. *Women from nomadic caste/tribes* : Many organizations of nomadic castes and tribes jointly held a conference in Pimpri-Chinchwad near Pune in 1983. Prominent Dalit thinkers/activists like Laxman Mane, Daulatrao Bhosale, Motiraj Rathod, Balkrishna Renke, etc. participated in the conference. Women from various nomadic communities like Kaikadi, Kanjarbhat, Dangat, Vaidu, Joshi, Kashikapadi, Gondhali, Vanjara, Bhat, etc. were there. I compered the group discussion and issues that came up after studying other literary sources. These were:—

   a) Insecutity and social contempt arising out of migrations give a dependency syndrome. This is narrated in many autobiographics by writers after 1960's.

b) Neglect of health, education, lack of legal support all contribute to a lower standard of living necessitating a living at somebody else's mercy.

Common experiences of humiliation include public parading of these women, harassment at the police stations, sexual assaults etc. The hold of superstitions, practices like child marriages continue. Laxman Mane reported a sinister practice prevalent in a few castes among nomads during one of women's conference (conference arranged by Stree Aadhar Kendra, Pune of Women from nomadic communities on March 25, 1986).

A newly married couple is made to spend the first night by sleeping on a white bed sheet. This bed sheet is inspected by a caste-*panch* and the relatives on the next day for blood stains—a proof of the bride's virginity. And if there is no blood stain, girls parents have to pay fine or marriage is broken. In Panchayat disputes, woman is termed as cow and child as calf ! Denial of rights due to discriminatory caste panchayats is a major issue.

c) The state has tried to rehabilitate the nomadic communities. Some of the communities have also tried to settle at a place. In both the attempts, there have been reports that the villagers where a new settlement would come up, tried to oust the new settlers. Sometimes the villagers are apprehensive because some of the communities used to indulge in criminal activities in the past and the stigma persists. For some other communities who presumably still make a living by thefts, it is reported that the goods stolen were forcefully taken away by the villagers and the momads driven out.

2. *Non-neo-Buddhist Dalit Women* : Caste continues its strangle hold even on conversion to christianity or Islam. Lower castes continue to be exploited and treated as inferior. Women from such convert castes and those from the Hindu-fold like Matang, Mehtar, Charmakar, Dhor etc. show some common characteristics :

(a) There is a dependence on traditional occupations. These may be sweeping a locality, collection of scrap, smearing the floor with dung, rope-making etc. Girls from educated households—both rural and urban are found to be emulating middle-class way of life. But they feel suffocation in the uneducated group and with educated upper caste women.

(b) Various forms of superstitions continue like worship of a local goddess with attendant dancing in the month of 'Ashadh' (to ward off evil), playing traditional band in front of a house in case somebody in the household is suffering from boils on the body, etc. There is also an attempt to glorify one's own community rather than any attempt to understand the link between exploitation sanctioned by the government resulting in lower status and miserable living conditions. Hence, there is no desire to improve the situation. Neither is there much awareness except in a few stray cases to join Mahila Mandals or participate in wider groups.

(c) There are many Matang women among Devdasi-muralis.

(d) Nomadic urban women and those who work have problems similar to those of other caste urban women. These are harassment at workplace and elsewhere, getting inadequate daily wages, struggle for civic amenities, addict husbands, paucity of health care facilities, etc. Education and employment are the two sectors where casteism operates both openly and subtly. All Dalits need come together to counter casteism.

3. *Women in the Ambedkarite Movement*: I worked then with Bharatiya Republican Party (Prakash Ambedkar group) from 5th May, 1984 to 10th August, 1990 as a General Secretary for Maharashtra and also as Women's Organizer for some time. I have had an opportunity of interacting with hundreds of Dalit women during this period. Since 1992 I am with Republican Party (Ramdas Athavale group) as a General Secretary for Maharashtra. The political position has been confrontationist

as well as co-operative with the powers that be. My findings are as follows :

(a) *Role and Participation in Decision making* : Dalit woman is pained to see the factionalism in Ambedkarite movement and differences arising solely out of personal ambitions and competitive narrow interests. Such divisions affect political participation adversely, especially at the *basti* level where leadership is to be groomed. Women also face an additional and constant apprehension about character assassination. (Dual norms for sexuality). Family decides the extent of participation of women in social and political programmes. Unfortunately, the organizations including political parties with an allegiance to Dr. Ambedkar's thoughts have inculcated the same culture as obtains in other political parties. Factors like late-night meetings, absence of commuting facilities, leadership's taking offence at plain-speaking etc. impede women's participation. Sycophancy has become a virtue which gets duly rewarded. Women can prove themselves only if the political leadership backs them consistently and strongly. This has been observed over years. Women come to fore during struggles as a collectivity and on specific issues. There is non-participation between two successive struggles due to economic pressure to earn and conflicts due to factionalism. There is neither energy nor time for a sustained movement, nor co-operation from men. Society always looks upon a woman working with men with suspicion. Same applies to political sphere too. As compared with the sphere of religion, different type of men are active in politics resulting in less participation of women in political affairs than in religious ones because women don't feel security within political circles. Yet 30% reservation for women has made many Dalit Women participate more actively in politics. Last 10 years have seen development of women's cadres who can work at district level in Maharashtra. They, however, do not enjoy decision-making positions commensurate with the commitment they have had. In the near future Dalit Women will have to create a network of women's organizations and raise resources. It is also necessary to hold training programmes for Dalit women. They will also have to get backing of non-casteist political leadership.

(b) *Participation*: Dalit women will have to have power of negotiation based on their philosophy, activities and strength. Some mechanism needs to be evolved for them to get such power. Bureaucracy can be of much help in this endeavour if it does not dampen the awareness and vigour of Dalit women and implements the state programmes in an egalitarian manner. Women have to be given continuous opportunities to work which alone can make up for their low level of education and lack of unity among them. At the village level it is desirable to have groups of women implementing various projects to ensure a more efficient utilization of resources.

There are many positive schemes launched by the government like Mahila Samakhya of Karnataka, WDP in Rajasthan. SEWA of Ahmedabad has made the impact of women's power felt at the national level. In Maharashtra there is a large number of Dalit writers and activists whose networking is important.

The issue is very relevant as in the political parties, numerical number which can be organized becomes important than space created for individual women's empowerment. Though the importance of collective struggle is very important, lack of information to Dalit women increases their dependence on men in the political process or on Non-Dalit women's group. Though there are many women's rights groups and feminist womens' organizations, very few Dalit women are part of the decision making process of these groups. Women's organizations like ours, who try to raise issues about patriarchy, caste & class together are isolated within women's movement and within Dalit movement. Very few men and women leaders understand our work. Sometimes both the groups feel secure in Ghettoization than taking issue together. Specially in the executive committees of political parties, where 90% are men members and most of them happy in traditional sexual division of labour within their homes, I have felt often very lonely and felt as struggling the lone battle.

Upto the time there is no democratic setup of parties where women will have opportunity to get elected from women, they will have to remain on 'mercy' of District and State leaders. Secondly Articulation of speech, Drafting political and ideological agendas are important skills, which can be achieved by practice, opportunity and studying political process. Here I can see role of educated Dalit women, being a strength for non-visible Dalit women in the decision making process. This is a challange to Dalit men also whether they can be de-conditioned and work for gender-justice.

Strategies also include having autonomous Dalit women's groups and having networks with other women's groups.

One feels a need of independent a political women's organizations to take up the task of emancipation of all and not *only* Dalit women. Such organizations can facilitate both a dialogue within and undertake a struggle without.

(c) Economic empowerment of Dalit Women: Dalits are mostly among landless in rural areas and live in slums in urban areas. Hence, middle class Dalit women have a special responsibility to be active and alert. Lack of market information restricts Dalits' entry in small scale industry or in self-employment. Activities like edible production or managing restaurants seem to be having potential for business. Dalits are slowly entering into transport sector. But to enter into sectors of economy like co-operative societies, manufacturing industry or tourism it is necessary to have good contacts, market intelligence, training, management skills and social commitment. One does not know whether all the four can really coexist. Consequently Dalit youth has to make his way through caste struggle and economic participation. The same applies to Dalit Women.

Certain traditionally produced articles like ropes, baskets, brooms have been rendered obsolete by industrialization. This has meant that a new castes like Vaidu, Kaikadi and others are left with no occupations to offer in the market.

Since neo-Buddhists are coming out of the jajmani system they no longer abide by the restrictions on occupations. But other castes do have these restrictions. This gives rise to a dilemma. Demands like extension of special facilities to traditional occupations may in fact strengthen the traditional division of labour. The caste system on the other hand, allows no access to other skills and competition is fierce. Therefore the state tries to give priorties to certain programmes, raises certain special funds. Dalit women's economic status is linked with the wider issue of exploited women's condition in the era of privatisation and the new economic policy.

With the liberalization policies, the private sector is getting more facilities and some of the Govt. or Semi-Govt. areas are also being given on contract system. In the unorganized sector, there are no reservations in the job. As Central govt. has announced additional incentives for farmers as compensation for negative impact of new policies, there is need to ensure interests of Dalit and poor section.

Justice for and development of Dalit women can only be attained through constructive Development activities, conscientization and struggle. It is possible to have a network of women's organizations having non-aligned decision making power. Gender and caste have reinforced each other in the prevailing division of labour for exploitation of women. These have to be changed both at the political level and in the mind-sets of the people.

In the ideological framework, certain issues taken by feminist movement are very relevant for Dalit women also. Issues like 'Personal is political', 'Control over our own bodies' can give lot of insights. At the same time, contradictions and isolation faced by women of upper caste

> within family system, may not be present, when husband and wife both are part of the same movement. Patriarchy may have different manifestations. These mani-festations of patriarchy may change depending upon legal and social status. Here role of state power should not be underestimated as provisions of freedom and 'Emancipation from fear' are basic rights of citizens offered as per Constitution of India.
>
> After Indian freedom's long struggle and with the era of post-independence period, perspective for women's development was within narrow framework of *'welfare state'*. In this framework women were looked upon as mere objects of pro-creation and as mothers. As citizens of India and human beings, women and specially Dalit women have right of development.

In view of this, state of Maharashtra has declared new policy for women. This policy along with announcing many new provisions, legal Amendments for giving share in the property, speaks for empowerment of women. The policy also assures measures to check violence against women, sensitivization of police force, and reservations in job for women. These reservations will be for women in each caste as per the particular percentage. The policy also gives due credit to 'invisible' toiling common women in Maharashtra and N.G.O.s working for women. When as member of State Women's Commission, I had raised the issue of Dalit women while responding to the final draft, the state of Maharashtra has assured that though the specific word 'Dalit' is not included, Govt. is committed to strengthen the role of Dalit women and Nomadic women in the development process. Regarding this, Chief Minister Mr. Sharad Pawar wishes to scrap the schemes from the govt. which give status to Dalit women as just "paupers" or 'beggars'. New schemes which will reduce dependence on the government and increase self help are being worked out. With the 30% reservation and new policy for women, there is more expectation and aspirations from women. Dalit women are taking a lot of initiative for literacy movement. Dalit women are also expressing powerfully in literature. More space needs to be created in the National and at State arena for Dalit women.

And though some of them cannot write in the language, which is acceptable to the middle class, they do understand politics. I remember, a discussion in a Buddha Vihar with an expert on social forestry from the world Bank. We were discussing whether Dalit women who are having the land or land available as traditional caste 'watan' land can be used for horticulture? And whether women's groups will be able to look after the trees? Women from Manchar village looked at each other and said, 'of course, instead of having a barren land, we will be happy to have trees? and suddenly one of them asked, but who is going to have control over the fruits? We the cultivators or labourers or men, who take them to market'. How we will get strength to own the fruits of the trees, which are cultivated by our energy and life?

Precisely, the issue of social development and Dalit women, is the issue of sharing the fruits and not only participating in labour as mere implementers. Realization and acceptance of this 'just' demand by Dalit women need to be understood on state power and political leadership including global women's movement.

12

THE LIFE OF A DALIT WOMAN*

Kumud Pawade

Introduction

What is the life style of a Dalit woman in the urban areas? I am not writing this as a sociological survey, but as an attempt by a social worker to evaluate the life. So instead of going into scientific details, I have tried to trace the life in a general way. (In some cases I have tried to give details in statistics also).

For this work I choose the Dalit areas and dalit subcastes from Nagpur and the period as from 6th Feb. to 10th Feb. 1993 (4 days). Dalits according to me means completely broken up and destroyed and downtrodden. Because of public prosecution—complete and in human neglect the group of human beings that are downtrodden and completely neglected, ignored like dust—may be called Dalits. In the traditional Hindu culture the group that has been designated as not fit to live as humans—the sense of identity, of self-respect of these groups of human beings is completely destroyed. They

* Translated by Nalini Pant.

cannot hope to raise their heads and look at other so called "people above them" and they have been deprived in every walk of life.

In the Indian constitution, their untouchability has been taken as the touch-stone of their being in the scheduled caste. Such people, the untouchables, are on one hand distressed by poverty, but also this basic concept of their being less than human gives them an enormous inferiority complex. The way they are treated less than animal makes them suffer more. The following seven groups have been choosen for detailed examination.

1. Nav-boudhas (ex-Mahars)
2. Mangs or Matangas
3. Chamars
4. Bhangis
5. Chattisgarh Dalits
6. Mang Buruds
7. Mang Garudis

Out of these 3, 4 and 5 are Hindi speaking. I talked to 10 women from each group and I tried to find out about their family, size of family, social customs, cultural heritage, infancy, financial problems, health consciousness, blind faith or superstitions, education, work, work ethics, political or social consciousness and their relationship to changing times.

To get at the truth, I visited their bastis and stayed with them and watched keenly their general habits, etc. The other condition I wanted to watch was how are these women following the tenets of Manu? Or are they free from all that.

Had the pronouncement of emancipation and state liberalization of policies towards women made an impact and changed their view of society in any way? Also, due to their conversion from Dalits to Nav-boudhas, was there any difference to the life style & basic thinking?

I also wanted to see whether exposure to principles of Christianity, Buddhist doctrine, Islam had led to any comparisons being made between these principles and Hindu tenets. Also whether they had grasped the basic ideas underlying these religions.

Therefore, I interviewed some Christian women. Muslims women did not respond at all. I also tried to see if Dalit movements and awareness of Dalit rights had any influence on these women.

In this group, I have not included those people whose better jobs and economic conditions set them apart. Only builders majdoors worker women, coir workers, dais (midwives), small vegetable vendors and fruit sellers, old cloth sellers and so on have been included.

The Women's Position in the Family

Like all Indian women, the women's position here is also secondary. Though she may be a wage earner, she has to consult her husband, father, son or an elder from her family or friends. As ours is still a male dominated family this is inevitable. The families were mostly joint families.

The families can be very large even upto 20-25 people. Sometimes they cook and share together, sometimes they have 3 or 4 different *chulas,* but all under one roof. Whatever the women earns she spends in the house. Family, illness, etc. are also looked after by her.

Housework the women do. The day is long from 5 in the morn-ing till late at night. Mang Garudi women first make the '*bhakris*' and then set out to work. Bhangi women start at 6.30. Men do not do any work as it is below their dignity. Like in all families the elders are respected, elder brothers-in-law and sister-in-law expect to be respected. Quarrels after drink, wife beating is common. Only in about 10% of the houses there is no drinking. Men can have outside relationship, also they can have other wives surreptitiously.

In a family fight usually the girls stand by their mothers but the sons do not. Some don't do any house work but the daughters do.

Generally, men can behave as they like. Men are supposed to be wiser than women. Whatever her earning capacity and the capacity of the work, the woman is inferior. Even the woman accepts this state of affairs. She is not permitted to talk to strangers or behave familiarly with them. She is under surveillance and generally torture and she is victimised. Even so she has a little more freedom than the so called "higher communities". They are free to remarry, the consent is taken, whether she is a divorcee or widow. Even in the children's wedding the consent is taken especially in the boy's wedding.

The average age of marriage of a girl is around 18 and the boy's age is 3 - 4 years more. Boy's side makes the first offer never the girl's side. There is no dowry system but if something is given it is appreciated. The boy's side makes all the expensive clothes, jewellery etc. The girl's side gives a big wedding feast, they give presents also. Nowadays among Nav-boudhas the expenses are divided equally. Some Nav-boudha women are also in favour of registered marriages and instead of so much being spent on weddings the money to go into the joint account of the bride and bridegroom.

If girls are decent and well behaved some women are prepared to accept them as brides for their sons even if they are not of the same caste, but most of them prefer to have daughters-in-law from the same caste.

Rituals, Festivals, Vratas

Most of the Mang, Mang Garudis, Mang buruds, Bhangi, Chamars worship the same deities as the Hindus do and observe more or less the same rituals. They honour all the saints and sadhus of the Hindu Dharma. Mochis worship saint Ravidas, Chatisgrahi's worship sant Ghasidas Maharaj. Mang garudis worship Muslim Pirs and go to the dargas. Nav Boudhas worship and observe Buddha Poornima and also Dr. Ambedkar birth and death anniversary. Mang garudi women also venerate Dr. Ambedkar.

Eating habits

These are as before. They are meat eaters and some special sweets like Manda, Bhatwa are common and a must.

Superstitions

This element is now a little lost but when doctors fail or even before, Bhagats and Babas are sought after. Some say that they believe because that is their experience. So the Dalit woman is still very much like other Hindu women as far as freedom in the house is concerned but she can be strict in choosing a bride for her son. One is afraid though that as Dalits get educated the bad aspect of 'civilization'—like dowry are growing and an increasing liking for rich clothes etc. may come in by the back door.

Economic Conditions

Though there is no restriction on her going to work the work sphere is still limited. So she does not earn much because the work she still does is only what Manu had ordained. The non-Dalit women may have some restrictions on going out to work but that is also quickly going.

Mang women make brooms and baskets. They also used to practise midwifery but now with the habit of going to maternity hospitals they do not get many customers. Most women clean vessels or wash clothes. The women whose husbands weave baskets help them in that work and often do better work. But this hard work does not have much demand. They get work in municipalities, earn well and live better. Nav buddhas have no traditional skills but they work on building sites, filling pots and pans, work in schools, etc. They mostly live on daily wages. Chattisgarh people again have no traditional occupation. They work at what they can have quickly. They are not sure of their daily bread.

According to the old Hindu tradition of Manu these women still do only unskilled labour and their earning capacity is thus limited. We have already discussed the work they do. They are mostly day labourers. Only women who are employed on a regular basis like municipality schools etc. earn a regular income and are comparatively well off.

In earning capacity the scale would be (1) Leather workers,

(2) Bhangis, (3) Nav bouddhists, (4) Mang garudis, (5) Mangs, (6) Chattisgrahi, (7) Mang garudis; in that order.

This means income scale are also in that order, regular earning is a rarity.

In housing also the above order prevails Chamars have better houses. Nav Boudhas are also not bad.

Clothing also followed a similar order. The upper strata had synthetic clothes. In the lower strata these are often repaired, from clothes obviously cast off collected from somewhere. Some Mang Garudi women told us that their families have not had a square meal for days together and for the last two days there was nothing to cook in the house. People no longer give alms. We are hungry from birth.

Even in this century the housing of such caste is away from the village. These areas are dirty and they do not have the wherewithal to keep it clean. No water in the dry seasons and puddles were inside their so called houses in the wet season.

The women were saying that for land people ask them from 5-7 thousand rupees. We have no food to eat so from where are we to produce this money. So we stay where no one else wants to live and from where we will not be driven away. We have to beware of snakes, "Dadas" make our life miserable. There is no safety of our lives, please do something for us. The last 10 years there is a possibility of getting loan for a house but who will give it unless there is some way of getting it back.

One thing is certainly true that because of various new laws and amendments in the government laws regarding society and particularly Dalits they don't have the acute problems about food, shelter, pay scale and daily wages as before.

However, in the villages where there are no industries the problem is the same as before. On some piece work or domestic type of work (work that can be done in the house) it is possible to get loans and there is a ready market for the product.

There is a grant of loan for making zachis while the raw material costs nothing except the time spent in collection. However, the turn-over being quick, in a town people earn more. The village worker has to move round from place to place to sell his goods. Either this costs money to travel or a lot of physical energy is expended.

Some women buy old clothes, repair them and sell them. This is possible only in a town. These women saw to know that loans are available for these businesses but only Navbuddha men and about 30%. Mang women know how to utilize it best. They understand that prices have gone up but do not understand anything about the new economic changes. The house holds also change but slowly. In some places we got dais to sit on, the other places only gunny bags. Only in one or two places there were chairs. There were stainless steel glasses everywhere. T.V. is a status symbol. In many places 5/6 houses share a T.V. Some have their own. T.V. Cinema going has therefore lessened considerably. The women seemed conscious of the unnecessary waste in rituals and marriage etc. but that becomes a caste issue and aspersions are cast on the people who do not do them or are stingy about it. They claim that rich people can do or not do things as they please, but if we do not observe the caste norms and spend money we are looked down upon. In spite of getting into debt, death rituals, birthdays, naming ceremony, marriage, all these are out-lets to spending money that we do not have and have to borrow.

Health Consciousness

Women in the town seemed conscious about health and hygiene. Having deliveries in hospitals, taking patients to doctors, injection and consultation are becoming common. They naturally prefer to go to government hospitals because the cost is too much in private. But now even in spite of government dispensaries and hospitals they are charged something which they object to.

Family planning is known, appreciated and practised but they were not in favour of operations and so prefer to have abortions done. There seems to be a different view point amongst women under 35 and those above 35. Women above 35 have about 3 children, women under 35 more children. The Nav Baudha women know more about health and eating.

Education

Among 70 women were interrogated: Mang Garudi and Chattisgarhi women were completely illiterate. Women under 35 may know the alphabet.

Mangs	: out of 10, 8 women were illiterate	
	one up to 3rd class	
	one up to 8th class	
Bhangi	: above 35, 5 women were illiterate	
	under 35, 5 women were upto 5th class	
Chamar	: above 35	2 illiterate
		2 upto 3rd
		6 upto 6th
Mang Burudi	: above 35	5 illiterate
		2 upto 3rd
		2 upto 4th
		3 upto 8th
Nav Buddha	: above 35	illiterate
		2-4th class
		3-8th class
		3-7th class

Average 62.85% illiterate.

Literacy rate of Dalit women is 37.15 and literacy of these women's (Urban) women is about 62.85.

According to Govt. of India statistics, Scheduled caste literacy rate is 35.91%.

Children's Education

Nav Boudhas are very conscious about childrens education. Even girls are made to study and given facilities to do so.

Other caste women are not that responsive about children's education. The Mang women are specially careless about this. "The boy was hungry so he did not go to school", "My children prefer to be around than to study", etc. Even after learning upto 3rd std. boys don't get jobs so what is the use. One woman said she didn't realize that the child had not studied enough.

Boys who go upto 12th std. look for jobs or business too. They do not realize that they can go to night school and carry on their education. The attraction Navboudhas have for education no other group seems to have.

In Bhangis girls go upto Matriculation. Nav boudhas go up to college and post graduation level. Others usually give up middle school. They are all after the latest trends, fashion, responding to what they see in Hindi movies.

There is a great understanding of social changes in Navboudhas. Other are not that aware. Nav-boudhas know about Phule, Gandhi, Baba Saheb Ambedkar so that they are more advanced than other women.

Among the other women in Mang, Chamar women about 50% know that they got opportunities to learn more through Babasaheb Ambedkar. They get reserved seats for schools and jobs and the women know it. Only Navboudhas know about Baba Saheb Ambedkar and Phule. Mang Garudi people also know but do not know what Ambedkar really did and they do not know about Phule.

Political Awareness

Political awareness seems to be common in all the Dalit women. Right to vote is exercised properly. Except Navboudha women others usually vote for the "Palm" (Congress). Voting by looking at the signs is more common than thinking of the person who is standing. The Nav boudhas women will choose a candidate according to his work. Everyone knows about Indira and Rajiv Gandhi but Narsimha Rao is not known. That the Maharashtra Chief Minister is Sudhakarrao Naik they did not know but the Boudha women know this. On this question one 65 year old uneducated women said "good people from all the parties should come together who can do good things for the people give them protection". There is a lot of goondaism in zopadpattis and all the political people are with them and no one looks after us. Everyone complained about the rising price.

The government is not for the poor, it is for the rich, they said how should we live? What has happened to the sense of justice which was there in the days of the English? This generally the older women ask. After the Ayodhya event the agitations took place everywhere. When questioned on this they said such agitations should not happen. We poor people have to go out every day to earn our bread, how can we live like this. There is always apprehension of whether our men and children will come home safely or whether we will be safe and not molested. Mang Garudi women were asking. We pray to the Muslim God's. Will that be held against us and will we be molested? The Bombay riots took place to get rid of the jopadpattis so will that also happen to us? That was the principal fear in the women's minds so that all this happens due to political motives was quite well known to Boudha women.

As we were asking questions regarding all these. Whatever they answered has been set out in short. Before that some Christian Dalit women were asked the same question. They were not ready to accept that their origins or forefathers were Dalits at all.

In Education these women are not very well educated may be upto 7th or 9th std. Christ is worshipped in their homes. Husbands income is above 1000 rupees. They have good houses. Women do not work. Children are educated. Political awareness is quite common. About riots, their views were like the other women. They want to live like cultured people that is why the children should be well educated and should be able to stand on their own feet. They were better situated and lived better than the Hindu Dalits. They read papers. Dr. Babasaheb Ambedkar they know as the leader of the Boudhas and the constitution maker of India. Mahatma Gandhi, Indira Gandhi, Rajiv Gandhi, P.V. Narasimha Rao, Sudhakar Naik were known. They are Indira Congress workers.

Muslim women do not talk openly but it seems that religious fanaticism is in both men and women. So they have no strong views about any social matters. "Allah Talah ne jo kiya apne bhale ke liya kiya" is their attitude. That is why all that happens is ordained by God. They are uneducated, poor, family planning not practised as men do not like it. Their whole life goes around not being 'talaqed'. Though they are Muslims they still have their jati divisions like Bhangi, Khatik, etc.

Conclusions

From this survey the following points have been emphasized (1) Dalit family system is patriarchal. (2) Dalit women's place in family is secondary even if she earns. (3) She does not take any independent decisions. (4) She can be sometimes quite firm. (5) She is a little more "free" than other women as remarriage and choice of husband is possible. She has economic independence but spends all the money for her family. She can go out to work. (6) She still does the menial and dirty work that Manu ordained. (7) Economic standard is low. (8) Food inferior state, etc. (9) Clothing - 50% women wear torn clothing. (10) Houses usually in very bad area of the village, dirty and mud constructions "kachhi". (11) Marriage and other social occasions they tend to follow caste restrictions. (12) During all rituals tendency is to spend more than what they can afford due to what people will say. (13) Better awareness of health. (14) Though all women understand importance of education only the Boudha Dalit women understand importance of education particularly girls' education. (15) Political awareness is quite a lot. (16) Boudha Dalit and Christian Dalits more advanced than Hindu and Muslim Dalits in their living and way of thought. (17) The Boudha women seem to have matured more and more conscious of their rights than even the Christian.

On the basis of these points one can draw certain conclusions. The life of a Dalit women is governed by certain rules and taboos as prescribed by Manu. Consequently, the Dalit women are subjected to inhuman behaviour and acute discrimination. They are not being treated as full human beings. For those who converted to Buddhism or Christianity, the life of women has undergone change. They are more conscious and are trying to establish their own identity in society. On the contrary, the Hindu Dalit women are still stuck to the tradition and superstitions. As a result, they (Hindu Dalit Women) are lagging behind in all spheres as compared to Nav Buddha women.

13

DALIT WOMEN : ISSUES AND REDRESSAL*

Ujwala Jadhav

Justice, liberty, equality and fraternity are the founding principles of the Indian constitution. The constitution grants all the citizens social, economic and political justice, equal status, equal opportunity, equality before law, freedom of thought, expression, faiths, beliefs, worship, profession, organisation, action, etc. The state constantly endeavours to attain political, social and economic equality. We have attained political justice but have yet to attain social and economic justice. Inequality reigns in many spheres of the country's life. The need of the time is to end inequality between man and woman in various fields. Inequality breeds many social and economic problems and these problems are a hindrance to women's liberation and development. Within women too, there is inequality e.g. between Dalit Women and non-Dalit women. If women are considered as a category, then all women face the same problems of discrimination and denial of natural justice. Women are fragmented in different groups based on caste, religion, occupation, cultural tradition, family background, literacy and economic

* Translated by C.K. Purandare.

development. This fragmentation has also created numerous problems. Fragmentation means women are not a homogeneous category. The type and gravity of problems of women in different groups are different and these demand different solutions. Taking into account this variety, only Dalit women are considered here. As mentioned above, they are in a different group and their problems too are more serious necessitating different redressal measures.

This paper attempts to club problems of Dalit women and suggest solutions. The term Dalit is used here for all Scheduled Caste and Scheduled Tribe women who are backward socially, economically, educationally and politically, who have been exploited for centuries and who have been denied natural justice.

The paper is based on statistics from the Census of India and field survey information. Statistics from other parts of the world and other written sources have also been considered.

In the pre-independence period many social reformers like Raja Ram Mohan Roy, Iswarchandra Vidyasagar, Keshav Chandra Sen, Mahatma Phule, Dr. B.R. Ambedkar, Gopal Krishna Gokhale, Pandita Ramabai, Dhondo Keshav Karve, etc. worked towards bringing about equality in the society. In the post-independence period, this mission has been continued by the state. Through its 5 year plans, through provisions in the Constitution and by other social reformers or voluntary organisations. Yet there remain a plethora of problems of Dalit women. The paper attempts to state the problems and relevant solutions.

Education

Low level of education is a problem in itself and, in turn, gives rise to many other problems. As per '81 census, all-India literacy rate for men and women put together was 36.17%. It was 46.79% for men and 24.82% for women. In Scheduled Castes, it is 21.38% for men and women, 31.12% for men and 10.93% for women. In Scheduled Tribes, the figures are 16.35% for men and women, 32.39% for men and 11.14% for women. This means that compared with non-Dalit women, Dalit women have the literacy rate of one-third and compared with non-Dalit men it is one-fourth. Put differently, in every 100 Dalit women, 11 are literate and 89 non-literate. If this is the level of literacy, that of higher education is best left to imagination. Non-literate women and those lacking higher education among the literate cannot contribute to nation-building. They also miss out an various attendant benefits.

High incidence of non-literacy is a major cause of prevalence of superstition among Dalit Women to a larger extent than among other women. Dalit women, prisoners of such beliefs, therefore, have no inclination to rebel against the harmful traditional practices. Rest of the society exploits them on account of their ignorance. Lack of education has resulted in their lower social status.

To quote Dr. Ambedkar, "Mal-nutrition would make a person weak in body and would result in a premature death. Likewise if she/he is not educated, she/he is reduced to slavery. Due to lack of education women have become living corpses. Mentally, they are slaves". And further,—"The real problem of backward castes is to get rid of the inferiority complex arisen out of their arrested development and resultant slavery. It is also to conscientize them to prevalent social practice which exploits them and make them aware of implications of the exploitation to themselves and to the nation. This task can be addressed only by higher education". If Dalit woman is conscientized she can contribute substantially to the upliftment of untouchables. She can work towards reducing evils in the society. Freedom of thought is the only real freedom. A person with a shackled mind is only formally free but a slave in fact. She/he is as good as dead. Freedom of mind is a sign of life. We can conclude that the inferiority complex among the Dalit women is detrimental to their development. In effect, non-literary is the major issue and mere granting of facilities will not serve the purpose. They will have to be made conscious about education which will make them capable of converting facilities to tangible benefits.

Sex-Ratio

The sex-ratio in Dalits is adverse to women. There are about 950 women per 1000 men. This imbalance sustains many ills like child marriage, prostitution etc. It is necessary to reduce infant mortality of girls by giving her equal attention as is given to boys in the early childhood. Women too have to stop hankering after a son and adopt family planning.

Employment

Among Dalit women rate of self-employment is quite low. Mostly they are wage labourers in unorganised sector thus not getting any benefits that workers in the organised sector are entitled to. Exploitation increases as they are not organised. They have to work in jobs with low status and there is no cartainty of work round the year. Times of shortage of labour bring them in the labour market. In the absence of permanent employment they are mostly dependent upon family members and do not have economic freedom. Women work for longer hours than men. They work alongwith men and additionally on domestic work, fuel collection, lending the cattle etc. Their health is neglected under the heavy working schedule and they are prone to frequent illnesses. Wages for men are higher than those for women for the same type of job. This exploitation can only be stopped by conscientizing women. Women have also to be provided many more opportunities of self-employment. Training, financial inputs, tie-ups for raw material supply and marketing of finished goods that they may produce, have to be provided for, by some agency. Co-operative industries generating permanent employment will have to be created. The state has to intervene for training and supply of credit. 'Women's only' co-operatives are coming up in India in a large number but the number of those for Dalit women is negligible.

Lower economic status and widespread non-literacy result in poor upbringing of the children. Children accompany women to their work places where hardly any facilities are available, least of all education.

Health

Dalit woman's daily diet is the leftover of the family meals-inadequate in quantity and inferior in nutritional quality. Health services are either not available in case of illness or unaffordable, if available. This results in premature deaths due to malnutrition and poor health. Improving economic condition may be the only remedy.

Reservations For Women

The state announces many schemes for holistic development of women. Recently 30% reservations for women were announced (in Maharashtra) for posts in co-operative societies and local self government bodies. The reserved seats have, however, been mostly occupied by upper-caste women and among them too by those whose family members are or were already associated with these offices. In co-operative banks, for example, only those women have been elected whose male relatives are or were already office bearers. Other women stand no chance of participation. Same obtains for local self government bodies. We feel that 50% seats of the 30% reserved for women be earmarked only for Dalit women.

A similar proposal for 30% reservations for women in Central services is also under consideration of the Central government. We suggest that reservations for Dalit women be proportionate to their population within this 30%. Otherwise such posts too will again be appropriated by upper caste women increasing the social and economic gap between them and the Dalit women. This would mean a skewed development of women at the cost of public money through government schemes.

Atrocities against Dalit women: Mass rapes, public parading of naked women etc. are reported day in day out. Justice in such cases should be speedy and the guilty punished severely. A separate body may be created for disposal of such cases. In a few large cities there are legal advice centres run free of cost for women. Women's vigilance committees also work in some places from Taluka level upwards with the help of police and women. They highlight atrocities against women. But this system fails to reach rural women in most of the cases. Cities have cells dealing specially with crimes against women. In rural areas, however, a woman has no such help available neither does she know where to get it from. Legal awareness among Dalit women, therefore, has to increase. This again points to educating them and improving their economic conditions.

Addiction of Men

Addiction to alcohol has ruined many families. De-addiction of men is a major task. Women's organisations, like in Andhra Pradesh, have to be formed and voluntary agencies and the state have to actively intervence.

Conclusion

To quote Dr. Ambedkar: "It is not that there are no merited persons in lower castes but it is the Hindu religion which hammered this notion of inferiority in the lower castes. Hindu society itself has been a loser in the bargain as merits of women and untouchables are lost". Women's lot would not improve, nor would society a whole progress if only men progress.

According to G.C. Vippal, a nation does not prosper only on fertile soil, dense forests and everflowing rivers. It is the healthy people who make a nation. A society is made up of both men and women. If women are weak and exploited, it is not a healthy society. And if a society is not healthy, a nation cannot march ahead.

14

DALIT AMONG DALITS : SCHEDULED CASTE AND SCHEDULED TRIBE WOMEN

A.S. Jadhav

The constitution of India guarantees equality of rights and opportunities to women. In reallty, it remains mostly on paper and not only glaring inequalities exist in education, health, social status and employment but status of women in general and SC/ST women in particular has become identical with that of a commodity or pro'perty of man, even today. Women are discriminated against in the family itself in terms of distribution of income, consumption, assets and education. They earn but have no sole power over the use of their income. Women are deceived and dominated by vested interest groups like employers, Government officers, political leaders, contractors and even family members in every field. Scheduled caste and scheduled tribe women are the most vulnerable group to such discrimination so far as education, employment and social status are concerned.

Public debate on the question of equality between the sexes usually tends to centre on quesiton of education and employment for women. The question of their education and employment is fundamnetal to their enjoyment of equality and status. Employment and education give a woman not only earning capacity but also enhances the social status. It is important for their personal advancement and status in society. They should equally participate in the economic activities as that of their male counterparts in the country's advancement which is an essential precondition for the advancement not only of the women but country as well (Singh 1987).

In the present paper inequalities existing in literacy rate and employment in SC/ST and upper caste women is analysed at district level in Maharashtra State. Most of the problems encountered by SC/ST women spring from lack of education and nature and rate of work participation, hence only these two components are considered tc highlight the SC/ST women's problems. An attempt is also made to suggest some measures to bring up SC/ST women at par with men and upper caste women, and bridge the gap and disparities existing in SC/ST women and upper caste women.

The study is based on the primary as well as secondary data. The primary information regarding problems faced by SC/ST women wage earners was collected personally by conducting interviews. For analysing the spatial pattern of literacy rate and work participation at district level, the data were obtained from the primary abstracts of 1981 census, such as general population tables, scheduled caste tables and scheduled tribe tables.

Literacy Rate and SC/ST Women's Problems

The SC literacy rate is lower than the general literacy rate in Maharashtra State and same is the case at national level. The table 1 reveals that there is a wide disparity in literacy rate between the SC/ST female and upper caste females. Parbhani, Nanded, Beed, Aurangabad, Usmanabad, Solapur and Buldhana are the districts where SC female literacy is remarkably low. Higher rate of female literacy among SC is observed in Amravati, Wardha, Thane, Bhandara, Raighad, Nagpur and Greater Bombay.

The tribal literacy in Maharastra is far higher than the literacy rate of this section of population at the national level. Not only this, but the male and female literacy rates of scheduled tribe population in the State are also higher than the corresponding male and female, literacy in the country as a whole. But in general the level of literacy rate among the ST is very low as compared to general literacy rate at State level as well as national level. Table 1 also reveals that there are significant inter district and inter caste variations in literacy rates of SC/ST female and upper caste female.

Table 1.
Female literacy Rate in Maharashtra State

Sr. No.	District	% of Female Literacy Rate		
		SC	ST	GEN.
	Maharashtra	21.53	11.93	38.50
1.	G. Bombay	38.42	36.75	62.23
2.	Thane	31.97	6.29	50.83
3.	Raigarh	34.66	9.36	37.84
4.	Ratnagiri	26.98	6.86	38.42
5.	Nasik	26.91	8.04	40.47
6.	Dhule	20.58	6.72	40.93
7.	Jalgaon	18.01	8.97	38.00
8.	Ahmednagar	20.32	7.11	32.28
9.	Pune	27.98	14.78	44.53
10.	Satara	24.84	19.18	36.11
11.	Sangli	25.51	25.06	35.09
12.	Solapur	15.16	17.68	29.20
13.	Kolhapur	18.85	20.05	26.97
14.	Aurangabad	9.10	5.83	21.19
15.	Parbhani	7.28	5.06	16.56
16.	Beed	8.50	8.38	14.74
17.	Nanded	7.77	7.41	17.89
18.	Osmanabad	11.45	10.68	23.57
19.	Buldhana	15.61	13.27	31.79
20.	Akola	19.96	20.30	37.52
21.	Amravati	28.29	16.59	47.84
22.	Yavatmal	20.11	12.96	31.39
23.	Wardha	30.18	23.87	44.22
24.	Nagpur	34.88	30.62	47.93
25.	Bhandara	33.32	17.99	31.53
26.	Chandrapur	20.04	11.28	26.88

Source : Census of India, 1981 Part-II B (I i, ii, iii).

An overview of the table 1 shows that SC/ST female literacy and upper caste female literacy vary widely in Maharashtra State.

In every district upper caste female literacy rate is higher than SC/ST. It means large chunk of SC/ST women is illiterate.

In brief it can be said that the literacy rate among SC/ST women varies from district to district and SC/ST female illiteracy is concentrated in certain regions and socio-economic groups. The literacy rate of women is low and differs to great extent between depressed caste women and upper caste women and very significantly between rural areas and urban areas as well. The rural female have the lower literacy rate. The low literacy rate or illiteracy is one of the major causes for below mentioned problems of SC/ST woman.

Since women have less access to education and training they lag behind in exploiting instruments through which they can attain equality.

The lack of literacy detracts from women their dignity, keeps the women economically poor and mentally isolated and does not allow them to play dominant role in society. It acts as breaks on the social development, economic progress and political maturity of the women. Therefore, it can be said that SC/ST women are socio-economically backward.

Due to illiteracy SC/ST women could not develop their children properly. They could not educate them properly. The inferiority eomplex is developed among them and they are incapable to build confidence in themselves. Their latent capacity is not used properly for national development.

Lack of awareness due to low literacy among SC/ST woman prevents them from taking advantage of facilities provided by government and safeguard their interest with the help of constitutional provisions and laws.

Illiteracy has given rise to rampant ignorance and lack of scientific attitude which ultimately results into superstition and belief.

In short, low literacy is responsible for low social status, superstition, gross ignorance regarding law and constitutional provisions, their right, their very slow socio-economic development, education development and lack of confidence or inferiority complex.

Work Participation Rate and SC/ST Women's Problems

An inspection of table 2 of female participation of SC/ST and upper caste women compiled from the census of India 1981, brings out the wide range of variations in aforesaid classes. It is needless to say that male participation rate is always higher in all sections of society. It can be observed from table 2 that female participation rate in upper caste women is generally low whereas in the case of SC/ST women the participation rate is very high. At the State level, the participation rate of female is 21.88% and for the latter, 29.08% and 38.78% respectively. The high rate of SC/ST female participation is found in Central Maharashtra. It is revealed from the table 2 that females of SC/ST engaged in non-agricultural sector is very low as compared to the proportion of upper caste female, in other words it means most of the SC/ST female labour force is engaged in agricultural and allied sectors because the literacy rate is relatively low among SC/ST females as most of them are poverty striken. In short it can be said that inter district and inter community disparity exists in Maharashtra State.

Owing to illiteracy and poverty among SC/ST people, as an economic necessity women belonging to these communities have to seek work outside their poverty striken households, whereas higher caste women are rarely seen working outside. The reasons are: Social stratification based on caste system, poverty, landlessness, decay of traditional occupation, absence of occupational mobility, ignorance, fatalistic attitude due to lack of education.

SC/ST women mostly perform agricultural jobs. Their low social status, illiteracy, unskill, force them to undertake manual jobs. SC/ST women can be grouped into four categories of workers viz. domestic and home workers doing household work, cooking, washing, cleaning home, looking after children: servicing type workers in agricultural and cottage industries; manual and unskilled labourers in factories, mines, plantation, construction and building work; skilled and professional workers in legal, medical, administration, managerial, military and other professions. In urban area, most of the house hold work is done by SC/ST women and very few are professional workers. In rural area, SC/ST women work on agricultural field. In short, most of SC/ST women are manual and unskilled labourers working on farm, cottage industries and performing domestic work in the houses of rich people and have to perform filthy jobs of menial services. Thus they have to do all types of inferior jobs for earning money to support their poverty striken families. Problems faced by downtrodden SC/ST women are manifold and can be summed up as below:

Table 2.
Female Workers in Maharashtra State

Sr. No.	District	% of Female workers to total female population			% of Female workers in Non-Agricultural sector to total female workers		
		SC	ST	Gen.	SC	ST	Gen.
	Maharashtra	29.08	38.78	21.87	20.72	08.58	16.82
1.	G. Bombay	11.08	14.31	08.36	99.47	98.47	99.73
2.	Thane	13.55	41.34	12.45	76.33	07.90	45.19
3.	Raigarh	23.92	34.98	25.17	44.55	28.32	11.38
4.	Ratnagiri	29.92	41.35	26.67	25.43	74.39	08.64
5.	Nasik	28.35	43.19	23.62	21.68	03.54	16.82
6.	Dhule	28.89	33.67	15.41	16.78	03.49	15.69
7.	Jalgaon	35.06	42.43	25.38	13.07	04.63	06.09
8.	Ahmednagar	32.62	43.20	29.08	13.18	05.23	05.00
9.	Pune	20.24	31.34	18.48	45.92	08.94	26.19
10.	Satara	25.35	28.73	21.08	22.89	31.45	10.96
11.	Sangli	21.91	16.62	15.12	17.40	12.93	13.30
12.	Solapur	28.64	21.34	20.75	15.06	18.13	25.17
13.	Kolhapur	23.74	21.15	20.02	13.67	23.33	09.74
14.	Aurangabad	36.29	41.08	27.68	13.41	03.84	07.55
15.	Parbhani	41.68	46.38	29.53	10.85	04.51	06.66
16.	Beed	35.52	30.57	19.83	07.94	10.25	07.63
17.	Nanded	33.37	36.73	23.45	06.34	02.84	09.09
18.	Osmanabad	33.73	28.93	21.31	04.05	04.77	06.97
19.	Buldhana	49.02	50.15	37.19	08.89	02.97	03.55
20.	Akola	43.15	45.84	29.54	09.85	02.96	04.91
21.	Amravati	37.23	40.23	24.30	12.22	04.49	07.15
22.	Yavatmal	41.28	48.87	32.83	09.14	02.79	05.24
23.	Wardha	23.31	44.33	29.21	16.79	04.79	06.90
24.	Nagpur	24.72	28.60	19.27	16.35	16.05	24.17
25.	Bhandara	42.58	42.66	37.52	51.01	19.05	12.51
26.	Chandrapur	28.46	37.65	27.91	16.98	07.71	08.87

Source : Census of India, 1981 Part-II B (i, ii and iii).

SC/ST women are often discriminated against wage employment programmes, they do not get continuous assured work which they need badly but generally find work in times of scarcity of workers.

SC/ST women's access to basic goods and services and to productive assets, the right to sell their own labour is contingent in a way men's is not. It is embeded in the interlocking religious, economic and kinship structure. These women are most vulnerable to seasonal fluctuations of labour demand.

The labour market is not neutral to men and women. Gender inequalities exist in almost all sections. The division of labour is highly sex-biased. Gender inequalities are also marked in acquiring education and vocational skill.

There is a high degree of discrimination in a wage rate. In most of the state SC/ST women workers are paid unequal wages for equal work; it means SC/ST women are paid lower wage for similar work than that of male workers. In most of the State minimum wage act is introduced but minimum wage rate is not provided to SC/ST women workers. The terms and conditions of work are not in favour of SC/ST women.

Women work for longer hours than their male counterparts. Most of women spend a greater deal of time working outside the home, they fail to fulfil the responsibility towards their children and cannot take good care of their children as compared to upper caste women. More than 80% SC/ST women work in agricultural sector. This sector is unorganised and does not have facilities of social securities as found in other industries and organised sector. They are not benefited by leave, medical support, P.F., gratuity etc. Even as labourers of industrial sector enjoy many schemes of social securities, SC/ST women have to go to field for work with their infant children because in villages there is no faci-lity of creches. Hence they have to bring their children in open fields. In fields there are no facilities of shelter, pure drinking water and other minimum requirements. Some times women are not allowed to go to their children for feeding them during work hours. Some times land lord/employers do not prefer such women as agricultural labourers.

New agricultural technology, technological changes and modernization have affected SC/ST workers adversely, number of women are thrown out of job.

Women engaged in professions, small entrepreneurs or self employed SC/ST women face difficulty of marketing their produce, loan facilities as well as consistent supply of raw material.

Girl's labour is needed for agriculture and household work like cooking etc. It is difficult for the poor people, agricultural labourers, to incur expenditure on education of women as a result that drop-out rate of girls is very high as compared to girls of upper caste and boys. It has become quite difficult and problematic to reduce the drop-out rate of SC/ST girls due to precarious economic conditions of SC/ST. All these socio-economic conditions and backwardness of SC/ST women in every respect have aggravated the Socio-economic disparities between SC/ST women and upper caste women.

Hygienic conditions are poor in SC/ST women owing to their poor economic conditions. 90% of SC/ST women take nutrient deficient food as most of them are below poverty line, and women are the last claimant of food. Their diet is protein deficient and gives low calories. Many a time the SC/ST women have to starve themselves. There is a glaring inequality in health status of female and male. SC/ST women marry at early age.

In spite of hard work, inside and out side, they are humiliated, beaten up by their husbands. Although women work for long hours and add to their family income, they are not perceived as workers by others, women themselves or the men. Her contribution to family income and national income remains largely invisible and under valued. A woman's plight is pitiable. Women's lack of land ownership, bars them from access to credit.

Though women work for long hours in field as their counterpart, responsibility for fodder and fuel collection in rural area rest largely with women.

Growth of women's share of employment in industries and services in India is very meagre and has lagged behind even in south Asian Countries.

Suggestions

SC/ST women face many problems and lead miserable life owing to lack of education and nature of their work. Here an attempt is made to suggest and discuss measures suggested by different commissions and individual researchers to inhiliation of illiteracy and improve their working conditions and socio-economic status.

The author would like to suggest that the areas of high concentrations of illiteracy should be identified all over the India. Whole India should be divided into three regions on the basis of literacy rate as low, medium and high. Secondly, some castes of SC/ST be identified which are having very low literacy rate. Thirdly, areas of high concentration of agricultural labourers be delineated and grouped into three concentration zones i.e. low, medium and high concentration zones, finally, an attempt be made to identify the castes which constitute maximum agricultural workers.

Having delimited regions of concentration of illiteracy and agricultural wage earners and castes with high illiteracy and high proportion of agricultural labourers, a phased programme should be chalked out to remove illiteracy and improve economic conditions of labourers. A priority be given to the areas and castes with high illiteracy and high agricultural labour force. Having attained expected progress or the literacy rate and work participation rate identical to national level, the next region and caste be given priority and the programme be continued till all come at a par.

Some of the suggestions given by different commissions and individual researchers to reduce illiteracy and ameliorate Socioeconomic conditions of SC/ST women are summarised below:

It is stated earlier that lack of education is one of the major reasons which keeps SC/ST women away from sharing national development in different sphere like economic, political, social and so on. So to educate them in every aspect is the way to their upliftment, by educating them properly important values of life can be imparted to them, they can develop thinking skill, they can earn money. Honesty, self-confidence, punctuality, scientific attitude are the values of the life to be imparted through education among SC/ST women, it will help make SC/ST women aware of their rights, constitutional provisions and laws. It will also help them orga-nize themselves. Education is the potent instrument that develops scientific thinking and eliminate superstition which is one of the main hindrances in the progress and development of SC/ST women. Educated women can educate their children properly and take care of them properly. Education will help build confidence among SC/ST women and remove inferiority complex and uplift them in all spheres of life so that they can fight against molestation, suppression and oppressions.

In short, SC/ST women's education is means of weakening the inside/outside dichotomy and expanding opportunities for women, it gives new ways of thinking and new perspectives on existing information, situation, health, hygiene etc. Hence the priority to educating SC/ST women should be given top place in the planning.

Government has been providing educational facilities in the form of fee concession, free education, scholarships, reservation of seats in courses, etc., and economic opportunities have been created for SC/STwomen through statutory provisions, commissions and programmes, but expectation of attaining complete upliftment has not been realised. On the contrary, in spite of visible development or progress, certain inter regional, inter caste disparities are seen every where. Widening gap between boys and girls in education, regional imbalances, women's enrolment in limited fileds of higher education, concentration of women in certain faculties are witnessed. The Government is not alone responsible for this state of affairs and disparties. As education spreads the knowledge, awareness and enables to adopt economic modernization, SC/ST Women should be enlightened on the significance of education. The most significant aspect of the education policy should be enlightening women about the importance of educations in all walks of life so that awareness be created among them about education which help reduce disparities.

It is found that most of SC/ST women are wage earners in non-organised sector like agriculture and domestic cleaning and cottage industries wherein they are paid lower wages than their male counterparts. There are minimum wage acts but these are not properly implemented, hence it is suggested that the Government must evolve and introduce such a machinery for the perfect implementation of the minimum wage act in those sectors and it to be scrupulously implemented. The firm steps should be taken by Government to remove discrimination in wages, working conditions and other facilities.

The policy should be designed so that better education, vocational, technical and professional trainings should be imparted so that SC/ST women become self reliant and independent.

Government should provide credit to these women and banks should be instructed to earmark some amount for giving loans exclusively to SC/ST women.

The latent capabilities of men of SC/ST must be utilized. They must become self dependent and self reliant economically. Economic successes for women will improve their own lives and those of all Indians. For that some sectors of cottage industries should be exclusively reserved for women. Some incentives should be given to SC/ST women to form cooperatives. The stress should be given to income generating units for example poultry, dairy, canteen, dress making, banking etc.

Women's groups can be formed to solve their problems like in western countries.

Government is spending a lot of amount on upliftment and development but benefits are not percolating down to SC/ST women and it is a widening gap between different sectors of society. Every agency of the Government should be responsible to ensure that planned resources and programmes benefit all sectors equally. Besides fixing the responsibility, there should be monitoring cell in each agency which should be able to monitor and evaluate the utilization of the resources and implementation of the programme. SC/ST women should be mentioned specific target group for all agricultural development and other developmental programme and efforts should be made to involve them in decision making at all levels.

The National Commission recommends that to enlarge the areas of employment for women, to improve their working conditions to reduce their drudgery, and to provide social security a holistic and integrated approach be adopted as women do not perform one action. It can be recommended that along with existing development corporation, co-operative societies and other government programmes there should be an Independent Integrated Development Programme specially for SC/ST women.

Destitude women should be rehabilitated with shelter, training, apprenticeship and helping hand for economic stability.

It should be worthwhile to note that no substantial improvement in their economic conditions is possible without bringing about an improvement in the conditions of the poor masses of the society, SC/ST people as a whole including men and women. The appalling ignorance of the SC/ST women is often a hindrance to their advancement in the social and economic spheres. Their extreme poverty, backwardness and social disabilities conspire to prevent them from making full use of the existing educational facilities. This vicious circle must be ended.

Finally, most important is the change in the attitude of upper caste privileged group towards these poor toiling masses of backward caste.

References

Ahmad, K. (1979): "Studies of Educated Working Women in India, Trends and Issue" *Economic and Political Weekly*, pp. 1435-1939.

Census of India, (1981: Primary Abstract, General Population, Part-II B (i), New Delhi.

Census of India, (1981): Primary Abstract, Scheduled Caste Population, Part-II B (ii), New Delhi.

Census of India, (1981): Primary Abstracts, Scheduled Tribe Population, Part-II-B (iii), New Delhi.

Chitnis, Suma (1975): "Education of Scheduled Caste" *Jour. of Higher Education*, Vol. I, No. 2, pp. 167-75.

Gulati, L. (1975): "Female Work Participation: A Study of Interstate Differences" *Economic and Political Weekly*: Vol. X, No. 1 & 2, pp. 35-45.

Jain, L.C. (1981): "Emancipation of Scheduled Castes and Tribes: Some Suggestions", *Economic and Political Weekly*, Vol. 16, pp. 325-32.

Nath, K. (1968): "Women In The Working Force In India", *Economic and Political Weekly*, pp. 1205-13.

Nayak, D.K. and A. Ahmad, (1984): "Female Participation In Economic Activities - A Geographical Perspective with Special Reference to Rural Areas in India", *The Indian Geographical Journal*, Vol. 59, No. 2, pp. 263-67.

Nayar, R. (1987): "Female Participation Rates In Rural India", Economic and Political Weekly, Vol. 22, No. 51, pp. 2207-15.

Singh, M.K. (1987): "Participation of Women in Economic Development - Trends and Issues", Indian Journal of Industrial Relations, Vol. 23, No. 1, pp. 93-96.

15

DALIT LITERATURE AND DALIT WOMAN*

Jyoti Lanjewar

On 14th October, 1956, Dr. Babasaheb Ambedkar along with his followers embraced Buddhism at the sacred initiation site at Nagpur. After this conversion, the Bouddha community underwent a revolutionary change in its thinking. This revolution found an ally in the literary pen. Taking inspiration from Dr. Ambedkar, who exemplified rebellious, old tradition-negating Dalit literature came into existence. This literature expanded the horizons of Marathi literature. It challenged the Brahmanical dominance and contemplations. Dalit literature with its rustic dialect gave a fierce jolt to the established Brahmanical language and the Sanskrit-suffused ornate literary style.

Scorching life experience is the price of Dalit Literature. Anguish, revolt and negativism are the distinctive features of this literature. When anguish leads to revolt, then the will to totally negate is born. Dalit literature has nurtured this will. Shaped out of the philosophies of the three great humans - Buddha, Kabir and

---

* Translated by R.N. Kulhalli.

Phule - but, altogether new and self-sufficient, Ambedkar's philosophy is at the root of this literature. Dalit literature descended into the field of Marathi literature as a new current of spirited literature that rejected all the traditions of literature, and negating the traditional values, it burst forth the new values. In fact this event should have happened long back. Though, first *Satyashodhaks* ("truth-seekers") and later Ambedkar *Jalsa* ("traditional musical concerts") and *Tamasha* ("traditional folk plays") continued to be produced, there was no significant impact of these on Dalit literature. This does not mean that Ambedkar's philosophy alone and not the Jalsas awakened the masses and the Society. But then the true nature of Ambedkar's impetus has been revealed by the Dalit youth through their respective literature and works. Because of the impress of education and their inborn capacity for literary creation, they have portrayed their own experience in flaming words.

Who are Dalits?

Scheduled Castes and Tribes, Buddhists, toiling masses, workers, landless labourers, poor cultivators, nomadic, denotified tribes, tribals, all come under the term Dalit. Those who fight against the varna and caste systems and those who raise their voices against the political, social and economic oppression, are dear to Dalits. The seekers of power, wealth and prestige, landlords, capitalists, the practitioners of religion and caste-based politics, those who wish to continue the tradition of injustice and atrocities against Dalits, and the government in power which supports and protects these, are the enemies of Dalits. Such a stand has been taken by the prominent workers of Dalit Panther movement, Namdeo Dhasal, Raja Dhale, J.V. Pawar and others who side by side the movement nursed their pen as poets and writers. Through Dalit literature, they relentlessly placed before public meetings and conferences Dalit questions and Phule-Ambedkar vision. Truly, the culmination of Dalit Panther movement is Dalit revolt literature. Dalit literature is the flowering of the live coals kindled by the inspiration of a great leader. Because of that, this literature fostered the movement and carried it forward.

In its very beginning, Dalit literature was neglected by the established literature. But the blow dealt by the creation of revolt literature and Dalit movement was so powerful, its leap so high, the form of its spark so original, its experience so alive and burning, the mode of its expression so natural, the rage against the caste system and inequality so volcanic, that the Marathi literature had to take a welcoming stand. A new awareness and a new form of pain, of world and reality, never expressed before in Marathi literature began to appear in Dalit literature. The voice of this literature was so thundering that the people behind the closed doors of the respective monasteries and the custodians of the respective religious scriptures, Vedas and Puranas, were forced to open their closed doors and take cognizance of this literature. It is by smashing the closed mighty gates of All-India literary conferences that the Dalit literature has secured its entry.

The experience of life expressed in Dalit literature is so spirited, its agony so mind-distressing as to make the eyes of the white-collared people death pale. Because of this, though Dalit literature continued to grow, in the early stages critics did not dare to come forth to review it. Perhaps, who knows, they felt that the negativistic stand of Dalit literature was extremist. But the surging cascade of Dalit literature did not stop, nor could anybody impede it. The shaping of Dalit revolt literature and the Dalit movement occurred simultaneously. Thus, the literature strengthened the movement and in the same way the movement made the literature powerful. Even today in the creation of revolt literature, Dalit writers are so much in the forefront, so much ahead, that we do not find anything comparable in other groups. Dalit movement and Dalit literature have given an impetus to rural literature, folk literature, Muslim literature, tribal literature, or Gondi literature of fellow-suffering communities. It has given intellectual support to them.

A flourishing substream of Dalit literature is Dalit poetry. If we look into Dalit stories, novels, dramas, intellectual writing, all Dalit literature, we find that all these sub-streams have aggressively negated the caste system and inequality. Dalit literature which touches each and every facet of the withered, ravaged, mutilitated, life of ordinary people has to be recognised as a stage in one historical movement in the surging current of Ambedkarism.

Dalits produced literatu re even before religious conversion. But there was a difference: the objectives of literature before the conversion seem to have changed after the conversion. Because of the impact of Ambedkarian thought, a turmoil took place in the traditional literature. Instead of soaring in the imaginary world, an attempt was made to move closer to life. Dalit literature, which stands opposed to the four-fold varna system and capitalism, appears to be engaged in the retrospection of ideas regarding women, women's liberation, struggle for women's liberation, the human relationships that transcend woman-man relationship, equality of opportunities and an egalitarian way of life. Rebellious women like Sona, Sai, Mangala and Harana of Annabhau's novels provide inspiration to present writers.

Woman Portrayed in Dalit Literature

The Dalit woman depicted in Dalit literature by Annabhau Sathe down to this day is envisioned as a rebel only. But the forms of her rebellion are many and different. One encounters rebellious heroines in Dalit literature women, who seeing the mud thrown on her honour, injustice perpretated on her as poor, lover or husband fighting for society, the betrayal of nation or society, the injustice being inflicted, or likely to be inflicted on her as Dalit, more so as female Dalit, gnash their teeth in rage and are ready to charge. The woman one comes upon in the novels of novelists like Bandu Madhav, H.G. Bansode, Haribhau Pagare, N.B. Jadhav, Shankarrao Suradkar, Shankarrao Kharat, Baburao Bagul, Arjun Dangle and others has been depicted as one who is combative by nature, takes an aggressive stand, inflamed by injustice fights and is immersed in struggle.

With the exception of a handful of Dalit writers, the rest have portrayed Dalit woman as competent, as capable of overcoming the situations, as far removed from the habit of day-dreaming, and as conscious of subjective reality. In N.R. Shinde's novels, an attempt has been made to seek harmony between woman and nature. N.R. Shinde, through his novels, endeavours to shape woman as a deity by viewing her as a force of nature and to make her an object of worship or to give her an ideal form by recognising her as pure energy. In depicting her struggle as a woman, in portraying her social and emotional conflicts, some writers seem to have been niggardly.

While portraying the oppression and rape of Dalit women, some writers have become ungenerous, and by presenting her as weak and helpless have shown her as a victim of the circumstances. One discerns, that barring a handful of such exceptions, the woman shaped in Dalit literature is 'indomitable'.

Dalit woman, featured in some very recent novels, has been portrayed as extremely forceful. In the novels of Madhav Kondvilkar, B.S. Shinde, Bhimsen Dethe, Uttam Bandu Tupe, Yogendra Meshram, Sharankumar Limbale, B.S. Hate, Sudhakar Gayakawad, Namdeo Dhasal, Keshav Meshram, Nivritti Sheshware, Ashok Vatkar, Aravind Sonvale and others, Dalit life and Dalit woman's pain'—her plight have been expressed. In the novels of some prominent novelists of Marathi Dalit literature, woman does not come out solely as a creature of sympathy. She comes rather as harbinger of struggle. Women in Annabhau's novels, forsake tradition and emerge with strength to fight against adverse incidents. Whether she is Radha, mother of "Fakira" or "Vaijayanta" who loves art more than life, or Chandan who, tying a 'remindful knot' "Who stops, is finished", casting of her weakness, leads a life that is crushed by circumstances and rendered lonely by widowhood, or Durga of "Makadicha Mal" ("Monkey's Hill"), the familial social and mental conflict of all these women has been responsible for the birth of revolt. Some women characters in Annabhau's or Kharat's novels, sell their honour because of helplessness and poverty. Because of that they do not become depraved or accept this condition as their duty of life; but they search for a way of escape from this. They are consumed by the fire of repentance. They read the "almanac" of their actions to themselves and question themselves. All these women characters contemplate on the good. Whether it is Girija in "Hathabhatti" ("Home Brewery") or Sona in "Chitra", they discard their ugliness and struggle to lead a happy life. The draught of frustration does not touch them nor do the portents of failure depress them. They are not made to live in the fence of traditions nor are they made to give up their desire for change.

The female characters in Dalit literature are dynamic and not static. Dalit writers do not look upon widows, prostitutes, depraved women, as Dalit, the exploited, with compassion alone; but they make them valiant, create commotion in their inner minds and take them towards radiance. In the stories and novels of Annabhau, Shankar Rao Kharat, Baburao Bagul and others, though the nature of the struggle of woman in the beginning is individual, later on it becomes class conflict. The individual mind's conflict takes the form of group mind's conflict. As a consequence of this, Dalit female characters end the journey of deep darkness and behold dreams of sunrise. In the uncivilized world, they accept the civilized path. They fight for truth and for themselves. They revolt to protect their self-respect. They do not brood over the injustices perpetrated on them, nor do they just rave against it, but take up arms and prepare for fight. The revolt of Dalit women is not person-centred but society-centred. The fight for values by these women, who refuse to sit in the shadow of evil persons to avoid starvation, is important. The courage to fight, resoluteness, rebelliousness are the very essence of their life. That is why Dalit writers do not portray Dalit women as hollow idealists, overflowing with love, embodiments of sacrifice. Accepting the bitter truth of "to error is human", Dalit writers have depicted the various facts of human nature; "first error, then progress".

Womanhood, too, is Dalithood

The attitude of Dalit writers to Dalit woman characters and to Dalit women in general is not one of excessive idealism or intemperate exaltation. Beca[illegible] there are Annabhau and Bagul who accept womanhood also as Dalithood, Dalit writers while depicting the contempt with which the past society and even the society today looks down upon women, the way she is tortured, skinned and plundered, and the way in which her sentiments, feelings, her ver[illegible] womanhood are trampled down, instead of painting her as an '[illegible]s' or as a slave for enjoyment, have sounded a note of warning that till she is accorded a status equal to that of man, Mangala, Harana, Guna, Janaki of 'Sood' ('Revenge'), Nandini of 'Aghori' ('Monstress'), will be one step ahead of man.

The dual conflict of non-Dalit and Dalit women finds, its expression in Dalit stories and novels. They are not engaged in external conflict, only; an internal conflict also goes on. The heroine of 'Bhavin' ('Devdasi') by B.B. Borkar or 'Sevasadan' ('House of Service') of Munshi Premchand are not entangled in inner and outer conflict. Occasionally, they compromise with the situations. Both Annabhau and Premchand are the first commentators on the perception of life of women, who sensitively expressed in their respective novels the joys and sorrows of Dalit and exploited women. Broadly, 1920 to 1935 is the era of Premchand whereas Annabhau commenced writing novels from 1957. In addition, many important writers in Hindi, Amritraj, Vitthaldas, Swami Gajananda and Padmasinh have portrayed exploited, tormented women. The women depicted by Premchand-Loungi, Nirmala, Zunima, Silias, Suman, Jouhara, Bholi—become victims of social system. We come across women being exploited sometimes by society, sometimes by men and sometimes even by women themselves. Even then they take refuge with mind and heart in the Hindu culture of worship of the dead. Some are engaged in conflict, but the conflict does not become important even for themselves. Hence the women characters become self-centred. Both the event, the fall as well as rise of women characters, occur in the depiction of woman by Annabhau and Bagul.

Non-Dalit Marathi Novel and Woman's Life

The heroine, of Vibhavari Shirurkar's novel 'Bali' ('Victim') is ensnared in prostitution. There is no struggle in her life excepting the strife for food and thirst. Conceding that food at times is important, is 'sale of body' for that the only alternative? In course of time why should she not be able to give it up? Aba's mother in 'Bali' ('Victim') Benva's mother in Jayavant Dalvi's 'Chakra' ('Wheel'), for both of them their life is not worth repudiating. They have no grievances against life, no reaction, no effort to come out of this kind of life. Should hunger, poverty, servility and submission to the circumstances be the ultimate end of life of the Dalit, toiling, labouring women in the slum? Whether it is Radha of 'Garambicha Bapu' ('Bapu of Garambi') or the women penned by writers like P.B. Bhave, P.S. Rege, G.N. Dandekar, C.T. Khanolkar, Uddhav Shelke, Bhau Padhye, Jayavant Dalvi, they all represent middle class life. Though the agony of Koutika in 'Dhag' ('Scorching Heat') and of Girija of Kharat's 'Hathabhatti' ('Home Brewery') is the same, Girija is an ostracized Dalit; society has accorded respect to Koutika as a tailor.

Janaki of 'Sood' ('Revenge') of Baburao Bagul who has made Marathi Dalit literature flourishing, is an exceptional woman bestowed upon Marathi literature. Janaki comes into the world as the child of a beautiful Dalit 'Murali' (Devdasi). She becomes a victim of her mother's helplessness, misery and the perverted social order. She becomes disgusted with bodily function, bodily enjoyments and lives the life of a renunciate. Demanding that her womanhood should be replaced by a male body, she nurtures in her mind feelings of revenge. From the point of view of subject matter, Bagul's intent is totally different. The life of woman or Dalit woman presented in Marathi literature has emerged by affirming white-collared mentality and thinking. While depicting, out of sympathy and compassion, the neglected strata, woman has been considered as an 'object of pleasure' and shaped accordingly. But Dalit writers, while portraying these strata and Dalit women, have done so on the experience of life lived on the same plane. From the writings of Dalit writers one clearly understands their pain and commitment regarding life. As the main strand of thought in Dalit literature considers human being as greater than God or nation, the Dalit woman figuring in Dalit literature takes a down-to-earth form. Dalit novels, stories, dramas, poetry, have never been entertainment-oriented or dreamful. A woman, inflamed by feelings of revenge, finally accepts exalted intellect and compassion of Buddha. Conquest of the desire for revenge is true human liberation. But a Dalit has to constantly nurse self-awareness to take a fiery stand against injustice. Even then, revenge is considered as violence in Buddhist Philosophy.

Dalit women portrayed by Keshav Meshram, Bhimsen Dethe, Yogendra Meshram, Waman Howal, B.S. Hate, Namdeo Dhasal,

P.I. Sonkamble etc. is not egoistic or conceited. Though they come with varied strands of thought, the principal strand is made up of Ambedkar's thought. Dalit writers have not used Dalit women for political purpose. It is to demonstrate how people look at women that writers like Shankarrao Kharat present an objective perception of the life of female teachers, female village level workers etc. in the village. That is why though 'Simhasan' ('Throne') continued to be recorded in 'Mumbai Dinank' ('Date line Bombay'), Dalit pen has succeeded in noting on the minds of ordinary Dalits and readers the envy and friction in village in all its minute details.

By nature, Dalit woman is rebellious, change-oriented and thoughtful. She is the one who herself sets her own goal and herself discovers her own path. In spite of this, even today, quite a many Dalit women appear to be beyond the reach of the pen of these writers. Rural Dalit women are dealt with in the stories and novels. But urban Dalit women, employed women, educated Dalit women caught in the vortex of old-new ideas, the handful of women participating in meetings, conferences, processions, demonstrations etc. and, in this context, the attitude of society towards them, her social, familial conflict, problems of educated Dalit women, the agony of Devdasis, 'andhashraddha' ('blind faith'), the revival of old customs and morals, ignorance, tribal women, Banjara ('a tribal community') women, women in rural and urban areas toiling in sundry work, female village level workers, nurses, teachers etc. in the rural areas - the life of all these women has become insecure and problem-ridden. There is a need to give justice to these women through their writing. Dalit writers have not uptill now touched many such themes. Only injustice, atrocities, rape, have been painted. Even today, her combative spirit, her aggressive stand and her rebellious encounters have not been presented amply in the literature. A tigress is also brave like a tiger; when hungry she does not eat grass and is in the forefront of fight. There is need for Dalit writers to be aware of this. From this point of view, the limited writing of Dalit women has been proved to be several times more valuable than that of Dalit men.

Dalit Women's writing

In any society, woman is a slave of man. Even the tribal, who leads a free life, lords over his wife in his hut. In this context, even if women writers as a whole have not done justice to women, Dalit women writers have done justice not only to women but also to men. The attitude of women in viewing women has not changed even today. As a man consideres woman as enticing, in the same way woman looks at her as a character of hate-jealously and sympathy. Non-Dalit women writers have not yet realised that if the attitude of society towards women is to be changed, one has to produce powerful literature. Hence woman emerges from non-Dalit women's literature as helpless, pitiable, weak, 'pati-vrita' (religiously faithful to husband), fatalist, sorrowing or dozing on the swing of happiness, capitulating to the circumstances and a dreamer. Barring one or two exceptions which deal with the development of her stunted personality or its perception, woman has been presented as worthless. There are women who live under the illusion that an earning woman is an independent woman. If a capable and affluent woman lives a life free from attachment to man, leave along society, how many women have held her in high esteem? If all that one continues to get from women is suspicious, crafty glance and non-recognition of her living, then it is better not to expect literary creations from women. Accepting love, separation, lamentation, restlessness, Marathi writers have been ensnared in the self-centred, self-absorbed, emotional, intensely sentimental, love-lorn, soulfully overflowing relationships of wife, beloved, sister, friend etc. They have consistently neglected the fact that there is production of a literature which transcending these relationships fights, and with a new hope plunges into the struggle and makes the discerning reader also take a jump. Giving expression to individual experiences, they sketched a superb emotional poem—emotional life. But they could not perform the task of carrying forward their genuine deep feeling for woman beyond the threshold of the home and give it a social consciousness. This task has been accomplished by the Dalit literature of Dalit women writers.

Discerning accurately the psychology of Indian social system, Dalit women writers have shown not just indifference to the ideal values which have proved to be worn out and worthless from a cultural point of view, but instead of muffling the misery of neglected women, they have given woman the courage to overcome it.

Hira Bansode through her Dalit poem lodges not just her personal complaint but that of all women communities.

"Oh people, in your court,
I have brought a complaint,
Will you then, give me justice?"

She thus poses a candid question. Further, Jyoti Lanjewar dares to declare that the hand obstructing the bringhtness of the sun of new culture will be severed and used as a pen.

"You! Provide not clothes to cover the body.
But... the hand that pulls the cloth,
Chop it off from the root at least;
Or else,... write we shall,
On green grass, a red declaration"

She thus expresses her mental resolve. There are Dalit poetesses who endow women with courage and strength, and prepare them for battle in Kurukshetra. The poetry of Meena Gajabhiye, Kunda Gaikwad, Gipal Gimekar, Surekha Bhagat, Asha Thorat, Pratibha Gedam, Usha Bhalerao etc. is reflective. These Dalit poetesses have broken the existing framework and have brought to Marathi literature and the pysche of the society, for the first time, an awareness of a different sorrow.

From a comparative point of view, Dalit autobiographies are extremely important as an inevitable journey of the social, economic and cultural change among the Dalits. But, even then, they are not adequate. Quite a many experiences have yet to be placed before the readers. When they are depicted exhaustively, there is no doubt that the realm of Dalit literature, or alternatively Marathi literature, will be expanded.

In Daya Pawar's 'Baloot' ('Baloota'), Laxman Mane's 'Upara' ('Outsider'), Madhav Kondwilkar's 'Mukkam Post Devache Gothane' ('At Post Devachi Gothane'), P.I. Sonkamble's 'Athavaniche Paksi' ('Birds of Remembrances'), Shankar Rao Kharat's 'Taral Antaral' ('High and Low'), Nanasaheb Jhodage's 'Phanjar' ('Thorny Bush'), Uttam Bandu's 'Katyavarachi Pot' ('Thorns as a source of Livelihood'), Keshav Meshram's 'Hakikat Ani Jatayu' ('Narration and Jatayu') Sharankumar Limbale's 'Akkarmashi' ('Bastard'), Rustam Achalkhamb's 'Gavaki' ('Village Duty'), in all these autobiographies, Dalit woman has been portrayed as suppressed and shattered. Dalit writers, with a few exceptions, have not paid attention to the fact that Dalit women's life is worth contemplation. Because women have not got the justice they wanted, the autobiographies of these Dalit writers have become self-centred. In the development and shaping of every man, woman has a very major and important share. She comes in the form of wife, beloved, colleague, mother, etc. But in the autobiographies of Dalit men, nowhere there is a mention of her different identities, of her capability, her inner and outer conflicts. He expresses an awareness of how Dalit male was made, how he struggled, how he advanced. But there is no expression of how, because of wife or beloved, he reached that stage. On the other hand, the character of 'Mother' has been unduly glorified. In some autobiographies even when then there was ample scope, a limited and conventional picture has been presented; for example, Shashi of Laxman Mane's 'Upara' ('Outsider') Shashi, a caste Hindu, who loves and later marries Laxman belonging to a Kaikadi tribe, is really extremely, daring. She gives unstinted cooperation to Laxman. She endures anguish and humiliation. There is no true depiction of her conflict on the personal or social plane and the rebellion emerging from it. On the other hand, all the four autobiographies of Dalit women have done justice to Dalit men. They have delineated the support received from men in their relationship as father, husband, colleague etc., in succession and candidly. That is why Dalit men's autobiographies have proved spacious. They have accorded justice, not to women, but only to themselves. In their autobiographies, there is no social message which can give an impetus to society. Kumud Pawade's 'Antasphota' ('Inner Explosion'), Mukta Sarvagouda's 'Mitaleli Kavade' ('Closed Doors'), Bebitai Kamble's 'Jeen Amucha' ('Our Living'), Shantabai Kamble's 'Mhajya Jalmachi Chittarkatha' ('The Disjointed Story of my life'), in all these four authobiographies, while narrating how they fought with the circumstances, they have given an inspiring message to the society. In all these four autobiographies, the women emerge riding conflicts on different planes. They have developed philosophy of life of those respective characters. Their life itself has become their philosophy. Autobiography is an honest attempt at looking, from settled life, at the past life with detachment and seeing as far as the sight goes. Dalit autobiographies discover the past along with the present and penetrate into the future. From this point of view, though the literary output of Dalit women is scanty, it is precious.

Dalit poetry is a flourishing segment of Dalit literature. Even the woman presented in poetry is impressive. In the poems of Daya Pawar, K.B. Shinde, J.V. Pawar, Vaman Nimbalkar, Yashwant Manohar, Damodar More to Lokanath Yashwant and others, beloved, wife and mother figure, not in ideal forms, but in Dalit forms. Her misery, Dalithood and womanhood themselves are the very basis of impediments. Even then there are many more such themes to be taken up.

New challenges of changing times, casteism, sectarian mentality, political hypocrisy, stunted growth of woman resulting from male-oriented politics, the mentality of Dalit poets to form their own narrow clan and institution of disciplines, sub-casteism, egoism to preserve their eminence—all these have been burrowing Dalit life. As long as writers, unorganised, fragmented, strutting with totally false claim of being heirs to Phule - Ambedkar legacy, keep in moving in the realm of questions based on a narrow view of Dalit woman's life, Dalit literature will continue to be self-centred and self-destructive. For broadening it, societal awareness and reflective thinking are as important as the profuse enhancement of Dalit concerns. That is why, Dalit literature got world-wide publicity in India and abroad, translations were undertaken and University level recognition was accorded. This leap is very great and the one which validates the differentness of Dalit literature. From this point of view, if the woman shaped in Dalit literature herself remains neglected, it will create a hurdle in the rich growth of Dalit literature and Dalit literature will be considered as one-sided. Dalits should heed this.

16

THE DALIT WOMEN'S DUAL FIGHT: FIGHT FOR CASTE ERADICATION AND FIGHT FOR WOMEN'S LIBERATION*

Jaideo Gaikwad

The Brahmanical tradition did maximum harm to women and Dalits. Just as the untouchables were at the receiving end of the Varna based caste system, so were women belonging to all castes. Many years later Mahatma Phule launched a campaign against this caste-ridden social order.

Women and the untouchables had been denied the right to education and access to learning. Against this back-drop, Phule broke the stalemate and opened the first school for women in 1847. After that, in the last 100 years, many social reformers like Agarkar, Ranade, Lokahitwadi, Karve raised their voices against the injustice meted out to women.

Issues like widow remarriage, child marriage, deserted women, dowry, women's education were raised and women's progress was focussed on.

* Translated by Sadhana Natu.

In the post independence era; equal rights in the areas of education, employment, development were accorded to women by the Constitution. But in reality, women were not given an equal status.

In fact as more and more women came forward; gained education, started getting organised; the anti-women establishment started baring its fangs in overt and covert forms.

Women started perceiving how male domination had influenced the social psyche, social transactions and social thinking. Many rituals and customs proved this—giving dowry to the bridgegroom during the marriage ceremony, the practices of male-headed households, males owning the property, males controlling the decision making process in families.

In contrast the woman has an inferior and secondary status. She has to live as a counterpart of the male, her individual personality and existence is not recognised. Her husband is her god, lord and master who is her legendary 'protector' for seven life times.

Hence even in the social milieu the male is the omnipotent controller. He has the privilege of education, political clout, power, freedom of setting his sights on any goals, while the female is to be his mere shadow.

It was considered the woman's duty (dharma) to suffer all kinds of torture, acquisce to physical violence, to live amicably and keep serving the household.

In recent times women started questioning the existing social order, started thinking and articulating about their personhood, their individual personality their right to aim for the sky/all horizons, to live independently. They could do all the things that males could do. Man-Woman relationship should be based on equality. Women should be treated as equals both in the family and in society.

The Woman's movement and its efforts to shake off the patriarchal norms has gained momentum now. A lot of Women's organisations have been established in our country. Women's wings of political parties have also come up.

The women's movement, known as the Women's liberation movement has focussed primarily around patriarchy and for equality, but within the movement there are ideological differences and debates. Also various new organisations are coming into existence by prioritizing issues which they want to fight for viz. - the question of women from the toiling classes, the issues related to the educated, middle class women etc.

Against this background, for the women from the Ambedkari movement, their work does not end by fighting for the women's cause solely; for them the fight for a casteless society takes priority.

The Non-Dalit feminists have not gone beyond paying lip-service to Phule and Ambedkar. On evaluating their ideology one feels that they have not been able to give a definite sense of direction to the movement. Their work has remained restricted within the parameters of issues like women's education, employment, security, legal issues and problems of women affected by natural calamities.

The Non-Dalit Women's organisations and groups do not dare to question or bring about a change in the system which has bestowed a victim - status on them. On the contrary they pay obeisance before the political powers created by this very system which has enslaved them.

This movement is led by the well-educated, elite category of women from the higher echoleons of society. Due to this the women's movement is becoming brahmanial and classist instead of becoming an all encompassing progressive movement for social change.

The Brahmanical women's organisations try to attract Dalit and working class women to join them and to some extent, one does see Dalit women getting education and changing. But this change remains merely at the level of sanskritization. Because these educated Dalit women, then become alienated from their poor and working-class counter parts. They are seen pursuing the goals of individual progress, individual freedom, development of the family, their job, or chasing material dreams like owning a flat, referigerator etc.

Against this backdrop the goals of the women in the Ambedkari movement are fundamental, well-defined and clear in relation to bringing out a complete transformation in society. They want to bring about a change in the entire system because they realise that they cannot gain liberation for women until other inequalities remain in society. I would say that the Dalit women are an indivisible part of the women's movement. The existing social and familial conditions have taught them to fight, and they are seen battling on these two fronts simultaneously.

Though they give the first priority to social issues, in this social agitation the institution of family is also affected when men and women fight side by side in the Ambedkari movement, the man-woman relationship is transformed to an idealistic and warmer plain. In comparison the man-woman relationship in non-Dalit families remains confined within the parameters of the family. Hence Dalit women seem to be more aware of social issues.

We have witnessed that Dalit women have cast aside the idols of gods and goddesses from their family places of worship as mere stones, on Babasaheb Ambedkar's say so. At the same time they cast away their superstitions.

But we also have to remember that the Hindu culture (the culture of the majority) and the Hindu institution of family is found to influence Dalit families. The established pattern of society continues to be predominant.

In spite of all this the Dalit woman is seen escaping from the clutches of male domination easily; and hence the divorce rate is high among Dalits.

An important question which emerges is why could not the Ambedkari movement throw up a large number of women leaders. I feel the entire Dalit society was a victim of the domination, injustice and exploitation of the majority Hindus for a long time.

It is only in the last 50 years that they have cast aside their chains and this process is also going on under duress from the established society. Hence the Dalit is fighting this battle on a community level.

Similarly the women's participation in the struggle too, though large, is on a community level. Hence independent women leaders have not emerged. We have to work to create a secure and fearless atmosphere in the Ambedkari movement in the near future, whereby independent and capable women leaders will emerge. At this juncture the Dalit women's participating in the movement should be treated as a part of community leadership.

It is important to change the present inequality ridden society, and in order to do this we will have to move forward in the direction of formation of a new society envisaged by Mahatma Phule and Dr. Babasaheb Ambedkar.

When a new order based on the new values of equality, liberty, fraternity and justice is created; women will definitely have an equal status in it. Dr. Ambedkar made sincere efforts to gain an equal status for women in his life time. Women had participated in large numbers in his agitations (Mahad Satyagraha, Kalaram Mandir Satyagraha). Many women faced imprisonment too.

Looking at his struggle in retrospect Dalit women give the fight for social equality preference over the fight for women's liberation. Dalit women have to fight on dual fronts. The Non-Dalit Women too have a secondary status and are victims of social inequality.

In fact all women are Dalit and hence it would be possible to build a new society which brings together all women and whose foundation is based on Phule and Ambedkar's ideology.

17

THE DALIT WOMAN: THE TRIBAL PERSPECTIVE

Shashi Minz

Much has been spoken from various forums on the "Status of woman" in India over the past few decades; what actually is her status in India today, what is the position she occupies in the society and in her household, in her family varies from race to race and from society to society. Recently studies and researchers have voiced out that the word "Dalit" and "women" have become almost synonymous. But in the tribal society of Chotanagpur, it is not exactly the same. It is also true that the situation is fast changing and a different picture emerges today with the influx of other cultures, in gross violation of the principles of Panchsheel, as enumerated by Pandit Jawaharlal Nehru. We are witnessing the gradual Dalitization of the tribal women today.

The real meaning of the word "Dalit" is oppressed, suppressed and a person who is not allowed to develop and grow as is the right of every human being on earth and the word "Tribal" or "Adimvasi" *Or original settler - the indigenous people* - is a generic term used to denote a distinct ethnic group of people, speaking a distinct language and having a distinct culture of their own.

But this generic word has been misused and distorted and the connotation is now used disparagingly to speak about the deprived, the down trodden, the poor and now the powerless in our society. The causes are not far to seek - availability of limited resources which man tries to limit or appropriate only for himself be it material or spiritual. But man and woman have been made biologically and spiritually interdependent. This defines their position or status in society today, hence we find the varying position a woman enjoys in every society in all climes and also its evolution down the ages. Historically, women were not always oppressed and I quote from Gail Omvedt - "We will Smash This Prison-Indian Women in Struggle". "In the stage of society called primitive communal, men hunted, and fished, while women cared for the sprawling house-holds and the handicrafts. At that time women had equal status, because all production was social. While men hunted together women cooked together. Households were communal and so were families. When the mode of production slowly changed, when agriculture was discovered and men settled on land, the concept of private property as distinct from communal pro-perty, slowly arose. With this, lands, animals and children came to be owned by men. This in short is the origin of the oppression of women."

I. The Status of Women in the Tribal Society

Today I am going to speak about the status the tribal woman enjoys in the Indian Society - with specific reference to the tribals of Chotanagpur. The Oraons-Santhals-Kharias-Hos & the Mundas have a distinct ethnic identity. These tribes were driven into the forests by the marauding hordes of invaders over the centuries and lived in isolated communities for a long time.

i) Tribal folklores and songs have eulogised the role a woman plays in a tribal household down the centuries. She is the homemaker as it is she who dicides where should be the hearth and which should be the bedroom for the family. The Wordsworthian philosophy - "The hand that rocks the cradle rules the world" is deeply ingrained in the psyche and the spirit of tribal woman - as she enjoys equal social rights and duties in rearing up the children with her husband. Workload is not defined as such, but a tribal male is ready to help his female counterpart in all areas of work. No work is demeaning. It is she who organises the details of all the activities at home or the community and enjoys the final say in social events - be it birth, marriage or death in the family - and her wish, desire or suggestion is respected by all despite it being a patriarchal society.

ii) The rules that govern the tribal woman's dress-pattern speaks highly of the attitude and the purity of mind of the men in her society. The concept of "rape" never did exist amidst the tribal world. So much are the people in harmony with nature—the mother earth—the trees—the rivers and the hills amidst which they dwell. It is for this reason that a tribal woman is not allowed to touch the plough—as the act of ploughing symbolises the sexual-relationship; hence homosexuality or lesbianism is an unknown concept in the society.

There is no "parda" or the concept of "Ghunghat" as is seen amidst women of other cultures before the elders of the family or even outsiders - however, there is reference relationship—distance that is maintained; e.g. the eldest brother in the family is respected as the patriach is—and the womenfolk of the younger brother shall keep a respectful distance from him - both in address in social patterns of behaviour. While the reference relationship between the "Salis" "Salas"-brothers and sisters of the bride or the "Bhatu" or the brother-in-law "Jijaji" is of a healthy teasing joviality.

iii) There is freedom of movement for a tribal woman in the village anytime of the day and night—as there is no concept of illegal or free-sex as is insinuated and is visualised by some outside anthropologists. Respect and dignity is ingrained in the tribal culture; so much in tune is the tribal woman with nature that she responds to the stimuli of the stage of puberty and the natural growth and development into womanhood as part of nature. She is educated on the importance of healthy sexual relationship and control of the natural instincts in the "Dhumkuria". Between the age 13 to 18 the elders of the village educate the youth and they emerge well versed in the art of life and learn great respect for the human body and its purity. The symbol of women as the creator of the future generation who should herself be pure and holy to give birth to a in the feast of "karm" wherein the branch of the Karm tree is venerated in the absence of the husband. Songs and rythmic dances mark the festivities during the pre-harvesting season and a message is conveyed in the "Tals" in beat of the tribal drum—"the mandar" so much in tune with nature is the concept of virginity in a woman that she becomes an embodiment of nature-creator of new life, new crop, and the values of purity and motherhood are celebrated in "Sarhul".

iv) This oneness in nature is enshrined in the belief system that the creation of the Universe, is by One Supreme God and the trees and rivers, hills and the earth, the sun and the moon and we human beings are co-creatures with these phycical elements of nature hence the symbolisation of woman in the new life and plant is inherent in the tribal culture. What is now called Environment Protection had been practised since long by the people who love nature as themselves.

The deforestation in the name of Nationalisation and the plunder of timber by misguided policies is heart rending and painful as one sees the bare hills stripped off its natural sources for selfish ends. Only a tribal heart can deeply mourn and emphathise with the brutal skinning of the hills of its glorious green wealth and the indescribable ache in the heart is carried to many a distant land wherever a tribal migrates in search of employment.

v) Equality of sexes is seen as the tribal woman works with her male counterpart both at home and in the fields, weeding and hoeing the fields with the sickle while she joins him in the forest with bundles of chopped wood for fire on her head. She enjoys the pleasures of selling the agriculture produce in the weekly market or "Haat" without making any distinction with her male counterpart or her contribution to the family.

It is the lurid looks of the non-tribal traders and forest-contractors who eye her with intentions other than respect that makes her feel self-conscious, shy, and she withdraws into a world of silence which she has to battle all alone—as in the real life situations well portrayed in most of the art films like *'ankur'*, *'Manthan'* and *'paar'*.

vi) Very often the simplicity of the tribal woman is misunderstood as docility and she becomes vulnerable to all the atrocities committed by misfits in the society. So alien is the culture of lust and marital deception in the tribal culture that a tribal male takes some time to react when he finds his woman afflicted by such embarrassing situations due to the influence/infiux of the outsiders and reactions are violent. Rabindra Nath Tagore has very rightly encapsuled this feeling in these lines of his in "Geetanjali", "Men going home glance at me and smile and fill me with shame. I sit like a beggar-maid, drawing my skirt over my face, and when they ask me, what it is I want, I drop my eyes and answer them not."

vii) The urgent need of the hour for all tribal dominated areas in the country is to develop entrepreneurship *by* the people, *for* the people, *of* the people. Even today it is not too late. Influence of the outside competitiveness, avariciousness of the materialistic world with all its latest technique of modern living has greatly affected the style of life of the people in the tribal village.

II. Proposed Solutions to the Existing Problem

(a) The Green Revolution of Punjab, if transported to the tribal belt of Chotanagpur, would solve much of its existing problems; death by starvation, malnutrition, lack of drinking water facility, proper sanitation and lack of employment can easily be solved.

(b) Operation-Blackboard coupled with Operation-Oilseed would change the face of the minerally rich Chotanagpur belt. People have been all the while plundering the mineral wealth without ploughing back any returns for the generous tribals who had to sacrifice acres and acres of their agricultural and forest land for open-pit mining of Coal, Iron ore, Bauxite and Mica and for the building of dams. This Ruhr Valley of India and its people would be very thankful for a total revamping of development programmes and projects for the tribals. My grandmother did four decades ago what Medha Patkar is doing today for the Narmada Bachao Andolan but to no avail; her cry was a cry in the wilderness!

Rehabilitation programmes well-implemented with the requisite-minimum requirement of housing, schools and medical facilities for the displaced families would certainly have contributed towards a better life-style with healthy sanitation facilities, as envisaged in the national programme of growth and development, but the interest of those in administration was miserably lacking.

(c) It has been 45 years since independence of our country but it has been reported by Members of the Planning Commission that all projects for the growth and development of the tribals by its numerous Sub-Plans were returned unutilised to the Centre due to the lack of political will to execute and implement the same. Illiteracy alone can buy votes blindly; hence the philosophy to eradicate illiteracy though flaunted through all media - is never executed - the only saving grace is a few missionary schools in the area.

(d) Today, the major tribal towns of Ranchi, Dhanbad, Hazaribagh, Gumla, Lohardga, Palamau and Siguhbhum hardly get a few hours of electricity at night, as the majority of the power generated by the Thermal Power Station, of Patratu and Damodar Valley Corpn. is used to supply electricity to cities of North Bihar and West Bengal. Such and many other forms of exploitation of tribal Bihar has proved a handicap for the development of the people of Chotanagpur and women as usual are the worst sufferers. Crime rate has increased and no one is in sight in the township after sun-set. It is sad to note that there is no qualms of conscience among those in power who pocket the money meant for the tribal education and health programmes. Lavish weddings and display of wealth, in form of ornaments for their daughters' dowry are only evidences of the plundering of illgotten wealth by the non-tribals of Bihar and the vanquished stand in stark poverty without a shred of decent cloth in their bodies. This systematic exploitation of the tribals is the Dalitization process.

(e) Despite the deprivation and abject poverty suffered by the tribals of Chotanagpur down the ages - Celebrations of festivals and commemoration of glory of the bygone days are exemplary and heart rending. There is joy and peace even amidst want; as the gift of contentment - a cherished value amidst the tribal is enshrined in their philosophy of life.

(f) The equality[2] respect and dignity which a tribal woman enjoys in her own community is unique. Alcoholic drinks are shared in common and even the hookah is passed around without any distinction. Dances to the beat of the tribal drum - *'nagara'* conjures up a vision of distant thunder rolling down the hills and the clash of brass cymbals blending with the melancholic tones of music/melody and the rhythemic steps of the dances display a harmonious community living. Men and women dance with dignity and grace and there is no vulgarity or taboo in entwining of the arms while dancing. Much plagarism in the hindi films have distorted the minds of the people by showing how one is seduced after a dance in the tribal 'Akhara' far into the moonlit night. Unfortunately, misuse of the liberty has crept in due to unhealthy notions of sex by influence from the outside world.

III. Need of Preservation of Value Systems and the Ancient Heritage and Tradition

i) Historical evidence well-chronicled in Britannica and Mundarica Encylopaedia have gone to show that the tribal women of Chotanagpur have over the past centuries contributed their mite for keeping their status high. They are looked upon by their society as Saviors. They enjoy a sense of freedom and dignity of labour; seldom witnessed in other societies.

ii) The tribal fort of Rohtas was saved thrice from Mughal invasion; like Lakshmi Bai, our women had fought and defeated successfully three times the foreigh invasion, and our society today commemorates the event every 12th year in their memory as *"Jani Shikar"*. Centuries ago the tribal womenfolk, dressed as men circled endlessly the fort to show the invaders the strength of their army - while their men folk were reeling under the influence of doped liquor - ministered by the milk-women who supplied milk to the fort on the 'Sarhul' festival and who betrayed them to the Mughal army. Many jumped into the well and river to avoid capture and dishonour.

iii) Even today in the field of games and sports tribal girls have not lagged behind in protecting the glory of their own society and of the nation. If we glance through the list of national hockey team for women - we shall find Purti, Topnos, Guria, Soy and Kerketta and Kujurs all hailing from Chotanagpur. Unfortunately, they have not been given any national recognition. Mr. Jaipal Singh in 1947 was the only tribal who could make it into the Olympics; there are several tribal women today who possess similar skill, stamina and talents but they are yet to be recognised and given the opportunity to prove their worth. Once sectarian thoughts and ideologies of caste and creed are surpassed by the human mind and the political will to-give all equal opportunity is ignited in the hearts of the people - there would be no height which a tribal woman would not be able to climb and conquer. There are many more talents, power and strength in the tribal women which needs to be fruitfully tapped. Lack of political will and faulty planning has seen the premature death of the skilful art of handloom and mat weaving and clay pottery.

iv) Cottage Industries to develop their skills could have been encouraged and markets to sell their products could be explored. Invitation to non-governmental organisation to start industries of agricultural produce could help to generate economic resources. Encouraging growth of cash-crops in the tribal belt and formation of co-operatives can be streamlined and re-organised. The concept of middle-men who have been lynching them dry over the centuries can only be eradicated by the spread of education and the use of ones' own language and mother tongue alongwith Hindi.

v) Linguistically the tribals of Chotanagpur are very rich and the Kurukh is of Dravidian Origin - while that of Ho & Santhali Austro Asiatic - an unique phenomenon. However, similarity in culture and belief system have kept the tribals together. Taboo systems and their monotheistic belief system have helped them to understand the concept and accept Christianity better. Self-employment schemes with the requisite subsidies can only be introduced by a local tribal Banking Management staff who can emphathise with the needs of the people. Hence the policy to post the natives of the place amidst the people of their own culture and linguistic origin would help genuinely in eradicating the poverty and corrupt forces.

vi) Introduction of Free Trade Zones can be contemplated in the field of electronics and agricultural produces in the Tribal dominated areas of Bihar, Orissa, Madhya Pradesh and West Bengal. This can give impetus to the local people's skill and traditional art and handicrafts as it is the nimbleness of the fingers that has made most of the tribal women migrate in search of work in the tea gardens of Assam and Bhutan.

IV. Systematic Dalitization of Tribal Women : Socio-economic Deprivation

(a) With the influx of North Biharis and people of other states there has been a systematic displacement of the people of Chotanagpur. However, a small percentage of educated women found working in the Government offices have met with such out bursts from their male Bengali Counterparts—

"We feel hatred and anger when we see these tribal women working with us and drawing the same amount of salary. They are inferior to men in all respects except in child-bearing". We can't blame the male psyche either, as contrary to the tribal culture. - men and women could never be at par with each other in Bengal. Education was a taboo to the women there for the men feared literacy would make them aware of their human and social rights and privileges.

(b) Even today the tribal women are facing this deprivation because of this fear. The work of the Christian Missionaries in the belt has been discredited because they have given education to the tribal poor and made them aware of their identity and also of their rights outside the tribal world.

(c) There still exists even today exploitation of the illiterate tribal women by forest contractors, block development officers and doctors who have invaded the place by faulty implementation of the Government policies. Posts required to be filled up by SC/STs never go to the right persons. Land grabbing by foul means has increased the poverty of the people of Chotanagpur. Actually the systematic exploitation of the people is a blot to humanity as a whole and this fact had been voiced in the International Forum of Human Rights for the Indigenous people. Incidently the United Nations had declared the year 1993 as the International year of the Indigenous People—. But this has had little impact in our national scenario perhaps it has more important issues on its agenda as is usually the case. But the voice of the Dalit tribal women today cannot be smothered or silenced - for the pain of deprivation and victimisation has reached the peak.

(d) Mass migration of tribal women in search of economic stability can be seen from the tribal belt as the economy has not been developed in their place of residence. Odd jobs as construction—workers and house maids are mostly sought after posts for the illiterate and semi-educated young girls in cities like Delhi, Bombay and Calcutta. Recent studies have revealed that many have been affected by veneral diseases and the spectre of AIDS is not far away for they often fall victims to crimes/vices inflicted on helpless women in a male-dominated society.

(e) Since this is a problem faced by the tribal society in the last few decades, concerted efforts should be made to contain the same. Economy generating industries should be started in the backward areas. Accountability factor of the builders and contractors and the officials incharge of projects should be increased. Infrastructure has to be improved - roads and bridges have to be built in reality and not on paper alone. The National Commission of SC/ST, New Delhi should be vested with more statutory powers to see the projects' policies of the Government implemented.

(f) Leadership qualities should be encouraged from among the women and industries indigenous to the people should be encouraged. Food preservation centres and canning industries e.g. fruits, vegetables, mulberry, gooseberry, bamboo shoot and mushrooms growing can be encouraged. Dried and smoked vegetables preservation methods can be modernised. The Tassure silk industry can be given a fillip and handloom industry can be encouraged.

(g) Co-operatives for vegetable farming and with easy loans can be introduced - as the illiterate tribals are cheated by the middle-men who buy their produce at cheaper rate not commensurate to their labour or capital used and supply to the states of Calcutta and other major cities of India. More and more income generating schemes can be introduced and also self-employment programmes can be encouraged. Forces to ensure that the tribal, agriculturists and entrepreneurs get his/her due can be ensured once the place enjoys even the status of a Union territory.

V. Conclusion-Role of Voluntary Organisations

Concerted efforts are required to be made by the affected people of the place or the well intentioned rulers of the state to combat this systematic Dalitization of the Tribal women. Non-governmental organisations can be formed and the youth force from schools and colleges should be encouraged to bring literacy to every household in the tribal village. The political conscience has to be rankled as Babasaheb Ambedkar did some decades ago. Educate, unite and agitate are the only recourse left to fight the twenty century old oppression. A time has now come to fight for survival of our value systems and the revival of our art and culture which has been brutally wiped away over the past by those who believed that Madhubani art was supreme and ignored and suppressed the rich and cultural tradition and heritage of South Bihar. A time has now come to give the women of Chotanagpur an opportunity to decide, organise and plan for themselves what future course of action they should adopt. The Indian bureaucracy has seen a few capable women officers but their plans and projects are swamped down or made ineffective by those below them who are not in consonance with the idea of liberation and change or upliftment of the tribal women. What we need in today's context is a trail-blazer in the likes of Helen of Troy and Mata Hari combined with the spirit of Mother Teresa - to really help this deprived section of the tribal society - to get back her former honour and glory which she once enjoyed in ancient India.

I wish to conclude with reflections by *Dag Hammarskjold*, Secretary General of the United Nations, in his "*markings*" in 1956.

"Before Thee, Father
in righteousness and humility,
with Thee, Brother,
in faith and courage,
in Thee, Spirit,
in stillness.
Thine-for thy will is my destiny,
dedicated-for my destiny is to be used
and used up according to thy will"

18

TRIBAL AND NOMAD WOMEN AND UNIQUE SUBJUGATION OF INDIAN WOMAN*

Saroj Kamble

The European woman is under the dual yokes of class-system and patriarchy. Indian woman is additionally under the oppression of caste-system. Caste panchayats, caste-based division of labour, rules governing family deriving from caste-system all contribute to subjugation of women. Marriage, divorce, remarriage, succession rules, all rooted in caste-system make a woman dependent on man and restrict her autonomy.

New currents of thoughts are emerging in India to address this issue. Sharad Patil[1] makes a few fundamental points:

(1) Notwithstanding Marxists' contention, a gender-egalitarian society did not exist in the primitive communities. This society was also based on gender discrimination and was inegalitarian. Women had rights in distribution of communal land, administration and priesthood because women invented form of agriculture. Women were privileged in the primitive

* Translated by C.K. Purandare.

society for her reproductive ability, essential for continuation of the society.

(2) In pastoral phase, succeeding the primitive phase, animals were introduced in agriculture by men. Increase in productivity due to this introduction started the first stages of patriarchy. Women began to be discriminated against in many areas. Their subjugation started right during the phase of communal property owning society. Varna system further subjugated women. She got some protection as she was no longer remained purchaseable and violable but her subjugation continued.

A struggle against the caste system is necessary to break the strangle-hold of caste on women. Liberation of women and anti-caste movement have to go hand in hand.

The campaigns against atrocities on women do not have numerical back-up or mass support today. There are women's organizations among domestic labourers, workers, nurses, agricultural labourers etc. But their impact and area of operation are limited. They have limited strength to pressurize perpetuators of atrocities or the government. Unless they have mass support of rural tribal and dalit women, these campaigns would not make much headway.

Caste-System and Subjugation of Women

Caste-system exploits dalit-tribal and Sudra women more than upper caste women.

1. Among agricultural labourers, tribal and dalit women are in a large number. Next come women from peasant castes. These women work more and earn less.

2. Low social status alongwith lower ranking in the village power hierarchy make dalit tribal women an easy prey of atrocities and rapes e.g. mass rapes in U.P., Bihar or rapes by government employees in tribal areas. In 1982, 15% of rapes in rural areas and 28% in tribal areas were committed by government

employees. An atrocity against a poor Maratha woman is taken up by members of her caste having social and political status. This does not happen in case of an atrocity against a dalit-tribal woman.

3. Caste-system forces many dalit-tribal women in prostitution in rural and urban areas. Poor Maratha or upper-caste women are not drawn into this profession to the extent that Dalit women are. In Pune area there are 12,000 Nepali prostitutes and in Bombay 40,000. Mahars, Mang and Chambhar women are in a majority as *Jogtinis* of *Yallamma devi*. Tribal woman has less protection than upper caste woman in matters of marriage, divorce, post-divorce compensation and polygny. Caste-system denies them the protection making them more vulnerable to prostitution.

4. During the last and beginning of this centuries upper caste women had to face shaving of head on widowhood and ban on widow remarriage. Those who took reformist position and tried to alleviate miseries of women suffered from social boycott and other forms of punitive measures initiated by Brahmin orthodoxy. Some reformers were driven to suicide. Evidences of such harassment are cited by S.G.Malshe and Nanda Apte[2] in Vidhawa Wiwaha Chalwalicha Itihas (in Marathi) ('A History of Widow Remarriage'). Caste system was perpetuating the subjugation of women.

5. Literacy rates vary as per the caste. Dalit women have 11% literacy and tribal women 1%. This imbalance has arisen because women's education and their participation outside the home have changed according to caste-hierarchy.

6. Operations of patriarchy in a community are manifested most starkly in nomadic tribes. Dr. Prabhakar Mande's[3] *'Gavgadya Baher'* ('Outside the Village System') gives instances of such patriarchal caste practices:

   1. *Mang garudi* : Caste-panchayat has set rules regarding marriage. A fine of Rs. 100/- is to be paid by the offender violating these rules.

   2. *Peacock dancing communities of Dakkalwar* : Once a marriage is decided in the presence of caste panchayat, it cannot

be cancelled. In the event of cancellation, girl's father has to pay an amount demanded by boy's side and obtain 'release' of the girl.

3. *Rairand* : Dowry or bride price is decided by the caste-panchayat. A wife seeking divorce has to approach the caste-panchayat for approval. Caste-panchayat gives a certificate to that effect.

4. *Gopal* : A girl is excommunicated from the caste for immoral behaviour. The punishment is met only to a girl, never to a man.

5. *Kolhati* : Caste-panchayat permits sale or purchase of a girl for prostitution *Chal* (anklets) are put on her feet during a ceremony to seal this entry into prostitution.

6. *Kaikadi* : Rules ragarding sale or purchase of a woman are set by the caste panchayat. Kaikadis have a tradition called *'Agu'*. For a woman desiring second marriage, her second husband-to-be has to pay the first husband a certain amount to 'release' the woman from her first husband and his relatives. However, her earnings during the first marriage and her children from the second marriage remain the first husband's property.

In short, not class but caste-system decides a woman's position in nomadic tribes. This uniqueness of Indian woman's subjugation is found all the more vividly among nomadic tribes.

Social Reformist Movements

1. Historically, the movement addressed the issues of upper-caste women only shaving of head on widowhood, ban on widow remarriage, etc. were the problems of these women. But the untouchable or Sudra caste women suffer more due to restrictions on social participation and on education.

2. It is to be noted that only such social reformers who attached the caste system supported reform for women. Mahatma

Phule, himself from a peasant caste, started the first school for women. Dr. Ambedkar an untouchable and their leader, drafted laws giving protection to Hindu women to some extent. As against this a caste system supporter leader like Lokmanya Tilak opposed the mutual consent bill for marraige and instigated attacks against Agarkar, a reformer, with the help of orthodox groups. In Delhi there were protests against Hindu Code Bill by upper caste women. Sankaracharya Katpatriji expressed fear that this bill would help 'impure' castes contaminate the 'pure' ones, through marriage. Supporters of caste-system have always been supporters of subjugation of women.

Therefore, Indian women's movement has to decide its course of action carefully with respect to caste-system.

Social Movement among Nomadic Women

1. Various organizations of nomadic castes have launched movements in Maharashtra. The demands range from employment to habilitation. But never has there been a demand to improvise upon caste rules which control family behaviour and make a woman more insecure. This is so because the male activists operate in a capitalist society and caste leaders have patriarchal bias. Women's liberation is struck off the agenda by many leaders for personal gains from powers that be.

2. Left movement in Maharashtra (except Satyashodhak Kashtakari Mahila Sabha) never raised the issue of caste rules as affect life of nomadic women. This is due to the fact that women's movement with leftist inclination is urban-centred and has no legacy of anti-caste movement. Therfore, their agenda does not include tackling of rules governing nomad families.

3. Tribal and nomadic women can still be organized against the patriarchal system. Hindu laws apply to nomadic women. But her caste rules do not allow her to go to court of law. Patriarchal

social control is also quite strong. Brahminical women's liberation movement does not allow anticaste programme to be taken up. But caste system remains the unique feature of subjugation of Indian woman. As a result, women's movement in India has reached an impasse.

References

1. Patil Sharad *Das Shudra Slavery*, Allied Publishers, New Delhi, 1982.
2. Malshe, S.G. & Apte Nanda *Vidhawa Wiwaha Chalwalicha Ithas* (in Marathi), Stri Sanshodhan Kendra, SNDT University, Bombay, 1978.
3. Mande, Prabhakar *Gavgadya Baher*, (in Marathi) Parimal Prakashan, Aurangabad, 1983.

19

ATROCITIES ON AND AGONIES OF GUJARAT DALIT WOMEN

Devyani Punalekar

I

Dalit women suffer on two counts, being Dalit and being women. Newspaper reports and some scattered studies inform us about the atrocities on the Dalit women in rural and urban areas. These accounts give us the glimpse of their sufferings and agonies, their problems and struggles. However our senses are so burtalised that the rapes or naked parading of the women in the village streets do not stir us immediately for action; whatever that action can be. These events are treated as any other ordinary news bereft of social contents. This is indeed an alarming situation.

Suffering of Dalit women is depicted in popular literature. Short stories, novels and poems by the Dalit writers do reveal the inner social and cultural tensions experienced by the Dalits, including their womenfolk. We shall mention one such story in this essay later. Also some studies have brought out the disadvantages and multiple sufferings of Dalit women in different parts of India. But there is no systematic attempt to put together these narratives in coherent manner and weave a pattern out of these episodes. Such exercise is necessary and vital to deepen our understanding and perceptions on the status and conditions of Dalit women in India.

In this essay my purpose is to outline briefly some cases relating to harassment and victimisation of Dalit women in Gujarat. We can also look into the problems they face, harassment they undergo, treatment they receive and the insults they have to swallow. The perpetrators of crime against Dalit women are members of upper caste society including their women; the petty officials and also the politicians. Incidents vary from place to place; and often it happens that though a target is Dalit men or Dalit community as a whole, often Dalit women become the victims.

II

The problems Dalit women face are of the varied types. Inadequate water facilities in a village still constitute a major source of problems for a Dalit community. Their womenfolk suffer the most on this count. How did Dalit women suffer in this respect in a village called Sambarda in North Gujarat? This is only one aspect but there are many more disadvantageous features which make survival for Dalit community difficult. There is humiliation and insult for members of Dalit community in this village. But there is always some human limit to tolerance; and if the situation goes beyond this limit, there is a possibility of some explosive reaction from the victims. Let us see what happened in village Sambarda.

Case of Sambarda Dalits

The story of Dalits of Sambarda village is a story of supreme struggle for 131 days of 60 Vankar (Dalit) families. This was essentially a struggle waged for asserting their dignity and self-respect. In Sambarda village, nearly half the population is that of Gadhavis, and the rest half is that of Vankars, i.e. Dalits. Gadhavis were against the Dalits of this village, though they were never economically dependent on them. Dalit men, women and children were publicly abused. They were harassed in number of ways.

Because of everyday problems and tussle with Gadhavis, the entire Dalit community decided to leave this village permanently. When the news of their forced migration or *Hijarat* reached the district and state headquarters, there were efforts to pressurise them to abandon this path. Also there were veiled warnings and threats. So the Dalits had to wage the battle against the government also. Dalits' decision to leave the village was not an easy thing. They had to lose a lot. In the village they had pucca houses and some immovable assets too. Even then, they were prepared to take this extreme step.

All of them including old men, women and small children gathered at the collector's office. They raised their temporary shelters in the premises of the collectorate. They stayed there along with their belongings and against all odds till their struggle ended. They were demanding that the separate place be given to them. They never wanted to return to this village. The struggle lasted long, but ultimately they succeeded. They were given an alternate place by the government. A separate colony of their own away from their original village was set up. This colony they named as "*swamannagar*".

There were number of situations and incidents where the Dalits were harassed, abused and humiliated. Here we would concentrate on some incidents concerning Dalit women. They are as follows :

— When Dalit women used to go for a natural call, idle Gadhavis were throwing away their water tumblers.
— While filling the water pots at hand-pumps, the upper case youth would put their tumblers used for latrine purposes in-between and thus prevent them from carrying clean water.
— Youth of this village used to pass indecent, lurid remarks when the Dalit women and girls used to pass through their settlements.
— The young persons used to call the Dalit women and girls in abusive language whenever they saw them on the village road.

Mithapurna Khara Pani

Now about the second case. This refers to the incident where

Dalit women had to face lot of difficulties in getting water. Village Mithapur, located in Dholka taluka, in North Gujarat, and other villages around have a perennial problem of drinking water, because the underground water sources are full of salinity owing to sea-ingress. In reality every one in the village suffers and has to undergo hardships. But the Dalits and particularly their womenfolk suffer the most.

In Mithapur, there is a water stand-post nearer the Dalit settlement. But the village elites including the Sarpanch deliberately did not permit the water to flow to this stand-post on which the entire Dalit settlement was dependent. As a result, the Dalits had to depend upon the tank located nearby where even the village cattle shared that water. It was dirty and muddy. But there was no way out. Not only that, during the peak agricultural season, the villagers threw crop waste and other refuse in that tank, and further contaminated that water source. The water also carried a bad odour due to this.

The hardships were indeed unbearable. But one day, a ray of hope was found. One Dalit inhabitant discovered a huge water-pipe alongside the highway. This pipe was leaking and the spilled water formed a pool. This was relatively better. Dalit men and women started filling their water pots from this new-found source. But even this 'convenience' of the Dalits became an eye-sore for the non-Dalits. They felt angry and enraged. "How could the Dalits have an access to good, potable water?"—they thought. As a revenge they forcibly pushed their cattle in this pond-like pool. Once again the Dalits were thrown into miserable position.

Especially the situation of Dalit women was unspeakably worse. Some idea can be had from the heated exchange of words that took place on the site between the savarna women and Babuben. Babuben, a Dalit woman, is literate and educated. She is a teacher. She has a high sense of self-identity and respect. She is aware of both, the language of struggle and its aftermath. She was prepared to face any consequences that follow from such encounters and engagements with the upper caste women.

Once she went to fill up the water at the public water-post. Her sister Maniben was with her. At that time, Sarpanch's wife Shyamba, her sisters-in-law Januba and Laduba were also at the stand-post. Seeing Babuben and Maniben, they lost their temper. Following was the conversation:

"You Dhedis: Why have you come here";—Shaymba began shouting at them. Babuben decided to keep quiet and hence pretended of not hearing this comment.

But when they found that others are still abusing them, Babuben politely said; "We have no other place to get water. So kindly serve us the water by your hands; or allow us to fill the water pot on our own."

These remarks were not taken as a request, but as an affront from lower untouchable caste women. Immediately they retorted in a stronger, authoritative tone, "You want to make our taps impure by your touch. Isn't it?"

Babuben, without losing her patience, repeated; "No. We just want to fill in the water."

Babuben and Maniben became aware that the situation would flare up because of the incalcitrance of upper caste women. The result was expected. Three upper caste women attacked Babuben and Maniben. Babuben suffered an injury and started bleeding. She came back home. She felt strongly that such highhandedness must be exposed. One day these things must come to an end. Why not today?, she thought. She narrated this incident to her husband, and they together decided to go to Dholka police station to lodge a complaint. There she could also get medical assistance.

The news that the complaint is being lodged at the police station reached the locality of upper caste; and soon the Sarpanch named Keshu Chhagan, his brother and others rushed to the Dalit settlement. They were in a devastating mood. Beating and looting started; and when they knew that Babuben and her husband are already on a way to Dholka, they decided to follow them.

They caught them midway and started shouting in abusive

language. "Wait. You Dheds. Today we won't spare you". And indeed they did not spare them. They pounced on them; mercilessly beating them with sticks and sharp weapons in their hands. Many were injured and bleeding profusely.

The attackers had followed them in a tractor. They shouted :

> "Tie them at the rear of the tractor and drag these Dheds; so that we are off the trouble forever in our village."

In the melee Babuben managed to escape. She caught hold of a passing truck whose driver sympathised with her. He reached her to a nearest police station. But the policemen on duty did not respond to her plea. He cold-shouldered the whole issue in the beginning. After repeated requests, he agreed to listen and accept the complaint.

After the complaint was lodged, few persons were arrested. However the upper caste families have not relented or feeling sorry for what happened. Instead they have resorted to other mechanisms to delay and dilute the case. Interestingly, one MLA who has got elected from a reserved constituency is taking undue interest in this matter and is bent on helping the Sarpanch and his allies. The case is filed; but the matter is dragging on and reportedly there are deliberate delays in collecting evidence. There is all possibility that in the end the culprits might get the benefit of doubt and let off from the clutches of law.

It is clear from the above narrative that in securing basic minimum needs, the Dalit women have to suffer untold miseries and hardships. In rural areas the brunt of such happenings is more sharp and acute. They have to quietly accept the indignities and remain submissive to the traditional forces and institutions. If they begin to rise against their dominance, they are left in a minority and in a lurch with arms of law not always apprehending those responsible for such disarray and misuse of resources. The case of Babuben is poignant enough.

III

Dalit women are increasingly becoming the targets of sexual

exploitation. Stories of such perversities are quite numerous, both in the rural and urban areas of Gujarat as elsewhere. We come across such cases occasionally because there is no quick and adequate reporting of such instances. Also the Dalit women face one additional handicap apart from the gender-based humiliation which other women from *savarna* community also face.

This extra handicap is that the Dalit women belong to the socially and economically marginal groups. The perpetrators of sexual crime are mostly from the dominant sections of society. They hold the reigns of social and economic power. Being the owners of main resources i.e. agricultural land, they are also the providers of wherewithal to members of Dalit community. If Dalit women proceed further in the matter of sexual harassment, and decide to book the culprit; not only her family would suffer from hunger and starvation; but the whole Dalit settlement would have to share the wrath of the dominant community. We have seen this happening in some places in Maharashtra, Karnataka and other states. Such hidden pressures emanating from the socially dominant *savarna* community need further investigation.

Case of Guntaben: Rape Victim

Here we shall briefly discuss the rape case involving a tribal woman who was a victim. The incident took place in 1986 and because of intervention of social activists and media persons, the news caught the national coverage. The incident took place in Devidav village of Sagbara taluka in Bharuch district. Guntaben belonging to Vasava tribe was raped by four constables in the presence of her husband in her own house. Not satisfied, they took both of them to a police station in a private truck, and again they repeatedly raped Guntaben in the police station.

There was a hue and cry all over the state. The social activists visited the village and contacted Guntaben. They took her report and carried a legal battle against the erring criminals. Expectedly the police department dragged their feet in this case and began covering up the case with disinformation and false propaganda against Guntaben, her husband and also others helping the couple in securing the justice. At long last, Guntaben's case was decided in her favour and a sort of justice was available to her. Four constables involved in the rape case were sentenced to ten years' rigorous imprisonment.

The Supreme Court also ordered the state government to pay Rs. 50000 to Guntaben within three months. The apex court has also passed strictures against the state administration and criticised them for delaying the justice in this case. The judgement came in 1993; while the incident took place in 1986. It was a long, traumatic battle for Guntaben with all humiliations and sufferings that went along with it.

Ayesha Pathan: Victim of Communal Orgy

As stated earlier the stories of atrocities on Dalit women are numerous but under-reported. These atrocities take place during the so-called 'peaceful or normal' times. But particularly when the social fabric is restive and beset with internal strife and tensions; the condition of Dalit women is particularly vulnerable. We have witnessed this happening in the war times when the vanquished community and their womenfolk are targeted. During the situations of civil strife also, this happens.

In the recent years, there are increasing incidents of crimes against women during communal tensions. This can be evident from the interviews and observation reports filed by Asghar Ali Engineer, Lancy Lobo, Kalpana Shah and others in connection with communal riots in Surat city in December 1992. In Bombay city also, similar instances have taken place.

Surat riots brought in its wake death, destruction of property and also humiliations and tortures perpetrated on the womenfolk belonging to minority community, i.e. Muslims. The Babri Masjid was demolished in Ayodhya on December 6; and the Surat city witnessed the rape, killings of Muslim women. They were thrown into the burning fire after being gang-raped. The case of Ayesha Pathan is particularly significant in this series.

The following account reported in *manushi* reveals how pathetic and inhuman was the situation. Ayesha was travelling with her family members to her native place in a train towards Bhusaval. The train had hardly reached a nearest station *udhna*, some five kilometres away from main *surat* junction, the unruly mob gathered there forcibly pulled the chain and stopped the train. The mob entered the compartment and started attacking the Muslim passengers. Many were killed. The family members got separated in a melee.

Ayesha was gheraoed by a group of some 10-15 persons. They started beating her. They tore away her clothes. Some four persons raped her in the train compartment itself, and later pierced a knife in her breast. Not satisfied with this inhuman, mindless torture, they inserted iron rods in her private parts; and then they threw her body in a burning fire. Later they took the body out from the fire and threw it on a railway track assuming that she was dead already. Luckily she survived this onslought and remained alive to tell this horror story. She was taken to the civil hospital in a state of unconsciousness and continued to receive the medical treatment for number of days.

Ayesha says that she can identify the people who have committed this crime. But the police have so far not produced anyone for identification. Maybe they have found none till this date. It was indeed a matter of grave concern that there was no widespread protest against this incident. Neither the women's organisations in the city nor the social service organisations have raised their voice of condemnation against this brutality and many other similar atrocities on women and children. Why? This is a question we must ask to ourselves.

Dalit Women in Literature

In social science literature, the question of Dalit women, their situation of marginalisation and miseries and their struggles for assertion of self-identity and self-respect are as yet not discussed widely. There is very little documentation of Dalit women's conditions in the mainstream social science literature. This consciousness has emerged only recently and it would take some more time to get it reflected through the social and cultural analysis.

All the same, there is another domain where the insights on this theme are already articulated in a powerful language. This domain is that of literature, namely short stories, novels, poetry and autobiographical narratives. In Gujarat as in Maharashtra and Karnataka, there is a distinct emergence of literature of the oppressed including that of Dalit women. The noted Gujarati writers who are covering this field with creative imagination are: Joseph Macvan, Dilip Ranpura, Dashrath Parmar, Nirav Patel, Chandu Meheria, Kisan Sosa, Mangal Rathod, and Atmaram Parmar. Their literary works document the hardships and agonies of Dalit women; including those belonging to nomadic tribes and other untouchable castes.

Their literature is the embodiment of social and cultural indignities heaped upon the Dalits including their womenfolk. In my view this is the first step signifying the cognition of the situation and its structural roots within society. One must welcome these experiments. And social science can benefit a great deal in acquiring insights from literature. Also our understanding of Dalit women can be enriched through the readings of the works of these writers many of whom are themselves Dalits. They themselves are a witness to horrifying experiences of manipulation, control and dominance.

A story entitled; "To Survive but with Determination" is worth recounting in this context. This story is written by Maria Shres Mitska, and was reviewed by a noted literati, Raghuvir Choudhari who congratulated her for this brilliant piece. The story centers around the Adivasi woman who is a labourer. Her name is Kamali. She is a widow and has five children to support. Not only that she is exploited economically, but she is exploited sexually also by her employers-contractors.

She faces this grim reality with equanimity and without losing her cool. Her attitude and outlook to life and perpetrators of exploitation are worth noting she says :

> "...I want to survive. So I have no other alternative but to accept your money. You can play with my body but me......You can never conquer me....when I was too young,

> I trusted you, I trusted even my father, but with that trust, I will die one day. But no, now I will not die because, now I know how to survive......I myself will survive and I see that my children also survive. You can do anything to me as you like, but you cannot dissuade me from my determination..."

While commenting on the story, Raghuvir Choudhari writes:

> "In this century, there is more clarity about chastity of 'sex'. Rape victim need not commit suicide because it is an attack, attack by an animal. One should learn to live normal even after being wounded."

Kamali wants to bring up her children by working as a labourer, but contractors grab major chunk even from whatever little amount she earns after hard work. And if their sexual demands are not fulfilled, they even threaten to dismiss her from the employment. How can Kamali and many others like her survive under such harrowing economic and sexual exploitation?

IV

The foregoing account is a brief narration of some typical cases. These events have taken place in Gujarat society, a milieu widely acknowledged for its liberalism, progressive outlook and tolerance. Why then these atrocities and miseries for Dalit women? Do other women from higher castes encounter better environment and treatment? Do the mainstream society in Gujarat observes dual standards with regard to the women in general and Dalit women in particular?

These questions require deeper investigation. My own view is that the mainstream women also suffer some injustices and humiliations, tortures and aggressive male world in variety of spheres. This is evident from reports available from some quarters, including stories of dowry deaths, foetus test or amniocentesis; and wife-beatings. We must begin to collect more comprehensive information on this critical sector.

Question of Dalit women and their handicaps reveal a different story; a story which is more gripping, pathetic and merits more concerted attention of all saner elements in the society. The sources of atrocities and disabilities of Dalit women lie in their multiple subordination levels; their dalitism, gender and other social and cultural handicaps. They are tortured or harassed within their own household. Patriarchy also plays the part in this case. But outside the home, they face unkind and cruel world of men steeped in authoritarianism, fundamentalism and sexism.

Our stories of Guntaben, Ayesha and Babuben amply reveal the social and cultural backwardness of Gujarat society despite its material progress. That the upper caste power elites including Sarpanch and the law-keeping agency like police constables themselves breach the order makes not only sad story, but makes an alarming reading on the state of civil society in Gujarat.

It is time to ponder over all aspects of this social and political behaviour of the powerful in this society and to evolve strategies to empower the women, particularly the Dalit women to fight back the virus of social fascism which is bared on such occasions like communal riots and also on other seemingly 'normal or peaceful' times.

References

1. Macvan Joseph; "Mithapurna Khara Pani", *NAYA MARG*, Number 15, August 1, 1991.
2. Chaudhari Raghuvir; "Ankh Ada Kan", *SANDESH*, August 27, 1993.
3. Shah Kalpana et al.; "The Nightmare of Surat", *MANUSHI*, January-April, 1993.
4. Tarafdar and Sarkar; "Struggle against Social Slavery".
5. "Samajik Gulamisameni Ladat: Sambardathi Swamannagar", *NAYA MARG*, Number 19, October 1, 1992.
6. Vaidya Gargi, "Ardhi Alam", *NAYA MARG*, Number 12, June 16, 1993.

Index